C000097377

OSTON &
EW ENGLAND

SPIRALGUIDE

 AA Publishing

Contents

Original text by John Rosenthal, Kathy Arnold and Paul Wade
Revised and updated by Kathy Arnold and Paul Wade

Update managed by Lodestone Publishing Limited
Project Designer Lesley Mitchell
Series Editor Karen Rigden
Series Designer Catherine Murray

Published by AA Publishing, a trading name of AA Media Limited,
whose registered office is Fanum House, Basing View, Basingstoke,
Hampshire RG21 4EA. Registered number 06112600.

ISBN: 978-0-7495-5965-6

The contents of this publication are believed correct at the time
of printing. Nevertheless, AA Publishing accept no responsibility
for errors, omissions or changes in the details given, or for the
consequences of readers' reliance on this information. This does
not affect your statutory rights. Assessments of the attractions,
hotels and restaurants are based upon the author's own experience
and contain subjective opinions that may not reflect the publisher's
opinion or a reader's experience. We have tried to ensure accuracy,
but things do change, so please let us know if you have any
comments or corrections.

A CIP catalogue record for this book is available from the British
Library

© AA Media Limited 2000, 2005, 2007, 2009, 2011.
Content revised and updated 2011.

Cover design and binding style by permission of AA Publishing
Colour separation by AA Digital Department
Printed and bound in China by Leo Paper Products

Find out more about AA Publishing and the wide range of services
the AA provides by visiting our Web site at theAA.com/shop

A04413
Boston maps in this title produced from mapping
© MAIRDUMONT/Falk Verlag 2011
Transport map © Communicarta Ltd, UK
New England maps in this title produced from map data supplied
by Global Mapping, Brackley, UK. Copyright © Global Mapping
(except pp132–133, 184–185)

The Magazine

A great holiday is more than just lying on a beach or shopping till you drop – to really get the most from your trip you need to know what makes the place tick. The Magazine provides an entertaining overview to some of the social, cultural and natural elements that make up the unique character of this engaging region.

Birthplace of a
NATION

New England is where it all started. The seeds of America's 200-year-long experiment in democracy were sown here, and reminders of those days stand proudly in this northeast corner of the United States.

Name a landmark event in colonial American history, and it almost assuredly happened somewhere in New England. The Pilgrims' landing at Plymouth Rock, the Salem Witch Trials, the Boston Massacre, the Boston Tea Party, Paul Revere's ride, the first shot of the American Revolution, the Battle of Bunker Hill – they all happened here. You could spend a month touring the historic sites in Boston alone, not to mention those found elsewhere in the New England region. The best historic sites are linked by the Freedom Trail (➤ 44–47), a red line on the Boston sidewalk that seems never to run out of historically important attractions.

The Pilgrim Fathers

A new chapter of history began in 1620, with the Pilgrims' landing. Originally intent on Virginia, they landed first at Provincetown rather than brave a difficult storm, but found no source of fresh water, and so continued on to Plymouth. A rock – who can say for sure whether it is *the* rock? – marks their disembarkation spot in Plymouth (➤ 64). A stone tower memorializes their landing at Provincetown (➤ 81–82).

Almost half of the 102 Pilgrims who came over from England on the *Mayflower* died within the first year, falling victim to pneumonia, influenza, malnutrition and scurvy. The others survived, but only with the help of the friendly Wampanoag Indians, who taught the new arrivals how to live off the land. They planted corn and other native vegetables, and in the fall of 1621, legend has it that the Pilgrims and the Native Americans celebrated the first harvest, or Thanksgiving.

Building a Community

The first settlers arrived in Salem in 1626; Boston became the first capital of the colony in 1632; Boston Latin opened its doors in 1635, America's oldest public school; Harvard College was founded a year later, making it the first institution of higher learning in the United States; in 1638, colonists built their first printing press in Cambridge; and in 1639, Richard Fairbank opened the country's first post office.

The Puritan ethic, so valuable for building communities, was not as successful in abiding those who did not share the same views. Quakers, Baptists and other dissidents were persecuted and sometimes prosecuted. Religious hysteria reached its most fevered pitch in Salem, where 19 men and women were put to death for allegedly practicing witchcraft (➤ 62).

"No Taxation Without Representation"

The 18th century brought many more settlers, and fundamental changes to the colonial way of life. In their quest for more space, the colonists' once-symbiotic relationship with the Native American tribes turned hostile. At the same time, many residents began to feel the strain of ties to Britain. In an effort to pay off the debt amassed during the Seven Years' War (the French and Indian War), the British government levied taxes on colonial sugar (1764), stamps (1765), tea (1767) and other British imports. Each new tariff provoked greater outrage among the free-trade-minded colonists, who adopted the revolutionary slogan of "No taxation without representation." The King sent British troops to quell the unrest in 1770, but ended up fanning the flames of independence when the soldiers killed five colonists outside the Old State House (➤ 45).

In 1773, patriots disguised as American Indians snuck aboard a British merchant ship and dumped its cargo of tea into Boston Harbor as a protest against the tax on tea. Parliament responded in 1774 by imposing the Boston Port Act, which closed the port, and the Coercive Acts, which quartered soldiers in colonists' homes. A year later, full-scale revolution was brewing.

The "Shot Heard 'Round the World"

Early in the morning of April 19, 1775, Paul Revere rode west from Boston, warning the colonists that the British were coming. Later that day, Minute Men (patriots who were ready to fight at a minute's notice) and redcoats skirmished in Lexington and Concord, and the first shot in the conflict, a "shot heard 'round the world," was fired. This was the beginning of the American Revolution.

On July 4, 1776, the colonies declared their independence from Britain – the document was read to the citizens of Boston from the balcony of the Old State House 14 days later – but the Revolution raged on for six more years. However, most of the important battles were fought outside of Boston. One significant battle took place in Bennington, Vermont. In August, 1777, a colonial militia confronted British troops seeking to seize arms and munitions stored at Bennington, and thoroughly routed the redcoats. The last British troops left America in 1783 and the United States officially became independent.

Costumed drummers at Boston's week-long July Harborfest

Literary Renaissance

The new nation set up its capital farther south, first in New York, then Philadelphia, and finally Washington, DC, and New England's historical importance waned. However, the region enjoyed a cultural renaissance in the mid-19th century, when Nathaniel Hawthorne, Herman Melville, Louisa May Alcott, Henry Wadsworth Longfellow, Ralph Waldo Emerson and Henry David Thoreau made it the "Athens of America" (▶ 28–30).

Celebrating the Past

Today, New England embraces its history while integrating it into modern life. Faneuil Hall in Boston, where the seeds of the Revolution were sown, is now the centerpiece of a bustling complex of stores and restaurants. The 1970s Hancock Tower reflects the 1870s Trinity Church across the skyline, rather than condemning it to the shadows. And homes where George Washington, John Adams and other Founding Fathers once slept are now museums or even bed-and-breakfasts.

Patriots' Day (the third Monday in April), when the events of April 19, 1775 are commemorated, is a public holiday in Massachusetts and Maine, and myriad activities take place around Boston. In Lexington and Concord, Revolutionary War *aficionados* in full period costume commemorate the battle at Concord's North Bridge.

Over two centuries, Boston has also developed a passion for sport, with three professional teams: the Celtics, Bruins and Red Sox. But it is the name of the region's football team that celebrates the proud past: the New England Patriots.

Modern-day Minute Men reenact events at Concord's North Bridge each year in April

SEASONS
to Remember

Anyone wanting to find the perfect image to illustrate the four seasons would do well to study New England, a region which glories in a variety of seasonal beauty.

Spring

In April and May, New England is bright and green, with buds on the trees, new grass taking root on lawns too long overwhelmed by ice and snow, and students shedding sweaters long before sane people dare to venture outdoors without an overcoat. Spring is preciously short, and usually encroached upon by cold winters and hot summers.

Summer

June, July and August are idyllic, with long sunny days, punctuated only occasionally by thunderstorms. The color of New England summer is blue – blue skies and blue waters ripe for fishing, swimming, sailing or simply for cooling your toes. Areas close to shore become hot and humid in July and August, making a dip in the Atlantic the perfect antidote. Everywhere in New England is best in summer, but Cape Cod and the islands of

SPRING FLINGS

- The Nantucket Daffodil Festival, held in late April, and the Lilac Festival at Vermont's Shelburne Museum, which takes place a month later, remind you that warmer days are on the way.
- In March, Boston welcomes spring with the Boston Flower and Garden Show at the Seaport World Trade Center.

Martha's Vineyard and Nantucket hold a special place in many people's hearts. Plan to spend as long as you can here. In the mountains of New Hampshire, Vermont and Maine, days are warm and nights are often cool. Maine in summer may be the finest place on Earth. Maine residents will tell you that their state has two seasons – winter and August – but that the glory of that month makes it worth muddling through the rest of the year.

Fall

The months of September, October and November mark New England's finest hour. From late September, the deciduous trees distinguish themselves from their evergreen cousins by donning fabulously gaudy coats of red, yellow and orange. The metamorphosis begins in the northern reaches of Maine and, week by week, descends upon the more

Springtime blossom in Massachusetts (far left); summer surf at Squibnocket Beach, Martha's Vineyard (below left); fall foliage (below) and winter snows (below right)

southerly states, drawing "leaf-peepers" to rural Vermont, New Hampshire, Connecticut and even Rhode Island to collect the last corn and first pumpkins, and to hike, bicycle, stroll, ride horseback or drive through the ocher-colored forests.

Winter

Winter, from December to February, brings subfreezing temperatures and attendant snow and ice to most of the region. New Englanders make the best of it, though, with skis, snowboards, skates or sleds. Cross-country touring centers lace the area, as do long stretches of ungroomed, and often

Above: Benedict Pond, Massachusetts State Forest. Left: Winter at Port Clyde, Maine

unvisited, forests, which visitors with their own skis can explore independently. New England downhill ski resorts may have a reputation for being crowded and expensive, but don't let that deter you: there are still a few places, particularly in Maine, where you can find an affordable weekend of skiing.

Mud Season

New England also has a unique fifth season known as mud season, which occurs unofficially at the end of March and the beginning of April. The snow and ice that cover the ground each winter melt under the warm spring sun during the day, transforming the ground into a muddy, sloshy ragout that solidifies at night when temperatures drop back below freezing. A late April snowstorm is never out of the question: in Vermont, New Hampshire and Maine, the big piles of snow by the side of driveways often don't disappear until the middle of May.

Mud season is when most New England innkeepers go on their own vacations. Occasionally, you can find a bargain price at this time, but quite often lodgings simply close down entirely for renovations and other yearly maintenance that can be performed only when the house is empty. However, this is also sugaring season, when maple trees are tapped for their sap, which is boiled down for maple syrup. In the old days, buckets were collected by hand, but nowadays, sap flows through plastic tubes down to the sugar house. Stopping to watch the process is really just an excuse to taste and buy maple syrup. So, if your idea of a vacation is days spent hunting for antiques or reading in front of a fire, and nights dining in a country tavern, then mud season just might be the perfect time for you.

DARN SOX

In Boston – as in most of New England – striking up a conversation with locals is easy. Just ask about the Boston Red Sox. The "Sox" inspire a passion that sports fans around the world understand. This baseball team represents the sporting hopes of almost all of New England.

"Almost all." Those two words are very important. There is a mythical line somewhere in Connecticut that splits residents' sporting loyalties between New York and Boston. In 1986, when the Red Sox faced the New York Mets in the World Series, a sports writer coined the phrase "Red Sox Nation," referring to the New Englanders whose very existence seems to depend on the fortunes of the Sox. What started as a newspaper quip has since been transformed into a real-life fan club. Since 2004, "citizens"

who have become members of the Red Sox Nation are entitled to their own particular set of privileges and even their own dedicated website: www.redsoxnation.com.

But this passion is not built on decades of success. If anything, it is built on decades of disappointment. And therein, as every Red Sox fan will tell you, hangs a tale. When the Boston Red Sox took on the St. Louis Cardinals in the 2004 World Series, few people – even their most ardent fans – anticipated that they would win. Yet, in an historic victory, the team took the World Series title, bringing to an end an 86-year period marked by defeat and ridicule. No wonder every New Englander can tell you exactly where they were on October 27, 2004.

"The Curse of the Bambino"
The team's misfortunes really began in 1920, when owner Harry Frazee sold star pitcher and slugger Babe Ruth to the dreaded rival New York Yankees for $125,000 (plus a $300,000 loan so he could finance a production of *No No Nanette*). Ruth, of course, became baseball's greatest player, leading the Yankees to four World Series championships in his career, and swatting a total of 714 home runs. The Red Sox, meanwhile,

Getting ready to rumble: The Red Sox play a home game at Fenway Park against the Colorado Rockies

THE GREATEST RED SOX PLAYER EVER

Ted Williams. Despite giving up three years of his playing days to fight in World War II and two more during the Korean War (he was a naval aviator), "Teddy Ballgame" hit 521 home runs in his career, just 193 fewer than Babe Ruth. His eyesight was so good he could read the commissioner's name on the baseball as it was hurtling toward him at speeds exceeding 90mph (145kph). Perhaps his finest hour was in 1941, when he went into the final day of the season with a batting average of .3996. If Williams had taken the day off, he would have been credited with an even .400 once his numbers were rounded off, a phenomenal accomplishment in a sport where .300 is considered excellent. But the "Splendid Splinter," as he was also known, wouldn't rest on those laurels. He played both games of a doubleheader, got six hits in eight at-bats, and finished the season with a .406 average, a mark that has never been equaled since.

Ted Williams, a Red Sox legend

fared less well. Prior to 2004, the Red Sox had made it to only four World Series championships, failing in each one. Each time, usually because of some bizarre twist of fate, they lost in the deciding seventh game. True Sox fans explained this as "the curse of the Bambino," a punishment for trading away baseball's greatest player. Baseball fans have long memories and the hows and whys of lost titles are handed down from generation to generation: in 1946, shortstop Johnny Pesky "held the ball;" in 1975, manager Darrell Johnson "pulled pitcher Jim Willoughby too soon;" in 1986, pitcher Bob Stanley threw away the tying run and first baseman Bill Buckner let the winning run between his legs.

GETTING IN

Red Sox games always sell out, and tickets are difficult to acquire unless you plan well in advance. For tickets, telephone the Red Sox ticket office at 877/REDSOX9 or check the website at http://boston.redsox.mlb.com. Be sure to ask about standing-room-only tickets when you call. The baseball season runs from early April to early October and ticket prices range from $20 to more than $100. If the game is already sold out, with money and luck you may be able to acquire tickets online or from scalpers at Kenmore Square on game day, but watch out for scams and expect to pay a premium price.

In 1999, in an act of sheer desperation, the management brought the Babe's daughter to a playoff game against the Sox's arch rivals, the New York Yankees, in an effort to exorcize the curse, but to no avail: the dreaded New Yorkers dispatched the team in five games and went on to win their 25th World Series.

A Change in Fortune

In 2004, as in earlier years, opening day in Red Sox country was full of hope, though little expectation. Players from the previous season returned to their positions, steeling themselves for another chance at glory; raw young newcomers were eager to play in a big-league game. As the season progressed, the Sox played well; excitement built with every pitch.

As the team inched nearer a place in the 100th World Series, the unspoken question on everyone's minds was: Would fall – as it had for almost a century – bring the inevitable? Collectively, the region dared to articulate the thought that "This just might be the year." But, as ever, the Sox kept their fans on the edge of their seats. Although three-nothing down to the hated Yankees in the American League Championship Series, the Sox bounced back to win four in a row. Yet again, they had made it to the World Series. This time, they triumphed, again winning four games in a row against the St. Louis Cardinals. Not only did they win, they set a record: eight straight post-season victories.

We Are the Champions

Having broken the curse, the Red Sox won the World Series again in 2007. Only one other team has won twice in the 21st century. Of course, it has to be those Damn Yankees.

The New England
LOBSTER

The lobster may not look like much at first, and it certainly does not look like food. Yet hundreds of New England restaurants make a whole year's worth of profits by serving lobster dinners for just four months in the summertime.

A Delicacy?

Lobster has not always been a gourmet treat. In 17th-century New England, they were so abundant that they were used to fertilize fields and appeared only on the tables of the poor. Legend has it that servants refused to eat lobster more than twice a week. Colonists enjoyed insulting red-coated British soldiers, by shouting "Lobsterback!"

My, how things have changed. Today, lobster restaurants, mostly in Maine, but also along the coasts of New Hampshire, Massachusetts (especially on Cape Cod), Connecticut, and Rhode Island, draw in customers by the droves, all eager to enjoy their succulent specialty.

Lobster dinners are served at simple lobster shacks all along the New England Coast

Is It Worth It?

You look at the prices on the menu and think no overgrown shrimp can be worth that much money. You see other diners struggling to crack open the hard claws and you think no food can be worth this much work. Your waiter ties a bib around your neck and you think no meal can be worth looking this silly.

Then your meal arrives on a plate as large as a hubcap, adorned with corn on the cob and boiled new potatoes. The smell of the melted

> ## "Could it possibly be as good as everyone says it is?"

butter alone may make you realize what all the fuss has been about. Some say the claws are the tastiest part of the lobster, others that nothing can compare to the tail. Attack whichever end you like first and come to your own conclusion, but don't worry about getting messy.

Finally, dunk the much-hyped morsel into the butter and deliver it into your mouth. Could it possibly be as good as everybody says it is? No. It's even better! Sweet and chewy, with a hint of salt, and a taste that can only be found in food that was alive minutes before it hit your plate.

TRAPPED!

Nowadays, you can go out aboard a traditional Downeast-style lobster boat to learn about the life and work of lobstermen. In Bar Harbor, go out on Captain John Nicolai's *Lulu* (tel: 207/963-2341; www.lululobsterboat.com).

A Maine lobsterman lands his catch, ready for sale in local markets and restaurants

ROOM AT THE INN

The welcoming innkeepers and romantic atmosphere of
New England's country inns are a heady combination and
many guests leave thinking: "We could do this, couldn't we?
It would be fun!"

Day In, Day Out

At the Notchland Inn, near Jackson, New Hampshire, Les Schoof has
heard it all. "I get chills when someone says, 'We're going to retire and do
this!' People think that they can kick back at 4 or 5pm and sip Courvoisier
with friends." Unfortunately, the reality is not quite so idyllic. Few potential
innkeepers realize the level of commitment required in what is usually a
two-person operation.

At Vermont's Inn at Manchester, the Hanes family are typical
innkeepers. Frank left his job at a company in North Carolina and moved
to Vermont. Now he is the chef, while his wife Julie is the handyman:
"Just as I was in the family home." But long office hours have been
replaced with longer innkeeping hours. Frank starts at 6:30am; Julie
finishes at 10pm.

New England style and hospitality: a cozy bed and breakfast (below left), a riverside
hotel (below right), and the colorful Woodstocker Inn (right, ➤ 126)

Expect the Unexpected

And, as every innkeeper knows, problems never happen on a quiet Tuesday. Leslie Mulcahy of the Rabbit Hill Inn, near St. Johnsbury in Vermont, remembers the power outage during Thanksgiving Dinner. "We put candles into loaves of bread, creating a Martha Stewart moment."

Keeping Business Busy

As for earnings, innkeepers never make a fortune. "Every dime is plowed back into the business," Leslie explains. The hospitality industry is very competitive. "We can't stand still. We constantly upgrade. Thirteen years ago, we had four luxury rooms. Now we have nine suites and eight fireplace suites." On the other hand – and this is when a gleam comes into innkeepers' eyes – there are compensations. "Every morning, I look out at the mountains, look at our beautiful inn, wave to guests we know personally," explains Leslie Mulcahy. It may be hard work, but many innkeepers cannot imagine doing anything else.

The Urban Alternative

Not all bed-and-breakfast inns are in the country; more and more are opening in cities. "We get a lot of Europeans here," says Reinhold Mahler at the Encore B&B in Boston's South End. "And Americans looking for something different from the cookie cutter hotel. Like other innkeepers, we live on property, on call." Visitors range from college students to business travelers. They need less pampering, "but we love to get flowers, wine, a cake for that special occasion."

MARITIME heritage

Some say that salt water runs in the veins of New Englanders. Certainly, the region boasts 400 years of maritime tradition: the first boat was built in Maine in 1607.

New England's love affair with the sea and with ships ranges from trading and fighting to whaling and racing. One of America's icons is *Mayflower II,* the reproduction of the ship that took the Pilgrim Fathers to the New World in 1620. But, 13 years before they arrived, the tiny *Virginia* was launched from a fishing colony at the mouth of the Kennebec River in Maine. Weighing just 30 tons, this was probably the first English-built ship in North America.

Ships for War

As Europe's navies grew, so Europe's forests dwindled. The success of Britain's Royal Navy was directly proportionate to its access to New England's virgin forest. The exceptionally tall, straight, white pine trees provided vital "mast pines" for faster, bigger ships. By the mid-18th century, one-third of Britain's ships were being built in the Colonies. After Independence, this industry played a major role in the development of the new nation. Learn more at the Maine Maritime Museum in Bath, Maine (➤ 165). Of all the warships built in New England, the most famous is USS *Constitution*. Launched in Boston in 1797, she is the world's oldest floating commissioned naval vessel. Now docked in the Charlestown Navy Yard, across from downtown Boston, she gained her nickname of "Old Ironsides" during her victory over the British frigate, HMS *Guerriere*, in the War of 1812 (www.ussconstitutionmuseum.org).

Trading With the World

When it comes to trade, one of New England's most important ports from the 18th to the early 19th century was Salem, Massachusetts. During the Revolution, she played a vital role, with her merchant ships turning to privateering. After Independence, Salem's skippers roamed the world "to the farthest ports of the rich East," as the city's seal still boasts (in Latin). Their tale is told in Salem (➤ 62) at the Maritime National Historic Site,

An early 19th-century whaling ship in dock for repairs in New Bedford, Massachusetts

where the *Friendship* is a faithful replica of a 1797 Indiaman. Nearby, the treasures brought back from these voyages are displayed at the outstanding Peabody Essex Museum (► 62).

Thar She Blows!

Whales have long been part of New England's maritime life. No New England port is more closely linked with whaling than Nantucket, off Cape Cod. Between 1800 and 1840, this was the "Whaling Capital of the World," with 88 ships hunting down the mammoths of the deep for their precious oil. To understand the industry, head for the Nantucket Whaling Museum (www.nha.org), with its whale skeleton and whaling memorabilia.

To see what life aboard a whaling ship was like, it has to be Mystic Seaport in Connecticut. Here, the star attraction is the 1841-built *Charles W. Morgan*. But, this "Museum of America and the Sea" has other historic ships, as well as a village, where hoop makers, a sail loft, a shipping office and more recreate life in a 19th-century seaport (► 145). Whales are still a prime target in the waters off New England. Nowadays, however, they are the focus of photographers rather than harpooners. A dozen or so ports along the New England coast offer whale-watching cruises.

To Sail the Ocean Blue

The great days of sail, whether for whaling, commerce or war, are long gone. But, the sport of sailing thrives, with boats large and small bobbing in marinas from Connecticut to Maine. As for competitions, nothing is more prestigious than the America's Cup, which took place off Newport, Rhode Island, from 1930 to 1983. Learn all about it at Newport's Museum of Yachting (► 143); even better, go for a sunset cruise aboard a former America's Cup winner, sailing in beautiful Narragansett Bay.

The best of
NEW ENGLAND

Be sure to enjoy the very best of what New England has to offer, from watching the sunrise to watching it set.

Best New England Experiences

- **Eating lobster** Chances are, if you have one lobster dinner in New England, you are likely to have another one soon thereafter. Maine is where the best-tasting lobsters are, but they are also good in coastal Massachusetts, New Hampshire, Connecticut and Rhode Island.
- **Biking** The flat topography in New England's beach towns makes them ideal for exploration on two wheels. Cape Cod, Nantucket, Martha's Vineyard, Newport and the Maine coast are full of places that rent bikes.
- **Leaf-peeping** The annual arrival of autumnal colors draws foliage fans from all over the world and traffic on Vermont's roads grinds to a virtual standstill. The driving tour (➤ 181–183) is an attractive route between Manchester Center and Woodstock, but an equally good way to see the scenery is to find your way onto some dirt roads and try to get lost.
- **Eating ice cream** Ice cream is a serious business in New England, with contests to determine who makes the best. Ben & Jerry's is widely sold, but there is no substitute for getting it freshly scooped at a local ice-cream parlor. Or take a drive up to Waterbury, Vermont, and tour the main factory where Chunky Monkey and Cherry Garcia are packed.

Best Place To Buy Antiques

- **Sheffield**, in the Berkshire Hills of western Massachusetts, is home to more antiques dealers than you could possibly see in a day. Go with something specific in mind, otherwise the endless possibilities of places to peruse could be dizzying.

Most Romantic Place To Watch The Sunset

- **Madaket Beach**, Nantucket (➤ 84). On North America's eastern coast, there are precious few places where you can watch the sun melt into the ocean. Trees, hills or buildings usually mar the view, but Madaket is west-facing, with 30 miles (48km) of open sea between it and the next landfall. Bring a bottle of wine and a blanket to complete the experience; it can get cool once the sun sinks.

Best Place To Watch the Sunrise

■ The top of **Cadillac Mountain**, in Maine's Acadia National Park (➤ 158–160). Get up early and drive up to the top of the mountain to see the first place in the US to greet the sun every day.

Best Viewpoint

■ **Top of the Hub** Sip a drink and enjoy unforgettable views of Boston from the 52nd floor of the Prudential Center (➤ 58).

If You Only Go To One . . .

■ **Restaurant** Legal Sea Foods (➤ 68) is the quintessential New England restaurant, with outlets all over Boston. The seafood is top quality and the atmosphere is warm yet sophisticated.

■ **Lobster shack** Make it Abel's Lobster Pound (tel: 207/276-5827) on Mount Desert Island, Maine. Sit at a table overlooking the fjord-like Somes Sound and enjoy their tasty lobster stew.

■ **Museum** Boston's Museum of Fine Arts (➤ 48–51) has one of the greatest and most varied collections in the world.

■ **Historic Home** Visit Rough Point (➤ 138–139), home of Doris Duke, philanthropist, a contrast to other mansions on Bellevue Avenue.

Bicycling is one of the best ways to explore New England

BOSTON ALFRESCO

Despite charmingly erratic weather, Bostonians are passionate about being outdoors. Year round, even a brief period of sunshine brings them outside in droves to enjoy the fresh air, filling parks, plazas and cafes with laughter and activity.

Outdoor Concerts

Bostonians love concerts, films and special events under the stars, and the Hatch Shell on the Charles River Esplanade is a perfect venue for a picnic on the lawn accompanied by excellent entertainment. The season's most popular performance is the annual Fourth of July Independence Day Boston Pops (www.bso.org) extravaganza complete with fireworks over the river. Harborfest is a week long celebration leading up to the Fourth of July which offers hundreds of special events and concerts. For big-name

summertime music it's hard to beat the pop music events at the Bank of America Pavilion. Copley Square lights up with free evening concerts. And the Museum of Fine Arts (▶ 48–51) offers an eclectic mix of jazz and ethnic music in lovely Calderwood Courtyard beneath the evening sky.

Emerald Necklace

Boston is rich with parks. In the late 19th century, Frederick Law Olmsted, America's greatest landscape architect, designed a chain of natural spaces. Nine parks, connected by parkways and waterways, form a 7-mile long (11.5km) string of green spaces known affectionately as the Emerald Necklace. This magnificent greenway extends from Boston Common (▶ 58) to Franklin Park, offering accessible spaces to play and picnic, go for a stroll or for quiet contemplation.

Walk Along the Harbor

Boston's new 47-mile (75km) HarborWalk (www.bostonharborwalk.com) is a beautiful pedestrian path that follows the water's edge past verdant parks, marinas, working wharves and even a sandy beach. Nearing completion, it is rapidly becoming one of Boston's favorite outdoor gathering places, with cafes, gardens and views of the island-studded harbor. Points of interest along the way include the Institute of Contemporary Art (▶ 57), the Boston Children's Museum (▶ 57) and the New England Aquarium (▶ 57).

Taking time out on the Charles River

LITERARY
GREATS

Concord, Massachussetts was home to some of the greatest names in 19th-century American literature, among them Ralph Waldo Emerson, Henry David Thoreau, Louisa May Alcott, Nathaniel Hawthorne and Herman Melville.

The Brook Farm Community

Transcendentalism, the philosophical belief that God is present in both man and nature, arose in the mid-19th century. Ralph Waldo Emerson, Henry David Thoreau and several other prominent New Englanders gathered periodically to discuss philosophy, religion and literature. From 1840 to 1844, they published their writings on these subjects in a journal called *The Dial*. They also helped to found Brook Farm, near Boston, an experimental cooperative community (1841–47) in which each of the 24 members participated in both the day's labor and the evening's intellectual discourse. In the end, they proved to be better thinkers than farmers, but the ideas that they exchanged at Brook Farm paved the way for John Dewey's progressive education movement, and sowed the seeds of the abolitionist movement.

> "In the end, they proved better thinkers than farmers"

Ralph Waldo Emerson

Emerson (1803–82) was the preeminent spokesman of the Transcendentalist movement in America. His 1836 essay entitled "Nature" was the first to espouse its principles. His belief in the mystical unity of nature originally drew scorn from those who thought he was repudiating Christianity (he was prohibited from speaking at Harvard, his alma mater,

Concord's Walden Pond, where Thoreau lived for two years, the inspiration for *Walden*

for nearly 30 years). But it attracted the attention of intellectuals up and down the East Coast, many of whom came to Concord to share their thoughts.

Henry David Thoreau

Thoreau (1817–62) was Emerson's most prominent protégé. At the age of 24, he went to live in Emerson's house, serving as handyman, assistant, editor, and later as author of several pieces of poetry and prose for *The Dial*. Thoreau's most lasting contribution to the movement, however, came in 1845, when he eschewed all material possessions and went to live in a small cabin he built for himself on the

Above: Henry David Thoreau

shore of Concord's Walden Pond (➤ 61). For more than two years, he led a largely introspective life, reading, observing nature and writing his thoughts in a detailed journal, which he published in 1854 as *Walden*.

The Alcotts

The career of Amos Bronson Alcott (1799–1888) is often overshadowed by his more famous daughter, Louisa May Alcott (1832–88). However,

 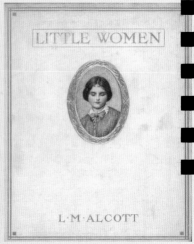

Louisa May Alcott (top) is renowned for her autobiographical novel *Little Women*

the younger Alcott's accounts of the experiment in progressive education would not have been possible without her father's tireless advocacy of educational reform. His Temple School, which stressed the importance of children's mental, physical and spiritual development, was ultimately a failure, though it met with greater success in England (Alcott House).

Louisa May Alcott's account of growing up in the unconventional Alcott household has conveyed the spirit of her father's philosophies to young girls ever since. Her autobiographical novel, *Little Women*, an account of daily domestic life in her home, became a best-seller and made Louisa the most highly paid author of her day. The trials and triumphs of sisters Meg, Jo, Beth and Amy have since been chronicled in five movie adaptations, the last in 1994. Visitors to Orchard House (➤ 61), the Alcott home in Concord, can glimpse her life through family mementos.

Hawthorne and Melville

Although they were writing at the same time as the Transcendentalists, Nathaniel Hawthorne (1804–64) and Herman Melville (1819–91) distanced themselves from the movement because they did not share its optimism (some might say idealism). Nevertheless, they moved freely among the group. Hawthorne's wife, Sophia Peabody, was a follower of the movement, and they lived for three years in The Old Manse, the house by the North Bridge (➤ 61) in Concord where Ralph Waldo Emerson wrote his famous essay, "Nature."

Finding Your Feet

First Two Hours

Arriving by Air: Boston

- Most travelers begin their New England vacations at **Boston's Logan International Airport** (www.massport.com/logan). International carriers arrive at Terminal E, as well as American and Delta Air Lines. Terminal B arrivals include North American carriers such as Air Canada, US Airways and Virgin America. Arrivals at Terminal C include JetBlue and United. At Terminal A, you'll find Continental and Delta.
- There are **currency exchanges** in Terminal A, B and E, as well as **ATM** machines both pre- and post-security in every terminal.
- You'll find **taxi** stands at all the airport terminals. Rates are metered and a ride from the airport to most hotels costs about $30, plus approximately $8 in fees and tolls depending on the route you take. Though relatively expensive, cabs are convenient and take up to four people in each taxi.

Public Transportation

- Boston has an extensive public transportation system, the MBTA, always referred to as "the T" (www.mbta.com). It includes buses, streetcars and metro lines. The **Silver Line SL1 bus route** goes direct from all airport terminals to Boston's South Station (approximately 20 minutes).
- To get to the Airport Station "T" stop, take the free **Logan Shuttle Bus** that travels between the airline terminals (arrival level), the Airport Station, the Water Transportation Terminal and Economy Parking.
- At Airport Station, follow signs for the **Blue Line Train Inbound** to get to central Boston. For details on major intersections ➤ 33.
- For **travelers with disabilities**, a free, accessible 24-hour shuttle bus service is available to and from the Economy Lot and Logan's terminals every 20 minutes. Disabled parking is available nearest the bus shelter. Massport provides Accessible Van Service to terminals, the Airport T Station (not currently wheelchair accessible) and to Wood Island T Station (which is wheelchair accessible). To request service, use the free "Van Phone" in terminal baggage claim areas or call 617/561-1770.

Arriving by Air: Outside Boston

- Several airlines operate services to **Providence**, Rhode Island and **Manchester**, New Hampshire. These two smaller New England airports are each about 1.5 hours outside Boston, but the low prices and efficient service make them an alternative worth considering.
- Visitors to Vermont or the Berkshires might consider flying into **Burlington**, Vermont; **Albany**, New York; or **Bradley International Airport**, 15 miles (24km) north of Hartford, Connecticut. Visitors can also fly in to **Maine** through Portland and Bangor, Maine.

Arriving by Rail

- Intercity **Amtrak** trains from New York, Philadelphia, Chicago, Washington and other points arrive at South or North stations; many stop at Back Bay Station as well. For detailed information on fares and schedules, call Amtrak (tel: 800/872-7245) or visit their website, www.amtrak.com.
- From South Station, it is about a $15 cab ride to most downtown hotels. The **Red Line** also stops at South Station.

Arriving by Bus

- **Greyhound** (tel: 800/229-9424; www.greyhound.com) provides a nationwide bus service, and can give you the names of several smaller regional carriers. Buses arrive at the South Station bus terminal.

Getting Around

Boston

Boston is extremely compact. Most of its attractions are within easy walking distance of each other, and those that aren't are linked by a simple, efficient subway system (the "T").

The "T"

- The "T" has five different lines, each radiating out from the city's center. The four major downtown stops are **Park Street** (the unofficial center of the system, where the Red and Green lines intersect), **Government Center** (where the Green and Blue lines intersect), **State** (where the Blue and Orange lines intersect), and **Downtown Crossing** (a pedestrian mall, where the Orange, Red and Silver lines meet).
- The system uses the terminology **"inbound"** and **"outbound."** Inbound always means toward Park Street, the center of the system, and outbound means away from Park Street. If you don't know which direction you need to take, just ask. It's not an uncommon question, and most people will be happy to help you.
- Note that many of the stops on the **Green Line** are so close together that it's almost faster to walk between them.
- The **fare** for most trips on the "T" is $1.70 with a **CharlieCard** or $2.00 with a **CharlieTicket.** You can purchase CharlieCards or CharlieTickets from the vending machines or from the ticket offices at any subway station.
- A visitor's **DayLink Pass,** which offers unlimited rides for a period of time, can be credited to a **CharlieCard**. It costs $9.00 for one day, $15 for seven days and $59 for one month and is available at stations such as Downtown Crossing, South Station, North Station, Back Bay Station and Harvard, as well as at some hotels and tourist information kiosks. Contact MBTA at 617/222-3200 or visit their website, www.mbta.com, for more information.

Cabs

- The "T" **stops running** after about midnight, but cabs can usually be found (or called) at most places frequented by tourists. You can try to hail a cab almost anywhere on the street: you will usually have better luck at official cab stands (in front of most hotels, popular restaurants and tourist attractions).
- Taxis are **metered** and they are not cheap, but no cab ride within the city limits should cost more than $20.
- The **initial fare** is $2.60, and you pay $2.80 for each mile. Tip drivers 15 percent of the fare.
- If you can't find a cab, try calling **ITOA** (tel: 617/825-4000), **Town Taxi** (tel: 617/536-5000) or **Boston Cab** (tel: 617/536-5010).

Driving

- **Don't even attempt** to drive in Boston. The traffic is blood-boiling, the one-way streets will drive you insane, and legal parking spaces are an endangered species. And, the old heart is a maze of tiny streets. If you are touring New England, start your rental at the end of your stay in Boston.
- If you have a car, by far the best option is to park it in a garage when you arrive and keep it there until you leave. If the prices at your hotel's garage seem too high, the large parking lots under **Boston Common** (tel: 617/954-2098) or under the **Prudential Center** (tel: 617/236-3060) may prove a less expensive alternative.

- The multibillion dollar construction project known as the **Big Dig** changed the heart of Boston dramatically. The old elevated expressway has been removed and traffic flows through an underground tunnel. New parks are being created between the harbor and downtown. Be sure to get a map which reflects the changes since 2007.

Outside Boston

To see the rest of New England, you'll have to have a car. Train and bus services (► 32) to the rest of New England are patchy at best and you'll find it next to impossible to get around the woods of Vermont, the beaches of Cape Cod or the small towns of the Berkshires without wheels of your own.

Driving

- If you're planning to do a lot of driving around New England, invest in a **good map**.
- **Reserve your rental car** at least a few days in advance and pick it up on the day you leave Boston.
- Most **major car rental agencies** have locations at the airport, as well as locations in town. For more information contact the companies direct:

Alamo (tel: 877/222-9075)   **Enterprise** (tel: 800/261-7331)
Avis (tel: 800/230-4898)   **Hertz** (tel: 800/654-3131)
Budget (tel: 800/527-0700)   **National** (tel: 877/222-9078)
Dollar (tel: 800/800-3665)   **Thrifty** (tel: 800/847-4389)

- To rent a car, you usually need to be **aged 25** or above and hold a major credit card in your name.
- An **overseas driver's license** is valid on all US roads, though it is helpful to have an international driving permit. Bring your passport, too.
- Check to see if your automobile insurance at home covers you for rentals. Otherwise, you'll have to pay the **hefty per-day surcharges** that all the rental companies impose for liability insurance.
- Call your credit card company to see if they will assume the **Collision Damage Waiver (CDW),** another per-day surcharge that absolves you of responsibility for damage to the vehicle in an accident. Most gold cards offer collision coverage to their customers, but do not cover liability.

Getting Out of Town

- **The Berkshires** Take the Massachusetts Turnpike (I-90) west to Stockbridge.
- **Cape Cod and the Islands** Take I-93 south to Route 3 south. Cross the Cape Cod Canal. For ferries to Nantucket, take Route 6 and then Route 132 to Hyannis. To get to Martha's Vineyard, follow Route 28 for Falmouth, then head for Woods Hole.
- **Maine** Take I-93 north to I-95 north.
- **New Hampshire** Take I-93 north.
- **Rhode Island and coastal Connecticut** Take I-93 south, then I-95 south.
- **Vermont** Take the I-93 north, then I-89 northwest to Vermont.

Admission Charges

The cost of admission for museums and places of interest mentioned in the text is indicated by price categories:
Inexpensive up to $10   **Moderate** $10–$15   **Expensive** over $15

Accommodations

New England in general, and Boston in particular, has some of the most luxurious hotels in the United States, and 19th-century inns with plenty of character.

Hotels and Inns

■ Though hotels in Boston and New England's other major cities tend to be expensive, they often offer **attractive discounts** for weekend visitors.

■ Victorian or colonial-style **country inns** offer guests a real New England experience. Inns vary in character and price: some are inexpensive family places, others recreate the grandeur of yesteryear, with prices to match.

Resorts

■ New England's mountains and beaches were the nation's first summer playgrounds. Today, **many resorts** are as grand as ever, offering a wide range of activities, from golf and swimming to spas and *haute cuisine*.

When to Go

■ Peak or **high season varies** from town to town. During this time expect elevated prices, with minimum stays required of two to four nights.

■ **Ski resorts** in the mountains of Vermont and New Hampshire are crowded on the major holiday weekends in winter. Bargains can be had in March.

■ Peak season in **Cape Cod** and the **Berkshire Hills** is in July and August.

■ With its plethora of colleges, **Boston** is busy at graduation time in May/June, and crowded in September at the start of the academic year.

■ Increased numbers of visitors during the **fall foliage season** make hotel rooms hard to come by. The Columbus Day weekend, the second weekend in October, is particularly busy. In Vermont some Chambers of Commerce coordinate lodgings in private homes to ease the strain.

Diamond Ratings

■ AAA Tourism Editors evaluate and rate establishments based on the overall quality and services. AAA's diamond rating criteria reflect the design and service standards, combined with the expectations of our members.

■ Our one (◈) or two (◈◈) diamond rating represent a clean and well-maintained property offering comfortable rooms, with the two-diamond property showing enhancements in decor and furnishings. A three (◈◈◈) diamond property shows marked upgrades in physical attributes, services and comfort and may offer additional amenities. A four (◈◈◈◈) diamond rating signifies a property offering a high level of service and hospitality and a wide variety of amenities and upscale facilities. A five (◈◈◈◈◈) diamond rating represents a world-class facility, offering the highest level of luxurious accommodations and personalized guest services.

Taxes

Lodging taxes vary between states and are not included in quoted prices.

VT 9 percent	**CT** 12 percent	**NH** 8 percent
RI 9 percent	**MA** 5.7–12.2 percent	**ME** 7 percent

Accommodations Prices

Expect to pay for two people sharing a double room, excluding taxes:

$ under $150	**$$** $150–$250	**$$$** over $250

Food and Drink

You can find sophisticated restaurants in even small New England towns and villages, as well as in Boston and the other major cities. Many country inns serve evening meals, and though you can expect to pay similar prices to those in an independent restaurant, it could be the highlight of your vacation.

Traditional New England Cuisine

- **Lobster** is the best-known New England specialty, though clams, oysters, and Atlantic and freshwater fish are widely available.
- The best place to eat lobster in New England is at a simple **lobster shack**, found in towns and villages up and down the New England coastline. They are open for lunch and early dinner in summer, but close in winter.
- Other **seafood specialties** include oyster stew and clam chowder thick enough to stand a spoon upright. Menus may feature steamers, quahogs (pronounced ko-hogs), cherrystones and littlenecks: these are all clams.
- **Traditional specialties** include baked beans (invented in Boston), brown bread (made with molasses) and Indian pudding (a dessert made from cornmeal and molasses).

Modern American/New England Cuisine

- Modern New England cooking uses **locally produced ingredients**: coastal seafood, trout and Atlantic fish. Maine produces juicy blueberries, New Hampshire grows apples and Massachusetts harvests tons of cranberries. Organically grown vegetables and salads are readily available. Vermont maple syrup and dairy products, especially cheeses and ice cream, are renowned. In the fall, game is plentiful, as are pumpkins and squash.
- Immigration has **influenced cooking styles** in the region. Boston's North End is the city's Little Italy, while Chinatown, although compact, is home to a large number of Asian eateries. Out on Cape Cod, descendants of Portuguese origin still bake Portuguese breads.

Practical Tips

- **Lunch** is usually served from 11:30 or 12 to 2 or 2:30 and **dinner** from 5 to 9:30 or 10. Some top-quality restaurants offer **special menus** for those dining early. Lunch menus are usually less expensive than dinner.
- Expect to leave a **tip** of 15–20 percent at the best restaurants.
- The dress code in New England restaurants is usually **smart-casual**.

Diamond Ratings

As with the hotel ratings (▶ 35), AAA Tourism Editors evaluate restaurants on the overall quality of food, service, decor and ambience – with extra emphasis given to food and service. Ratings range from one diamond (🏵) indicating a simple, family-oriented establishment to five diamonds (🏵🏵🏵🏵🏵) indicating an establishment offering superb culinary skills and the ultimate adult dining experience.

Restaurant Prices

Expect to pay per person for a three-course meal, excluding drinks and service:

$ under $20 $$ $20–$35   SSS over $35

Shopping

New England offers some of the most varied and best-value shopping in the United States. In addition to upscale malls, Boston boasts chic avenues such as Newbury Street. Although the region is known for its fine antiques and crafts shops, its numerous discount outlets make it popular with those in search of a bargain.

Farm Stands and Country Stores

- Throughout the six states, country lanes are studded with **stalls selling local produce**, from organic vegetables to jars of honey and maple syrup, even goat's cheeses.

- For pure nostalgia, nothing beats the traditional **Vermont Country Store** (► 129), which once supplied farmers and their families with everything that they needed. Today, customers can once again purchase long cotton nightshirts, a variety of patent medicines and wall-mounted can openers, and other old-fashioned essentials.

Antiques and Crafts

- New England is known for its antiques shops and collectibles. **The Old King's Highway** (SR 6A) on Cape Cod, is a fertile hunting ground, as is **Route 7**, running through Vermont, western Massachusetts and into Connecticut.

- The region also has a thriving **contemporary crafts** industry, with potters, jewelers, weavers and furniture-makers. Some states have craft associations with their own shops, such as the League of New Hampshire Craftsmen (eight, including those in Concord, Meredith, North Conway and Wolfboro) and Vermont's Frog Hollow (Burlington). In Maine, check out the Center For Maine Craft (► 171).

Factory Outlets

- In the past decade, factory outlets have become hugely popular. They sell everything from jewelry and books to designer-label clothes, shoes and bags, all at knockdown prices. **Freeport** (► 171), Maine is one of the best-known destinations, though **Kittery** (► 171), also in Maine, just a 90-minute drive from Boston, is also popular.

- Since New Hampshire has no sales tax, canny shoppers regularly hop across the state line in search of a bargain. The hikers and skiers who flock to the White Mountains usually leave time to stock up at the outdoors shops in **North Conway**, as well as seeking out more glamorous designer-label clothing. In southern Vermont, the outlet shops in **Manchester Center** (► 129) boast big names such as Escada, Ann Taylor and Armani.

- Not to be outdone, Massachusetts has a whole mall of outlet stores, south of Boston at **Wrentham Village Premium Outlets.**

Opening Times

- In towns, **stores** are usually open from 9 or 10 to 6 or 7. **Malls** usually stay open later, especially during the peak season.

Sales Tax

- In New England, a small sales tax is added to the price of the goods that you buy (though it is already included in the price of gasoline, tobacco and alcohol). Taxes vary from state to state. See also Taxes (► 35) for more information.

Entertainment

Winter

In Boston and throughout New England, the New Year is greeted with **First Night** celebrations (December 31), the last and best party of the year. Buy one First Night button and enjoy free music and theater, stand-up comedy and entertainment for all the family (www.firstnight.org). The **Winter Carnival** in Stowe, VT, is fun even when it's freezing. Think seriously creative ice-carving competitions and zany sports events, such as snow golf and snow volleyball (www.stowewintercarnival.com). In February the **Rhode Island Spring Flower and Garden Show** in Providence kicks off the year with more than 30 garden displays and 250 larger-than-life garden marketplace vendors (www.flowershow.com).

Spring

On **Maple Syrup Weekend**, March in New Hampshire, more than 60 sugar houses open their doors to show you how maple syrup is made (www.nhmapleproducers.com). In Vermont, the statewide **Maple Open House Weekend** is just as delicious (www.vermontmaple.org). **Boston** goes green for **St. Patrick's Day** (March 17). The South Boston St. Patrick's Day Parade is rated as the second largest in the country (www.southbostonparade.org). The start of the American Revolution is marked in Concord and Boston on **Patriot's Day** (April 19). Volunteers dressed in 18th-century uniforms march, and pipe and drum bands play (www.nps.gov/mima/patriots-day.htm). **WaterFire,** in Providence, RI, a unique mix of crackling bonfires and music, lights up the Providence River on evenings through October (www.waterfire.org). Across New Hampshire, the state flower is celebrated with **lilac festivals**, such as the Lisbon Lilac Festival and the Fields of Lupine Festival, in Franconia Notch (www.visitnh.gov).

Summer

Stately tall ships hoist their sails and gather for the annual **Windjammer Days Festival** (www.sailmainecoast.com) in Boothbay Harbor, ME, in June; city folk party at the **Old Port Festival** in Portland, ME (www.portlandmaine.com). The 10-day **Discover Jazz Festival** takes place at venues all over the town of Burlington, VT (www.discoverjazz.com). For wide-ranging culture, choose the three-week **International Festival of Arts and Ideas** in New Haven, CT: you'll find stunning music and dance, theater, and more (www.artidea.org). In the build-up to the Fourth of July, **Boston Harborfest** is a week-long jamboree with concerts, tours and a one-day **Chowderfest**, with restaurants vying to produce the city's best chowder (www.bostonharborfest.com). But it's up, up and away for 25 balloons in Stowe, VT, with the annual **Stoweflake Hot Air Balloon Festival** (www.stoweflake.com). In August, visitors consume something like 20,000 pounds (9,000kg) of lobster at the world's biggest **lobster festival** (www.mainelobsterfestival.com) in Rockland, ME. But in Newport, RI, thousands flock to hear the world's top musicians at the world-famous **folk and jazz festivals** overlooking the ocean (www.gonewport.com).

Fall

In September, the **Seafood Festival** marks the end of summer (www.hamptonbeachseafoodfestival.com) at Hampton Beach, NH, while in Vermont, autumn is welcomed with the annual **Fall Foliage Festival** in six towns across the Northeast Kingdom (www.nekchamber.com). At Mystic Seaport's annual October **Chowderfest**, visitors taste the best chowder anywhere (www.mysticseaport.org).

Boston

Getting Your Bearings

What makes Boston special? Talk to ten people and you will get ten different reasons. Its history – the capital of Massachusetts is the oldest city in the USA, with a 400th birthday coming up in 2030. Its location – the city is bordered on two sides by water: the harbor and the Charles River. Its walkability – as in European cities, everyone walks everywhere.

In addition, Bostonians love the cut and thrust of politics, just as their revolutionary forbears did. After all, the flames of independence were fanned here more than two centuries ago. As one friend put it, "When you see candidates for governor holding a debate at Faneuil Hall, where Sam Adams sowed the seeds of liberty, it makes you proud to live here."

The city has other charms, too. Boston is a college town of the highest order. Harvard, the Massachusetts Institute of Technology (MIT), Boston College, Wellesley and Boston University are just a few of the scores of colleges and universities that call the

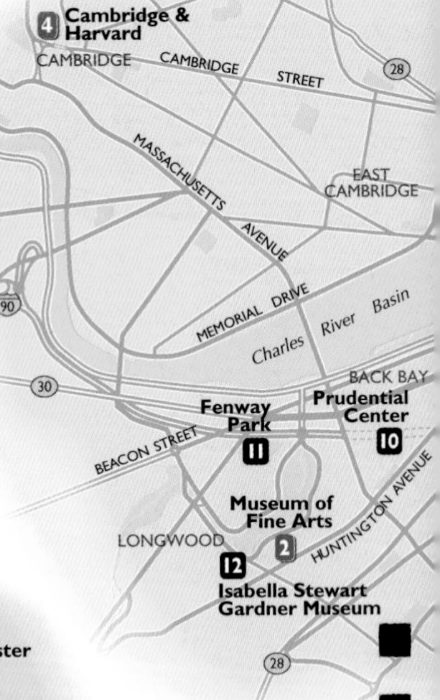

4 Cambridge & Harvard

CAMBRIDGE   CAMBRIDGE   STREET   28

MASSACHUSETTS   AVENUE

EAST CAMBRIDGE

90   MEMORIAL DRIVE

Charles River Basin

30   BACK BAY

Fenway Park   11   Prudential Center   10

BEACON STREET   HUNTINGTON AVENUE

Museum of Fine Arts   2

LONGWOOD   12

Isabella Stewart Gardner Museum

28

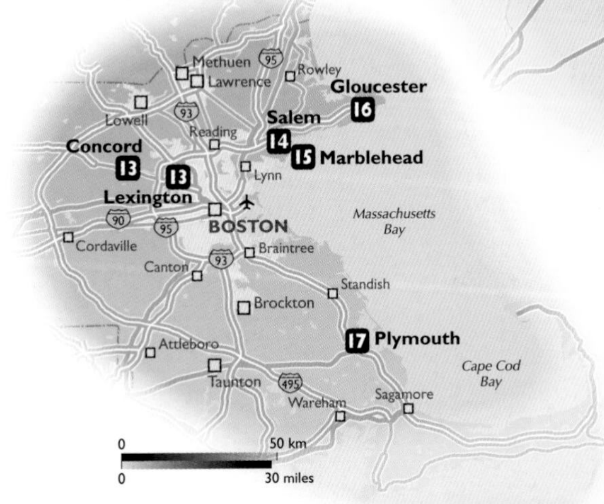

Methuen   95   Rowley
Lawrence
Lowell   Gloucester   16
93   Reading   Salem   14
Concord   13   Lynn   15   Marblehead
Lexington   13
90   95   BOSTON   Massachusetts Bay
Cordaville
Canton   Braintree
93
Brockton   Standish
Attleboro
Taunton   495   Plymouth   17
Wareham   Sagamore   Cape Cod Bay

0 ____ 50 km
0 ____ 30 miles

Previous page: USS *Constitution*, at the end of the Freedom Trail

area home. That means the city is full of thousands of undergraduates seeking enlightenment and entertainment. But it is also full of professors and other professional people who give the city a sophisticated air.

Most of the city's attractions are within easy walking distance, and the most significant Revolutionary sites are all linked by a red line on the sidewalk (the Freedom Trail). The historical flavor doesn't stop at the city limits, either. Plymouth, where the Pilgrims first settled, is less than an hour to the south. Within commuting distance to the west of the city are Lexington and Concord, where the first shots of the American Revolution were fired and where the Transcendentalist movement began a century later. To the north are Salem, infamous for its 17th-century witch trials, and the idyllic coastal towns of Gloucester and Marblehead.

In Three Days

If you're not quite sure where to begin your travels, this itinerary recommends a practical and enjoyable three days in Boston, taking in some of the best places to see using the Getting Your Bearings map on the previous page. For more information see the main entries.

Day 1

Morning
Beginning from Boston Common Visitors Center, follow the ❶ **Freedom Trail** (➤ 44–47) as far as Faneuil Hall Marketplace, soaking up some of the city's historic sights (including the State House, right) en route.

Afternoon
Wander around **Faneuil Hall**, Boston's old public meeting hall, and the surrounding Marketplace, crammed with shops and eateries, including Kingfish Hall (➤ 68), known for seafood. Follow the Freedom Trail over to Charlestown, then take the ferry back to Long Wharf.

Evening
Make your way to ❶❶ **Fenway Park** for a Boston Red Sox home game (➤ 59) if you have tickets. If the Sox aren't in town, check out the shops and restaurants along Newbury Street (➤ 71). Treat yourself and dine with a culinary star at No 9 Park (➤ 68).

Day 2

Morning
Take a leisurely stroll in the ❾ **Public Garden** (➤ 58) or go for a ride on one of the park's famous swan boats (left). If the weather won't cooperate, check out Filene's Basement, an attraction all its own, regardless of whether you're looking for a bargain.

Afternoon
Stop for one of the tempting sandwiches at the Parish Cafe (➤ 69), across from the Public Garden, then spend the afternoon at the **2 Museum of Fine Arts** (➤ 48–51). Afterward, if you have the energy, go to the **12 Isabella Stewart Gardner Museum** (➤ 60) two blocks away.

Evening
See the sun set over the city from the 50th-floor Skywalk (left) at the **10 Prudential Center** (➤ 58), then head to Top of the Hub (➤ 69) for a drink, followed by some of Boston's best seafood at Legal Sea Foods (➤ 68).

Day 3

Morning
Take the subway to the **3 Museum of Science** (below, ➤ 52–53), which kids will love and adults will enjoy more than they think. Be sure to catch a screening of whatever is playing at the gigantic Omni IMAX theater.

Afternoon
Head toward **Cambridge** and enjoy an alfresco lunch at Au Bon Pain on Harvard Square or sit elbow to elbow with the locals at Mr. Bartley's Burger Cottage (➤ 56). Take a self-guiding tour of Harvard Yard and the Tercentenary Theater at **4 Harvard University** (➤ 54–56), then visit one or more of the university's collection of art and science museums.

Evening
Stop at Harvest (➤ 70) for a meal, then take in Cambridge's music and club scene at any of a handful of local joints.

❶ The Freedom Trail

If you have time for only one Boston attraction, make it the Freedom Trail. This 2.5-mile (4km) walking tour not only takes you past several of the best Revolutionary War historic sites, but also gives a good orientation to the city as a whole. You will wander through the cemetery where patriots like Samuel Adams and John Hancock are buried, and navigate the narrow one-way streets they once walked. You'll see Faneuil Hall, named for Peter Faneuil, where the seeds of the American Revolution were sown, and the adjoining Quincy Market, a shopping complex that revitalized downtown Boston in the early 1980s. As well as touring the house in the North End where Paul Revere lived, you can stop for a bite to eat at one of the bustling Italian restaurants in Boston's Little Italy.

Toe the Line

There is no official "start" to the Freedom Trail, though most people begin at the visitor center on Boston Common. The red-brick line in the sidewalk links all 16 sites and the walk takes about three hours, depending on how many stops you make. Do it yourself with a map, join a tour led by a guide in historical costume or rent a hand-held audio player. Want a bargain? Head over to the Boston National Historical Park Visitor Center (15 State Street) and take a free guided tour with a Park Ranger.

Boston Common is the first attraction. Its 44 acres (18ha), set aside as parkland in 1634, are an oasis of greenery within the attractive, historic urban center of downtown Boston. On fine summer days, you will find people relaxing on the lawns or just soaking up the sun.

Walk up the hill to the gold-domed **Massachusetts State House**. Designed by architect Charles Bulfinch in 1798 – Samuel Adams himself laid the cornerstone – it's new only in comparison to the Old State House, erected some 85 years earlier.

The Massachusetts State House is also known as the New State House

Brimstone Corner

At the corner of Park and Tremont streets is **Park Street Church**. The church was known as "Brimstone Corner" not so much for the fiery sermons delivered within (although abolitionist William Lloyd Garrison did give his first antislavery speech here in 1829), but because gunpowder was stored here during the War of 1812. Next door is the **Granary Burying Ground**, the first (and best) of the small city cemeteries on the tour. The list of people buried here reads like a Who's Who of early American history: John Hancock, Paul Revere, Samuel Adams, Peter Faneuil and the victims of the Boston Massacre. There are many others, memorialized by gravestones that over the years have sunk halfway into the ground. The giant obelisk in the center marks the burial plot of the parents of statesman and scientist Benjamin Franklin.

Cross Tremont Street to the **King's Chapel and Burying Ground**. This was the site of the first Anglican congregation in Boston, and the adjacent burying ground is Boston's oldest.

Down **School Street** is the site of the country's first public school and Boston's old City Hall. The school's alumni include Samuel Adams, John Hancock, Benjamin Franklin, Puritan minister Cotton Mather and poet Ralph Waldo Emerson. The old City Hall is now a private office building, thanks to an ambitious 1973 preservation job that saved it from the wrecking ball.

Tea Time

At the end of School Street is the former **Old Corner Book Store**. Once the center of literary Boston (Emerson, Nathaniel Hawthorne and Henry Wadsworth Longfellow held forth here), it's now just a store, with no literary connections.

Half a block away on Washington Street is the **Old South Meeting House**, best known for the meeting on December 16, 1773, when 5,000 colonists congregated here to protest against the tax on tea, an uprising that resulted in the Boston Tea Party.

At Washington and Court streets stands the **Old State House**, built in 1713; the Declaration of Independence was first read to the citizens of Boston from the balcony. Although the new State House long ago replaced this building as the seat of government, the Declaration is still read aloud here every Fourth of July. In front of the State House, a ring of stones marks the site of the 1770 Boston Massacre, when British soldiers shot five colonists here, one of the fateful events in the buildup to the American Revolution.

Urban Renewal

Follow Congress Street downhill to Faneuil Hall Marketplace and **Faneuil Hall** (pronounced "FAN yull"). On your left, you'll pass architect Louis Kahn's brutally ultramodernist City Hall. Faneuil Hall itself is the public meeting hall nicknamed "the Cradle of Liberty" in honor of all the incendiary rhetoric that went on here in colonial times; Quincy Market is the collection of stores and restaurants that caters to locals and tourists alike. The entire complex is known as the Faneuil Hall Marketplace, the first, and still the best, of the Rouse Company projects across the USA that have turned abandoned waterfronts into successful visitor attractions.

Past Faneuil Hall, the trail takes you through a warren of lanes and historic buildings before crossing over to

North End, Boston's thriving Italian-American neighborhood, with dozens of restaurants lining the main drag, Hanover Street. **Paul Revere House,** at 19 North Square, is a highlight of the tour. For a nominal admission fee you can see the only remaining example of 17th-century architecture in downtown Boston; the house was 90 years old when Revere bought it in 1770. The short tour of the building's interior is informative and entertaining.

Bunker Hill Monument commemorates the first battle of the Revolution

To the USS *Constitution*

The next stop is **Old North Church**, best known for the two lanterns that shone here on April 18, 1775, to indicate that the British were advancing by the water, and not the land, route to Concord. In summer, there are regular "Behind the Scenes" tours, but you can just poke your head inside to see the closed pews encircled by 4-foot (1.2m) walls.

Up Hull Street on your right is **Copp's Hill Burying Ground**. See gravestones scarred by British bullets more than 200 years ago, and enjoy splendid views of Boston Harbor.

Faced with the prospect of a long walk across the bridge to Charlestown, tired legs often return to Hanover Street for a plate of biscotti and a glass of Chianti. Those intent on finishing the tour should cross the bridge and follow the red-brick road to the **USS Constitution**. "Old Ironsides" earned its nickname not during the American Revolution, but rather in the War of 1812, when British cannonballs bounced off the ship's oak hull. Try to get to the ship before 4:30, which is when the last free guided tour leaves, led by US Navy sailors in full period costumes. After that, you can take a self-guiding tour of only the top deck until closing. In the nearby museum, step into the role of a sailor and see what life aboard was like back in 1812.

Bunker Hill

From the *Constitution,* you can see the top of the **Bunker Hill Monument**, commemorating the first battle of the Revolution. If you still have the energy, you can walk the last quarter mile to the obelisk and climb all 294 steps to the top. Or you can just walk to the end of the pier behind the *Constitution* Museum and take the water shuttle back to Long Wharf, near the Aquarium T stop. The ferry journey is faster than walking back, cheaper than a cab (if you can find one), and prettier than a bus ride.

TAKING A BREAK

Faneuil Hall Marketplace is a good place to stop for lunch, a snack or just a cool drink on a hot day. Choose from seafood or Mexican fare; tuck into a sandwich or a full meal; eat indoors or outside. In fine weather, street entertainers liven up the scene.

➕ 196 C2 ❓ Begin at the Information Center on Boston Common, by Park Street Station

New State House
➕ 196 C2 ✉ Beacon and Park streets ☎ 617/727-3676 🕐 Mon–Fri 10–4 ✋ Free 🚇 Green Line or Red Line to Park Street

Park Street Church
➕ 196 C2 ✉ Park and Tremont streets ☎ 617/523-3383 🕐 Mid-Jun to Aug Tue–Sat 9:30–3:30; winter by appointment ✋ Free 🚇 Green Line or Red Line to Park Street

Granary Burying Ground
➕ 196 C2 ✉ Park and Tremont streets 🕐 Daily 9–5 ✋ Free 🚇 Green Line or Red Line to Park Street

Old State House
➕ 197 D2 ✉ 206 Washington Street ☎ 617/720-1713 🕐 Daily 9–5 ✋ Inexpensive 🚇 Blue Line or Orange Line to State

Paul Revere House
➕ 197 E4 ✉ 19 North Square ☎ 617/523-2338 🕐 Apr 15–Oct daily 9:30–5:15; Nov–Apr 14 9:30–4:15 ✋ Inexpensive 🚇 Green Line or Orange Line to Haymarket, Blue Line to Aquarium

Old North Church
➕ 197 E4 ✉ 193 Salem Street ☎ 617/523-6676 🕐 Daily 9–6 (telephone for winter times) ✋ Donations requested. Tours: inexpensive 🚇 Green Line or Orange Line to Haymarket

USS *Constitution*
➕ 197 D5 ✉ Charlestown Navy Yard ☎ 617/242-5670 🕐 Summer Tue–Sun 10–6; winter Thu–Sun 10–4 ✋ Free 🚇 Green Line or Orange Line to North Station 🚌 92, 93

Bunker Hill Monument
➕ Off map 197 D5 ✉ Monument Square ☎ 617/242-5641 🕐 Daily 9–5 (last entry 4:30) ✋ Free 🚇 Green Line to North Station, Orange Line to Community College

THE FREEDOM TRAIL: INSIDE INFO

Top tips Many people poop out before the last two stops of the tour, especially on steamy hot or blustery cold days. If you have your heart set on visiting "Old Ironsides," take a **cab or bus No 92 or 93** to Charlestown and start at the USS *Constitution*, then follow the trail backward into Boston.

■ **Plan ahead:** pick the sites you are really interested in. Choose, say, five of the 16 and do them in depth. There is a lot to take in so make sure that you don't try to do too much.

2 Museum of Fine Arts

The collection at the Museum of Fine Arts, Boston (MFA) encompasses the whole globe and ranges across the entire span of human existence. The quantity of its Asian and African art and artifacts is matched only by the quality of its European and American paintings. The holdings here are so vast and varied that you'll wish you had a week to visit, not just a mere afternoon.

The "New" MFA

Since the museum (always referred to as the MFA) opened in 1909, the collection has increased substantially. Not surprisingly, the building has seen several expansions over the years. Nothing, however, matches the massive five-year building project that was completed in 2010. The work of architects Foster + Partners, this transformation has resulted in a truly new MFA. Much of the collection has been reorganized and, with some 28 percent more space, works that were packed away are back on public view. So, even if you have visited the MFA before, go again.

There are many ways to "do" the MFA. You could concentrate on a single collection, follow the map from room to room, or wander at will. Or, join one of the free daily guided tours; some give an overall view, others concentrate on particular areas. Whether you enter via the Huntington Avenue Entrance or the State Street Corporation Fenway Entrance, head for the Sharf Visitor Center for ticketing, maps and other information.

John Singleton Copley's 1768 portrait of Paul Revere as silversmith

The Art of the Americas Wing

The focal point of the revamped MFA is the new **Art of the Americas Wing**. For the first time in its long history (the museum first opened in Copley Square in 1870), the entire collection of American art is shown together. It covers the whole of the Americas, from North to Central to South, with some 50 galleries spread over four floors.

Start on the Lower Ground Floor, where ancient and Native American art rubs shoulders with colonial American embroidery and silver. Peer at a **Mayan pottery vase** that dates back to around AD750; then admire the craftsmanship of a **1710 silver chocolate pot**. Of course, this wouldn't be Boston without a serious collection of 18th-century colonial art and Level 1 has some of the museum's star attractions. Pay your respects to Paul Revere, whose **portrait by John Singleton Copley** was unique in its time. Here, Revere the silversmith is portrayed as a craftsman at work, in plain white

shirt and open waistcoat, rather than in a formal portrait pose. The museum has several examples of his silver work, most famously his **Sons of Liberty Bowl**, an elegant tribute to fellow patriots. Both portrait and bowl date from 1768, seven years before Revere's famous ride from Boston toward Lexington, broadcasting the message that that British redcoats were on the march (➤ 61).

19th- and 20th-century Art

Level 2 is devoted to 19th-century art, with one large gallery a showcase for works by John Singer Sargent. His large painting, **The Daughters of Edward Darley Boit** (1882), is one of the highlights of the entire collection. Continue on to see paintings by Winslow Homer, such as **The Fog Warning** (1885), a classic depiction of a fisherman facing a dangerous trip home. Childe Hassam, on the other hand, is best known for his **Boston Common at Twilight** (1885–86), an evocative image of winter in the city.

Up on Level 3 is 20th-century American art, including **White Rose with Larkspur No. 2** (1927) by Georgia O'Keeffe, Jackson Pollock's large-scale **Troubled Queen** (1945) and Edward Hopper's **Room in Brooklyn** (1932).

The American collection also includes furniture, textiles, photography, drawings, prints and much more. As well as being beautiful, many of them have fascinating histories. Take the **Pictorial Quilt**, with 15 scenes from the Bible; it was stitched more than 200 years ago by former slave, Harriet Powers.

Top: The MFA's galleries are least crowded on weekdays during the winter

European Old Masters

The American collection alone makes the MFA one of the world's great treasure houses of art, but, there's more. For example, in the **Koch Gallery**, on the second floor of the Evans Wing, European painters such as Titian, Tintoretto, El Greco, Rubens, Poussin and Velázquez are arranged together in a single gallery (designed in the style of a European palace) by period, rather than by country, because their considerable influences crossed national, rather than chronological, boundaries.

Impressionist Paintings

One of the most popular areas of the museum is the second-floor gallery devoted to the Impressionist painters of the 19th century: Renoir, Cézanne, Degas, Monet and Pissarro. Students from nearby colleges congregate in front of Renoir's *Dance at Bougival* as part of their introduction to modern art. They compete for space with out-of-towners and folks from the neighborhood, who can come by anytime.

As part of the revamp, many works have been re-hung. Postimpressionists like Van Gogh and Gauguin are now grouped with Picasso and Matisse in the Rabb Gallery, devoted to 20th-century art.

Asian Collection

The MFA's Asian collection is particularly strong, with an exceptional selection of **Japanese art**. The range is tremendous, including wood-block prints by Japanese Ukiyo-e masters, lavish Samurai swords and Buddhist statues, paintings and ritual objects. Don't miss the Japanese Temple Room with exquisite examples of Buddhist art.

And There's More...

The photography collection includes works from the 1840s to the present day, with images by great names, such as Alfred Stieglitz and Yousuf Karsh. Children usually like the Egyptian rooms with their wonderful collection of mummies, statuary, gold jewelry and burial treasures from ancient tombs. The Nubian collection is notable, with monumental sculptures of Nubian kings.

TAKING A BREAK

The dining options within the museum are all good and priced to any budget. Least expensive is the serve-yourself **Garden Cafeteria**, which has a good salad bar and views of the Calderwood Courtyard. The **Bravo** restaurant is the most elegant and costly. For light meals try **The Galleria** or the **New American Café** in the Shapiro Family Courtyard.

Pierre Auguste Renoir's painting Dance at Bougival (1883) may be the single most recognized work in the museum

🚩 194 C1　✉ 465 Huntington Avenue　☎ 617/267-9300; www.mfa.org
🕐 Sat–Tue 10–4:45, Wed–Fri 10–9:45　💲 Expensive. Reduced-price entry for senior citizens and students. Children 6 and under free; aged 7–17 years inexpensive, but free at weekends and weekdays after 3pm; voluntary donation Wed after 4pm　🚉 Green Line E train to Museum of Fine Arts, or Orange Line to Ruggles　🚌 39 stops in front of museum

MUSEUM OF FINE ARTS: INSIDE INFO

Top tips As well as the 1-hour free guided tours, the museum offers a **"Three Masterpieces in Thirty Minutes"** tour, starting at noon Tuesday through Friday.
■ The Visitor Center has **"concierge" computers** that not only have everything you ever wanted to know about the MFA, but also access to a wealth of information on Boston. You can check out transport and travel sites, restaurants and historic attractions.

3 Museum of Science

This top-flight museum makes science not only palatable but fun for kids, science-phobes and even jaded adults. There are so many interactive displays that require you to pull, push, press, open, close, shift, slide, buzz, bang, hit or climb, it's practically a theme park.

You can crawl into a replica of an Apollo command module and pretend you're blasting off to the Moon. You can watch live presentations in the Gordon Current Science and Technology Center, in the Blue Wing, or mark the passage of time by counting the rings on a 2,000-year-old giant sequoia stump, or watch lightning being made in the Theater of Electricity (daily shows). Or you can simply see proof of the Earth's rotation in the form of a Foucault pendulum, which seems to rotate imperceptibly but actually swings in an unchanging direction as the earth rotates.

The museum is divided into three wings, the Red, the Green and the Blue. The museum is small enough for it not to matter which one you choose first; you can always go back and do the other two wings later. Just follow your nose to what interests you. Better yet, follow an enthusiastic child.

The most curious, and popular, exhibit is the **Archimedean Excogitation**, a 10-foot-high (3m) Rube Goldberg device that carries billiard balls up, down, in and around wire cages, over a stepped xylophone, through windmills, and back up again. The effect is mesmerizing, especially to young eyes.

The museum's exhibits explain science in an accessible way

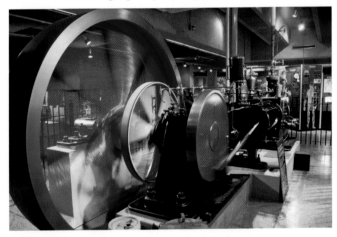

Youngsters will also like the **natural history dioramas** and realistic taxidermy animals in the Green Wing, while older brothers and sisters will gravitate toward an exhibit called **"Computing Revolution"** that covers the history of computers and lets you go "inside" one to see how it works.

Mugar Omni IMAX Theater

At some point during your visit, try to catch a showing at the oversized **Mugar Omni IMAX Theater**. The features here are shown on a concave planetarium-size screen that puts you right into the middle of the action, be it a climb up Mount Everest, a voyage under the sea or a trip through New York City. Features change periodically, but with two different films shown each day, there's usually something exciting for everybody.

Even the projection booth for the Omni Theater is worth a look. It is encased within glass, rather than tucked away at the back of the theater, so you can see each frame peel away from the gigantic 3-foot (1m) diameter reels. When you leave the theater, don't miss the **Soundstair**, which uses photo-electric sensors to play a different note each time a person steps on one of the steps. It can produce up to four sounds simultaneously, quite simply making music out of motion.

The Archimedean Excogitation captivates young visitors

TAKING A BREAK

Worth a visit just for the stunning view of the Charles River and Boston's skyline, the museum's **Riverview Cafe** (tel: 617/589-0125) is convenient and well priced.

➕ 196 A4   ✉ Science Park   ☎ 617/723-2500; www.mos.org
🕐 Museum: daily 9–5 (also Fri 9–9, and in vacation periods till 7pm).
Omni Theater and Planetarium: open until 9 or 10 most nights   💷 Museum: expensive. Omni Theater, the Planetarium and the Laser Light Show: moderate. Combination tickets that let you enter the museum and one or more shows are sold at a discount

MUSEUM OF SCIENCE: INSIDE INFO

Top tip Omni Theater **shows often sell out**, so make sure you ask for admission to the museum and a show (or two, if you have time) when you enter. Show up at the theater at least 20 minutes before show time to get the best seats.

Hidden gem The IMAX films are only some of the shows on offer; visit the stars in the Planetarium, and listen to great pop music bands at the laser shows. There are special prices for performances that begin at 6pm or later, offering savings of approximately one-third off the normal cost of admission. Make a reservation online via the website (www.mos.org) or telephone the main museum number (see above).

4 Cambridge and Harvard

Just across the Charles River from Boston is Cambridge, home to two major academic powerhouses: Massachusetts Institute of Technology (MIT) and Harvard University. Founded in 1636, Harvard is the nation's oldest institution of higher education.

Harvard University

Start your visit in Harvard Yard by the **statue of John Harvard**, in front of University Hall. Known as the "Statue of Three Lies," since it wrongly lists 1638 as the date of the university's founding, wrongly identifies John Harvard as the college's founder (he was a benefactor), and wrongly purports to be John Harvard. It was commissioned in 1884; undergraduate Sherman Hoar modeled for the statue. Rubbing John Harvard's left foot will supposedly bring good luck – notice how it's a lot more polished than the right one.

Above: Touching the left foot of John Harvard's statue is thought to bring good luck

Presidential Honors

Follow John Harvard's gaze across the Yard and you'll see **Massachusetts Hall**, the oldest building at the university, dating to 1720. During the Revolutionary War, it housed colonial soldiers. Today it is home to the offices of the university's president.

The remaining buildings on this quadrangle are dormitories housing most of Harvard's first-year students. If you visit during the school year, you can sometimes peer into first-floor windows and see what a freshman dorm room looks like. In all, eight US Presidents have studied at Harvard: the two Adamses, the two Roosevelts, Rutherford B. Hayes, John F. Kennedy, GW Bush and Barack Obama.

Below: Harvard University's Widener Memorial Library

Harvard is in Cambridge, just across the Charles River from Boston

The *Titanic* Connection

Behind University Hall is New Yard, a second quadrangle, known as **Tercentenary Theater** because that's where Harvard held its 300th anniversary celebration in 1936. Every June, the university's several thousand graduating students, their parents and all the graduate schools crowd into this space for Harvard's annual commencement ceremonies. The imposing building with the commanding stairway is **Widener Memorial Library**, named for Harry Elkins Widener, a 1907 graduate who perished when the SS *Titanic* sank because he was unable to swim in freezing water to a waiting lifeboat. According to undergraduate legend, as a condition of Widener's mother's bequest, she insisted that Harvard require every student to pass a swimming test before graduation.

Cultural Icons

Outside the confines of Harvard Yard, the architecture becomes more diverse, and visitors are often able to have a look inside. Some say Josep Lluis Sert's Science Center, across Cambridge Street at the north end of Harvard Yard, is designed to look like a Polaroid camera. The Carpenter Center for the Visual Arts, west of the Yard across Quincy Street, is the only building in North America designed by the French architect Le Corbusier (Charles-Édouard Jeanneret). Harvard also has several outstanding museums. Thanks to a major revamp, only one of the three art museums is open. The **Arthur M. Sackler Museum** has been reinstalled with some 600 of the finest works from the collections of the Fogg and Busch-Reisinger museums: Western art from antiquity to the present as well as Islamic and Asian art. The **Botanical Museum** (within the Harvard Museum of Natural History, 26 Oxford Street) houses the astonishing Glass Flowers exhibit, a collection of more than 4,000 replicas of some 800 different species of plants. Made of glass, they look like real flowers.

Harvard Square

No visit to Cambridge would be complete without an hour or two spent wandering through the neighborhood known as Harvard Square. This is not just a crossroads for undergraduates: everybody comes here, whether it's the chess players in front of Au Bon Pain cafe, the street performers in front of the Coop, the skateboarders who do tricks on the stairs in front of Out of Town News, or the young professionals in town for dinner and a movie at the art house theater. Harvard Square teems with life at all times of day and, in good weather, all through the night as well. Chain stores have elbowed out some of the family-run establishments that give Harvard Square its character but the vibrant pulse that comes with 6,000 bright, idealistic undergraduates remains.

Harvard's red-brick Botanical Museum

TAKING A BREAK

Mr. Bartley's Burger Cottage (1246 Massachusetts Avenue, tel: 617/354-6559), noisy, fun and full of students, is a classic among burger joints. If you like ice cream **JP Licks Homemade Ice Cream** (1312 Mass Avenue, tel: 617/492-1001) is local, award-winning and delicious, a stroll from the Harvard T-stop. Try Peanut Butter Chip: chocolate chips in peanut butter ice cream.

Events and Information Center

➕ 194 B4 ✉ Holyoke Center Arcade, 1350 Massachusetts Avenue, Cambridge, MA ☎ 617/495-1573 (events and information); www.harvard.edu 🚇 Red Line to Harvard Square

Harvard Art Museum

➕ 194 C5 ✉ 485 Broadway ☎ 617/495-9400; www.artmuseums.harvard.edu 🕐 Tue–Sat 10–5; closed public hols 💲 Inexpensive

Botanical Museum, at the Harvard Museum of Natural History

➕ 194 C5 ✉ 26 Oxford Street ☎ 617/495-3045; www.hmnh.harvard.edu 🕐 Daily 9–5; closed major hols 💲 Inexpensive. Free on Sun 9–12; also Sep–May Wed 3–5

HARVARD: INSIDE INFO

Top tip There are free student-led tours of the university, which depart periodically from Holyoke Center (tel: 617/495-1573), but they won't tell you a lot more than any guidebook. Instead, take the witty, tongue-in-cheek **Unofficial Hahvahd Tour** (www.harvardtour.com), led by students who mix facts with fun.

■ Avoid souvenir shops. Get **official Harvard T-shirts** at the Harvard Square Coop (➤ 71).

At Your Leisure

5 John F. Kennedy Library and Museum

IM Pei, who masterminded the controversial glass pyramid outside the Louvre in Paris, designed this glass and concrete structure, and JFK himself narrates the moving film that serves as the introduction to the short tenure of America's 35th president. Exhibits cover Kennedy's entire life, from the sailboat he navigated as a boy to the programs he initiated when in office.

The end of the self-guiding tour brings you to a room where news reports of Kennedy's assassination play in a loop, and to a glass pavilion, housing simply a bench, an American flag and quotes from Kennedy.

🚩 Off map 197 D1 ✉ Columbia Point, Dorchester ☎ 617/514-1600; www.jfklibrary.org 🕐 Daily 9–5; closed major hols 🎫 Moderate. Discounts for seniors, students and children 13–17; children under 12 free 🚇 Red Line to JFK/UMass, then the free shuttle (every 20 minutes)

6 Institute of Contemporary Art

Proof that Boston is not a city that looks backward all the time, this dynamic gallery is a major addition to Boston's 47-mile HarborWalk. The ICA displays ever-changing exhibitions of leading-edge works by national and international artists: visual art, music, film, video and performance. Cantilevered out over the waters of Boston Harbor, the building alone is worth the visit. The award-winning architects designed it both "from the sky down," as a contemplative space for experiencing contemporary art, and "from the ground up," with dynamic areas for public enjoyment. The museum also has a permanent collection, including works by Louise Bourgeois, Julian Opie, and Tara Donovan.

🚩 Off map 197 F1 ✉ 100 Northern Avenue ☎ 617/478-3100; www.icaboston.org 🕐 Tue, Wed, Sat, Sun 10–5, Thu, Fri 10–9; closed Mon, except hols 🎫 Moderate; free Thu 5–9 🚇 Silver Line to Waterfront

7 Boston Children's Museum

The giant 40-foot-high (12m) milk bottle out front lets you know that this museum is kids-oriented in every way, with touching encouraged (if not required). Joining in the fun is an inevitable part of every visit. Children can work off energy on the multistory climbing structure or carry out small woodworking projects at Johnny's Workbench, a workshop space for kids and adults. They explore the natural world in Science Playground: test the laws of motion with golf balls, create beautiful orbs in Bubbles. One of the most popular exhibits is still Arthur and Friends, where kids (and adults who aren't too shy) can see themselves on television. There are also exhibits replicating life in a traditional Japanese house, made from wood, paper and straw.

🚩 197 F1 ✉ 300 Congress Street ☎ 617/426-6500; www.bostonchildrensmuseum.org 🕐 Sat–Thu 10–5, Fri 10–9 🎫 Moderate. Reduced price admission Fri 5–9 🚇 Red Line to South Station, Silver Line to Courthouse

8 New England Aquarium

This harborside building is so much more than a tank full of fish and an IMAX cinema. Dedicated to conservation as well as education, it is a vibrant showcase for what lives beneath the waves, and is home to 40,000 creatures from 750 species. One highlight is the outdoor seal tank; another, the Caribbean reef set in a towering circular glass tank. From the dock outside, you can go on a Whale Watch (www.neaq.org) with a naturalist, or cruise round the harbor under sail aboard the *Liberty Clipper* (www.libertyfleet.com).

🚩 197 F3 ✉ Central Wharf ☎ 617/973-5200; www.neaq.org 🕐 Daily 9–5 (till 6 in summer; Fri, Sat till 7) 🎫 Expensive 🚇 Blue Line to Aquarium

The ever-popular swan boats in the Public Garden, an unmistakable sign of spring

9 Boston Common and the Public Garden

On a warm summer day, a crisp fall morning or even a bright winter afternoon, there is no better place to walk than Boston Common: Bostonians from John Adams to JFK have strolled this city-center oasis. There are scores of places for picnicking, sunbathing or daydreaming. At one time Boston's upper crust succeeded in closing the Common to the public, creating a private playground for the wealthy. But today it is inviting to all. Kids love to splash in the Frog Pond in summer or ice skate on it in winter.

The adjacent Public Garden, across Charles Street, may be even prettier than the Common. The season to be here is late spring, when the beautifully manicured gardens start to bloom and the famous swan-boat rides begin operating. The boats, which move at the same sedate pace as swans, are incredibly popular and you may have to wait in line around 30 minutes for a ride. Also in the Public Garden, close to the entrance at Charles and Beacon streets, are Nancy Schön's bronze duck sculptures, set on old Boston cobblestones. Inspired by Robert McCloskey's best-selling children's book *Make Way for Ducklings*, the statues represent the family of ducks that comes to live in the Public Garden. Mrs Mallard and her eight ducklings are a magnet for youngsters, who can't resist sitting on them.

196 B2 Bounded by Charles, Beacon, Boylston, Tremont and Park streets. (Public Garden bounded by Charles, Beacon, Boylston and Arlington streets) Swan boats: Jun 21–Labor Day daily 10–5; Apr 15–Jun 20 10–4; Labor Day to mid-Sep Mon–Fri 12–4, Sat–Sun 10–4 Inexpensive Red Line to Park Street or Green Line to Park Street, Boylston or Arlington. The Arlington stop is closest to the swan boats

10 Prudential Center

Until the Sears Building in Chicago was built, Boston's Prudential Center laid claim to being the tallest building in the continental United States (the taller Empire State Building being on Manhattan Island technically isn't part of the continental US and wasn't counted).

Although the Pru's boast about its size is mostly hot air, the 360-degree view from the 50th-floor Skywalk is nothing to sneeze at. On a clear day, you can get a bird's-eye view of the entire city, not to mention Cape Cod and southern New Hampshire. In a city built on 400 years of immigration, one in three of Boston's

The top of the Prudential Center is one of the best places from which to see the city

current residents was born abroad. Only New York has welcomed more immigrants. This is reflected in the Skywalk Observatory's Dreams of Freedom Immigration Museum. Journey through time watching the multimedia Dreams of Freedom presentation; appreciate how little immigrants brought with them for their new lives: a photo, a cup, just the clothes on their backs. See how a handful of English settlers were joined by Irish and Italian immigrants, and how that trickle turned into a flood. Boston now accommodates more than 160 ethnic cultures. Admission is included in the Skywalk Observatory ticket. For the best views, arrive about an hour before dusk, visit Skywalk for about half an hour, then go upstairs for a drink at Top of the Hub (➤ 69).

In the Pru's ground floor there is an upscale shopping mall, with a Saks Fifth Avenue, Lord & Taylor, and many other stores.

✚ 195 E2 ✉ 800 Boylston Street ☎ 617/236-3100; www.prudentialcenter.com ⊙ Skywalk: Mar–Oct 10–10; Nov–Feb 10–8. Stores: Mon–Sat 10–9, Sun 11–6. Restaurants stay open later than the shops 💷 Skywalk: moderate ⊙ Green Line B, C or D train to Hynes/ICA or Green Line E train to Prudential

⓫ Fenway Park

Built in 1912, Fenway Park is the oldest baseball field in the major leagues and one of only a few neighborhood ballparks remaining. It was carved into a square city block and, due to space limitations, the distance from home plate to the left field wall was too short for a legitimate home run. So a 37-foot (11m) wall, known locally as the Green Monster, was added.

The Red Sox play home games here between April and September and tickets are always hard to get. Fenway's tiny capacity means that there are no bad seats. Every seat is right on top of the field.

Take the "behind the scenes" tour to see everything from the trophies to the press box. The guides love

Fenway Park's small capacity means that every seat is right on top of the field

to tell the tale of Pesky's Pole, the dimensions of the Green Monster, and the significance of the numbers displayed high above right field. But you can never, ever tread on the grass. Tours (price: moderate) leave hourly every day, from 9am to 4pm, or till 3 hours prior to a game.

FOR KIDS

Children can quickly get bored at museums, but Boston has three that will appeal. **The Museum of Science** (➤ 52–53) and the **Boston Children's Museum** (above, ➤ 57) and the **New England Aquarium** (➤ 57) have interactive exhibits that practically beg to be touched, pushed, pulled or climbed on. A **swan boat** ride in the Public Garden (➤ 58) makes a welcome break from sightseeing (www.swanboats.com).

NEIGHBORHOODS TAILOR-MADE FOR STROLLING
- The red-brick and black-shuttered colonial town houses of **Beacon Hill** are quintessentially blue-blood Boston (▶ 174–177).
- **Newbury Street** is Boston's most fashionable shopping street. Its boutiques, stores, galleries and trendy restaurants are teeming with beautiful people and yuppies at all times, but especially on sunny Saturdays.
- **The South End** is the hippest area in town. You can see interior renovations going on from the windows along Tremont Street, which is now lined with bistros specializing in brunch and late suppers.
- Wander along some of the quieter backstreets of the **North End**, Boston's Italian-American district, around sunset and scout out the perfect restaurant for dinner.

✚ 194 B2 ✉ Lansdowne Street and Yawkey Way ☎ Ticket office: 877-REDSOX9. Tours: 617/226-6666 💰 Moderate for standing room, expensive for the best seats. Red Sox fans are passionate and tickets sell out fast. If you do want to see a game, the best option is to order tickets by phone, call 617/482-4SOX. On the internet, go to www.Redsox.com 🚇 Green Line to Kenmore

🔢 Isabella Stewart Gardner Museum

This museum owes its appeal almost entirely to the woman whose collection forms the basis of its exhibits; Isabella Stewart Gardner (1840–1924). She designed her home in the style of a Venetian *palazzo*, then filled it with 2,500 European and American paintings and sculptures. Her taste ran to Rubens, Rembrandt, Titian (*Europa*), Botticelli (*Virgin and Child with an Angel*), Raphael (he merits an entire room) and Giotto. She also displayed the work of personal friends like James McNeill Whistler and John Singer Sargent (whose portrait of Gardner hangs here), as well as Impressionists like Degas, Manet and Matisse.

As you walk through the museum, you realize that this was once a private home, and that one person amassed these rare treasures and actually lived amid them. The arrangement of the art remains as it was when Mrs Gardner lived here (but there are changing exhibitions). Sometimes it is hard to say which is more astounding, the house itself or the collection within it. The

manicured formal garden in the central courtyard is itself a work of art. On winter days, this bounty of flora is a reminder of lazier summer days gone by.

On Sunday afternoons from September to May, the museum hosts concerts, continuing a tradition established by Mrs Gardner when she first opened her house to the public in 1903.

✚ 194 B1 ✉ 280 The Fenway ☎ 617/ 566-1401; concert tickets 617/278-5156; www.gardnermuseum.org 🕐 Tue–Sun 11–5; closed public hols 💰 Moderate. Children under 18 free. Concert tickets $23 (reduced rates for seniors and children), includes admission 🚇 Green Line E train to Museum or Orange Line to Ruggles 🚌 39

The plant-filled central courtyard at the Isabella Stewart Gardner Museum is like a work of art itself

Farther Afield

🔟 Lexington and Concord

Both Lexington and Concord claim to be the birthplace of the American Revolution, but it was in Concord that the first shot was fired. On April 19, 1775, Colonial militiamen massed at the North Bridge and launched a volley into British troops who had been sent to destroy a cache of weapons in the town of Concord. On that day, the resistance officially became a revolution.

Today, both Lexington and Concord are prosperous Boston suburbs, with pockets of history sprinkled amid the modern drugstores, restaurants and other signs of 21st-century life. You can walk between most of the major attractions, especially in Concord. The Battle of Lexington and Concord is commemorated each year on Patriot's Day (April 19), but you can visit North Bridge any time.

The best place to soak up the colonial flavor, and to learn about the events of that fateful day, is at the Minute Man Visitor Center on SR 2A (between Lexington and Concord). Watch the multimedia program, which presents the British as well as the colonists' side of the argument, and walk along the Battle Road Trail that follows the route of the British soldiers in their famous red coats. The North Bridge, where the battle was actually fought, is in another section of the Minute Man National Historical Park, north of Concord.

Concord's second heyday came nearly 100 years later, when authors Henry David Thoreau, Ralph Waldo Emerson, Margaret Fuller and Bronson Alcott made it the center of their Transcendentalist movement. Houses belonging to each of them are open for touring. The most popular with many girls is Orchard House, where Louisa May Alcott grew up and upon which she based her best-selling novel *Little Women*.

South of Concord lies Walden Pond, where Thoreau went in 1845 in search of serenity. There is still beauty here (the park, the hiking trails and a replica of Thoreau's cabin), but the solitude Thoreau experienced is a thing of the past. Get here early on sunny summer or fall days, as parking is limited.

➕ 201 E1

Minute Man Visitor Center
➕ 201 E1 ✉ Route 2A, Lexington
☎ 978/369-6993; www.nps.gov/mima
🕐 Mid-Apr to Oct daily 9–5; Nov to mid-Apr 11–3 🆓 Free

Orchard House
➕ 201 D1 ✉ 399 Lexington Road, Concord
☎ 978/369-4118 ; www.louisamayalcott.org
🕐 Apr–Oct Mon–Sat 10–4:30, Sun 1–4:30; Nov–Mar Mon–Fri 11–3, Sat 10–4:30, Sun 1–4:30; closed Jan 1–Jan 3 and major hols
🆓 Inexpensive

Walden Pond
➕ 201 D1 ✉ On Route 126, Concord
☎ 978/369-3254;
www.mass.gov/dcr/parks/walden 🆓 Free

Visitors to Walden Pond can go hiking or simply enjoy the beauty that inspired Thoreau

🄴 Salem

Salem, less than 20 miles (32km) from Boston, is considered a day trip, but you might be tempted to spend the night because there is so much to do.

Salem's deep harbor made it a principal colonial port but it was the events of 1692 that gave Salem its place in American history: the infamous Salem witch trials resulted in the execution of 20 men and women.

Today, the city makes the most of its intolerant past, with several attractions revisiting some aspect of 17th-century life in Salem.

The best of the bunch is the **Salem Witch Museum.** The life-size audiovisual display gives a comprehensive account of the hysteria that engulfed the town during the late 17th century, including a re-creation of a victim being pressed by stones.

For a more interactive experience, be sure to catch a performance of "**Cry Innocent,**" a live re-enactment of the witch trial of Bridget Bishop, in which you play the grand jury.

As Salem was an important colonial port, it boasts a museum with a much grander collection than you would expect from a city of this size. The **Peabody Essex Museum** grew out of a society of sea captains who pledged to bring back items of interest – some might say loot – from their voyages around Cape Horn and the Cape of Good Hope. Admission includes tours of several historic Salem buildings. A highlight is the Yin Yu Tang, a complete Qing Dynasty house moved from China and assembled in the courtyard.

Finally, there is the **House of the Seven Gables,** which Salem native Nathaniel Hawthorne made famous in his book of the same name. It still has all seven gables, and is open for tours. The author's birthplace, originally on Union Street, has been moved here so that fans can do all their sightseeing in one place. The best place to begin a visit to Salem is the National Park Service Visitor Center at 2 New Liberty Street, or call the Salem Office of Tourism (tel: 978/744-3663).

➕ **201 E1**

Salem Witch Museum

✉ 19 ½ Washington Square ☎ 978/744-1692; www.salemwitchmuseum.com 🕐 Daily 10–5 (also Jul–Aug 5–7pm); closed public hols 💵 Moderate

"Cry Innocent"

✉ Old Town Hall, Derby Square ☎ 978/867-4767 🕐 Mid-Jun to Aug, Oct 9–31 daily; Sep Sat 💵 Moderate

Peabody Essex Museum

✉ East India Square ☎ 978/745-9500; www.pem.org 🕐 Tue–Sun 10–5; closed public hols 💵 Expensive

House of the Seven Gables

✉ 115 Derby Street ☎ 978/744-0991; www.7gables.org 🕐 Mid-Jan to Jun and Nov–Dec daily 10–5; Jul–Oct 10–7; closed early Jan 💵 Moderate

🄵 Marblehead

The self-proclaimed Yachting Capital of America, Marblehead attracts sailing enthusiasts from around the world, especially in July for Race Week. But the town offers much more than its famed harbor. Visitors can wander around the old town

The House of the Seven Gables was made famous by author Nathaniel Hawthorne

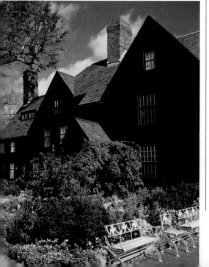

Gloucester was America's first seaport and fishing is still vital to the town's prosperity

and see its 17th- and 18th-century houses (many of which have a plaque identifying the original owner, builder and date of construction), shop in the quirky stores and dine in restaurants overlooking the water.

The best spots for a picnic (whether or not there's a sailboat race going on) are Fort Sewall, at the far eastern end of Front Street, and Crocker Park, at the western end. A walk from one to the other, even if you stop at every store along the way, won't take more than an hour. The town that once closed down after the summer is now less crowded and more attractive off-season.

🕂 201 E1 🛈 62 Pleasant Street; tel: 781/631-2868; www.marbleheadchamber.org

🔟 Gloucester

Founded in 1623, Gloucester was one of America's great fishing ports, as the tall "Man at the Wheel" fisherman statue on Stacy Boulevard recalls. Deep-sea fishing charters and whale-watching trips continue the nautical heritage, but, commercial fishing continues: the book and movie *The Perfect Storm* is all about the town. Gloucester is also home to the bustling Rocky Neck Art Colony, the oldest ongoing art colony in America. Winslow Homer, Fitz Henry Lane and Mark Rothko are just a few who found inspiration here in the past. More than 30 artists have studios here today; many welcome visitors.

Gloucester is the central town on the Cape Ann peninsula, and it has the best beaches. When Bostonians go to the beach for the day, they frequently choose to come here. Wingaersheek Beach, on the north side of town, is popular with families because of its gentle bayside waves. Good Harbor Beach, on the eastern side of town, fronts the Atlantic. Cape Ann Chamber of Commerce has information about all the towns on the peninsula.

🕂 201 F2
Gloucester Tourism Office
✉ 9 Dale Avenue and Stage Fort Park, where Routes 127 and 133 intersect (seasonal)
☎ 978/282-4101; www.gloucesterma.com
🕓 Daily 9–6

Cape Ann Chamber of Commerce
✉ 33 Commercial Street, Gloucester
☎ 978/283-1601; www.capeannvacations.com

The Man at the Wheel statue in Gloucester honors those who lost their lives at sea

🔢 Plymouth

On December 21, 1620, a group of 102 Pilgrims landed here, becoming the first permanent settlers in what was to become the 13 colonies. It wasn't their intended destination, nor was it their first landing (a lack of fresh water uprooted them from Provincetown, where they had stopped for about five weeks), and although the conditions at Plymouth proved less than hospitable, enough Pilgrims survived, with the help of the Wampanoag native people, who showed them how to grow corn.

The logical place to start a visit is Plymouth Rock itself, on the harbor at Water Street. The columned granite shelter that surrounds the rock was designed by the architectural firm of McKim, Mead and White in 1920. At first sight it may not look like much, but there are good historical displays here.

To see how the earliest settlers lived, visit **Plimoth Plantation**, a re-creation of the village as it was in 1627. Actors play the roles of 17th-century villagers, baking bread, planting corn, mending fences,

Right: At Plimoth Plantation, the life of the early settlers is re-created

Below: *Mayflower II*, a replica of the ship used by the first Pilgrims, was built in England and retraced the original voyage

splitting wood and shearing sheep. Even Governor William Bradford is on hand. A Wampanoag homesite is also on the premises.

The Plantation also runs the ***Mayflower II***, a full-size replica of the ship that carried the Pilgrims across the Atlantic. Located at State Pier, about a block away from Plymouth Rock, it is shockingly small – just over 100 feet (30m) long, or approximately one foot (30cm) of length for each passenger. Like the Plantation, it is staffed by costumed guides. *Mayflower II* sailed

from England on April 20, 1957, re-creating the Pilgrims' voyage. The journey shaved nearly two weeks off the 66 days it took the original *Mayflower* to make the crossing.

➕ 202 D2

Plimoth Plantation
✉ E Route 3 ☎ 508/746-1622; www.plimoth.org 🕐 Mid-Mar to Nov daily 9–5, 🎟 Expensive

Mayflower II
✉ Plantation, MA ☎ 508/746-1622; www.plimoth.org 🕐 Mid-Mar to Nov daily 9–5 🎟 *Mayflower II*: inexpensive; combined admission to ship and Plimoth Plantation: expensive

Where to...
Stay

Prices

Expect to pay for two people sharing a double room, excluding taxes

$ under $150   **$$** $150–$250   **$$$** over $250

▼▼▼▼ Back Bay Hotel $$–$$$

What was the Boston police headquarters in the heart of the Back Bay is now one of the city's newest hotels. The 222 bedrooms have high-quality showers and beds, CD players and internet access. Alongside the Stanhope Grille restaurant and the 154 cafe and bar is Cuffs, an informal Irish bar. Ideal for business or pleasure, with valet parking it is ADA accessible.

➕ 196 A1 ✉ 350 Stuart Street, Boston, MA ☎ 617/266-7200; www.doylecollection.com
Ⓜ Arlington Street

▼▼▼▼ Boston Omni Parker House $$–$$$

One of America's oldest hotels and close to the sights, the Omni boasts 150 years of hosting the rich and famous, from presidents and writers to movie stars. The lobby and the 550 rooms were renovated in 2008, blending modern amenities with historic styling. Parker House rolls and Boston Cream Pie were created here: both are still served in Parker's Restaurant.

➕ 197 D2 ✉ 60 School Street, Boston, MA ☎ 800/843-6664 or 617/227-8600; www.omnihotels.com Ⓜ Park Street, Government Center

▼▼▼▼ Bulfinch Hotel $$–$$$

Expect chic, contemporary styling at this mid-sized boutique hotel housed in a unique triangular-shaped building. The minimalist guestrooms are comfortable, with custom-designed furnishings and original art. The hotel is near the "T" and within walking distance of the North End, Faneuil Hall and Government Center. The hotel's Flat Iron Tapas Bar specializes in creative tapas with a range of international flavors.

➕ 196 C3 ✉ 107 Merrimac Street, Boston, MA ☎ 617/624-0202; www.bulfinchhotel.com Ⓜ Haymarket

▼▼▼▼ Charlesmark Hotel $–$$

Small and intimate, this European-style boutique hotel offers a great Copley Square location near the shops and restaurants along Newbury Street and Copley Place Mall. The 19th-century building was once a private residence and the 40 guestrooms are cozy and comfortable, with contemporary furniture in light wood tones. Amenities include free continental breakfast, wireless internet and satellite movie service.

➕ 195 E2 ✉ 655 Boylston Street, Boston, MA ☎ 617/247-1212; www.charlesmarkhotel.com Ⓜ Copley, Back Bay

▼▼▼▼ Commonwealth Hotel $$

Anchoring the revived Kenmore Square, this stylish hotel backs on to Fenway Park, and is close to Back Bay and cultural attractions. Among the luxurious 148 rooms, one is themed on baseball. Staff are professional, attentive and friendly. Eastern Standard (➤ 67), a Parisian-style brasserie, is fun, morning, day and night. Amenities include complimentary high-speed internet access.

➕ 194 C3 ✉ 500 Commonwealth Avenue, Boston, MA ☎ 617/933-5000; www.hotelcommonwealth.com Ⓜ Kenmore

ⓦⓦⓦ Fairmont Copley Plaza $$–$$$

One of Boston's architectural landmarks, the Fairmont Copley Plaza epitomizes the grandiose style of the early 1900s. The lobby glitters with gold, and huge crystal chandeliers hang from its ceilings. Over the years, presidents, high society and newlyweds have stayed here. Right on Copley Square, it is within easy reach of the main sights. The Oak Room is regularly voted one of the best steak houses in town, and the Oak Bar is famous for its martinis.

✚ 196 A1 ✉ 138 St. James Avenue, Boston, MA ☎ 866/540-4417; www.fairmont.com ⓜ Copley, Back Bay

ⓦⓦⓦ Hilton Boston Financial District $

Built in 1928, the city's first art deco skyscraper retains a feel of the past with all the latest innovations. Its business district location, 10 minutes from Logan Airport, makes it convenient for many Boston

attractions: the waterfront, Faneuil Hall Marketplace, the Freedom Trail, and the TD Garden.

✚ 197 E2 ✉ 89 Broad Street, Boston, MA ☎ 617/556-0006; www1.hilton.com ⓜ State, Aquarium

ⓦⓦⓦ Intercontinental Boston $$$

Sleek, 22-story twin glass towers face the waterfront, offering modern opulence with skyline and harbor views. Opened in 2007, this luxury hotel offers generously sized rooms with spa-like baths and the latest technology. Chic bars and restaurants include Miel, a French-style brasserie with a Provencal theme, and Sushi-Teq, serving sushi paired with vintage tequila. The 6,600-square-foot (613sq m) Spa & Health Club offers weight and cardio room, spa treatments and heated lap pool.

✚ 197 D1 ✉ 510 Atlantic Avenue, Boston, MA ☎ 617/747-1000; www.intercontinentalboston.com ⓜ South Station

ⓦⓦⓦ Residence Inn Boston Harbor on Tudor Wharf $$

On the water in historic Charlestown, this 168-suite, 8-story modern hotel is within walking distance of USS Constitution and Bunker Hill, TD Garden, the New England Aquarium, also the North End, Boston's Little Italy. Amenities include 12 allergy-free rooms, a heated indoor pool, exercise room, high-speed internet, coin-operated laundry and free Friday night Summer Movies on the big screen on the waterfront pier. A complimentary hot breakfast buffet is served daily.

✚ 197 D5 ✉ 34–44 Charles River Avenue, Boston, MA ☎ 617/242-9000; www.marriott.com ⓜ North Station

CAMBRIDGE

ⓦⓦⓦ Charles Hotel in Harvard Square $$$

The attractive rooms in this modern luxury hotel, a five-minute walk from Harvard university, are

decorated in Shaker style with plain furniture and hand-crafted quilts. Guests can use the fitness club, listen to jazz in the Regattabar, or try the Rialto restaurant, one of Boston's best. At the casual Henrietta's Table guests can enjoy an award-winning brunch.

✚ Off map 194 C5 ✉ 1 Bennett Street, Cambridge, MA ☎ 617/864-1200; www.charleshotel.com ⓜ Harvard

ⓦⓦⓦ Hotel Marlowe $$–$$$

This modern, eight-floor boutique hotel near the Museum of Science and Harvard Square overlooks the Charles River with some fine views of the Boston skyline. It is a great place for families to stay: rooms are funky and spacious with wireless internet and Sony Playstations to keep older children entertained. The stylish Bambara Restaurant serves American regional cuisine.

✚ 194 A4 ✉ 25 Edwin H. Land Boulevard, Cambridge, MA ☎ 617/868-8000; www.hotelmarlowe.com ⓜ Harvard Square

Where to...
Eat and Drink

Prices

Expect to pay per person for a three-course meal, excluding drinks and service

$ under $20 $$ $20–$35 $$$ over $35

🍷🍷🍷 75 Chestnut $$

Tucked between antiques shops, this neighborhood spot on posh Beacon Hill puts the emphasis on tradition and style. The room is intimate, with dark wood and comfy booths. Menus feature regional American dishes, with the best New England produce: chowders and crab cakes, thick sandwiches and beef stew. Yummy desserts are served in this popular bar. Reservations are essential.

➕ 196 B2 ⊠ 75 Chestnut Street ☎ 617/227-2175; www.75chestnut.com ⏰ Daily 5–10 (also Sat, Sun brunch Sep–Jun) 🚇 Park Street

🍷 The Beehive $–$$

A good example of Boston's bright, buzzy restaurant scene, the Beehive is in the Boston Center for the Arts. Part neighborhood cafe, part art gallery, there is regular live music. As well as a raw bar, the menu features modern American and Mediterranean-influenced dishes: cumin fried chicken tapas, a rich Portuguese fisherman's stew, grilled spicy tuna with couscous, and a popular brunch.

➕ Off map 195 F1 ⊠ 541 Tremont Street ☎ 617/423-0069; www.beehiveboston.com ⏰ Daily 5pm–2am, Sat, Sun jazz brunch 10:30–3 🚇 Back Bay

🍷🍷 Cantina Italia $

Celebrating 80 years in the North End, the Cantina has neon lights outside, a cheerful welcome inside. Order tried and tested favorites, such as *terrina di cozze* (mussels in a spicy sauce), home-made *bombolotti alla buongustaia* (Italian sausage, marinara sauce, parmigiano and goat cheese), and veal scaloppini with a wild mushroom sauce. Desserts include the ever-popular tiramisu and cannoli. There is a long list of Italian wines.

➕ 197 E3 ⊠ 346 Hanover Street ☎ 617/723-4577 ⏰ Mon–Sat 11:30–11, Sun 12–10:30 🚇 Haymarket

🍷🍷🍷 Clio $$$

In the Eliot Hotel, chef Ken Oringer creates dishes that would make New York foodies gasp. Take a starter such as roasted foie gras steak, which comes with spiced pineapple and a sweet-and-sour glaze. Entrees can be as simple as roast cod with figs or rack of lamb with a curry carrot broth. This is

one of the city's hot spots: prices are steep but service is attentive.

➕ 195 D3 ⊠ 370A Commonwealth Avenue ☎ 617/536-7200; www.cliorestaurant.com ⏰ Mon–Thu 5:30–10, Fri–Sun 5:30–10:30 🚇 Hynes/ICA

🍷🍷 Eastern Standard Kitchen and Drinks $$–$$$

The marble bar creates the feel of a Parisian bistro at this lively restaurant at Kenmore Square. The menu has something for everyone, from savory European entrees to shellfish and classic New England comfort food. Favorites include veal schnitzel, lobster crepes and juicy burgers. Desserts are rich, with cherry bread pudding, chocolate mousse and Boston cream pie. The bar offers classic cocktails, a range of beers and affordable wines.

➕ 194 B3 ⊠ 528 Commonwealth Avenue ☎ 617/532-9100; www.easternstandardboston.com ⏰ Mon–Sat 7–10:30, 11:30–2:30, 5–11 (Sat till 12), Sun 10:30–3, 5–12 🚇 Kenmore

Figs $-$$

One of four Figs restaurants, this has red-brick walls and a lively atmosphere. The freshly prepared Italian food includes salads, pastas, chicken parmesan, and an imaginative range of unusual pizzas, baked in the wood-fired oven. The fig and prosciutto pizza gets rave reviews, as does the white chocolate bread pudding with caramel sauce.

☐ 196 B2 ☒ 42 Charles Street
☏ 617/742-3447; www.toddenglish.com ◷ Daily 5:30–10, Sat 12–10, Sun 12–9 Ⓔ Charles/MGH

▽▽ Hamersley's Bistro $$$

The food here is what Boston's cooking revolution is all about. Chef Gordon Hamersley may be inspired by Europe, but the menu is pure New England, using seasonal and regional ingredients. Try the clam chowder prepared with smoked bacon, vegetables, wine and cream, or sticky toffee pudding with date-and-rum ice cream. The ambience at Hamersley's is less formal than a restaurant, but more plush than a bistro.

☐ Off map 195 F1 ☒ 553 Tremont Street (at Clarendon Street) ☏ 617/423-2700; www.hamersleysbistro.com ◷ Mon–Fri 5:30–9:30, Sat 5:30–10, Sun 11–2, 5:30–9:30 Ⓔ Back Bay

▽▽ Kingfish Hall $$

Celebrity chef Todd English's informal restaurant is a handy spot in Faneuil Hall Marketplace. His take on New England favorites includes local oysters, clams at the raw bar, classic lobster rolls, spit-roasted seafood skewers, as well as Thai bouillabaisse, wasabi-crusted tuna, house ceviches. Reservations are suggested.

☐ 197 E3 ☒ 188 South Market Building ☏ 617/523-8862; www.toddenglish. com ◷ Daily 11:30–10 (Fri, Sat till 11), Sun 12–9:30 Ⓔ Haymarket, Aquarium, Government Center

▽▽▽ KO Prime $$$

Chef Kenneth Oringer's trendy, sophisticated steak house transcends the ordinary. The modern furnishings and dark tones create a lounge-like atmosphere. The beef is top quality, with Kobe, succulent Japanese Wagyu and many more. If fish is more to your taste, try the King Salmon or Dover Sole. Rich spices, sauces and exotic mushroom side dishes create an adventurous culinary experience supported by an extensive offering of international and American wines.

☐ 196 C1 ☒ 90 Tremont Street ☏ 617/772-0202; www.koprimeboston.com ◷ Tue–Sat 5–10 Ⓔ Park Street

▽▽▽ Legal Sea Foods Restaurant $$

One of 35 nationwide in the Boston chain whose boast is: "If it isn't fresh, it isn't legal." The simple 40-year-old formula still works. The sawdust and bare tables of old have given way to sophisticated dining, and Cajun and Asian dishes sit alongside the New England clam chowder (served at presidential inaugurations), casseroled seafood, Legal's signature crab cakes and Boston cream pie. Reservations are recommended.

☐ 195 F3 ☒ Copley Place ☏ 617/266-7775; www.legalseafoods.com ◷ Mon–Thu 11–10, Fri–Sat 11–11, Sun 12–10 Ⓔ Copley

▽▽▽ No 9 Park $$$

An established star in America's culinary firmament, Chef Barbara Lynch draws on Italy and France for sophisticated dishes. Known for her depth of flavors and her skill at pasta-making, Lynch gives traditional dishes a modern twist: chicken with porcini marmalade, pork belly confit with curried pumpkin. The desserts are outstanding, and there's a good wine list. Lynch also runs hip (and less expensive) South End restaurants B&G Oysters Ltd and The Butcher Shop (at 550 and 552 Tremont Street).

☐ 196 C2 ☒ 9 Park Street ☏ 617/742-9991; www.no9park.com ◷ Mon–Sat 5:30–11 Ⓔ Park Street

Parish Cafe & Bar $-$$

Upscale sandwiches designed by notable Boston-area chefs are the draw at this casual eatery. Popular choices include the Schlesinger, created by Chris Schlesinger of the East Coast Grill, which is loaded with smoked ham, melted Monterey Jack cheese and mango chutney. Or try Joanne Chang's Flour BLT, with bacon, lettuce and tomato, on Texas toast with basil mayo. Soups, salads and a few entrees are available, along with martinis, wine and beer.

➕ 195 E2 ☒ 361 Boylston Street
☎ 617/247-4777; www.parishcafe.com
🕐 Mon–Sat 11:30am–2am, Sun noon–2am
Ⓔ Arlington

Sel de la Terre $$-$$$

You get three in one at this French-inspired restaurant near Faneuil Hall Marketplace: a restaurant, bar and boulangerie. In the restaurant, with its stone-flagged floor, expect Provençal classics such as Bouillabaisse, as well as New England produce prepared with a

French twist. In the bar, snack on pâtés and crab cakes, or just grab a coffee and a pastry from the bakery.

➕ 197 E3 ☒ 255 State Street ☎ 617/720-1300; www.seldelaterre.com 🕐 Daily 11–10 (also late-night menu Wed–Sat till 12:30)
Ⓔ Aquarium

Sonsie $$

When the weather is warm Sonsie's French doors open for alfresco dining on Newbury Street. The restaurant's eclectic menu includes monkfish scallopini and nori-wrapped salmon. Pizzas and focaccia are baked in the brick-oven throughout the day and as evening approaches the comfortable sofas in the lounge fill with martini lovers relaxing to the strains of classical music.

➕ 195 D3 ☒ 327 Newbury Street
☎ 617/351-2500; www.sonsieboston.com
🕐 Daily 7am–1am Ⓔ Hynes, ICA

Top of the Hub $$$

Fifty-two floors up, at the top of the soaring Prudential Tower, this is a

dramatic and romantic place to eat. The innovative American cuisine hops from prawns and shrimp with sugarcane and soma noodles to beef tenderloin and egg rolls stuffed with potatoes and lobster. Desserts include Grand Marnier ice, and warm chocolate cake. Sunday brunch is particularly popular; reservations essential.

➕ 195 E2 ☒ 800 Boylston Street
☎ 617/536-1775 🕐 Daily 11:30am–1am, Sun 11am–1am Ⓔ Prudential

BARS

Bleacher Bar $

Right under Fenway Park's bleachers in center field, the main draw is the big window looking onto the outfield. Filled with Red Sox memorabilia, this pub is a must for baseball fans year round. Go for the wide range of beers; all-American food: burgers, pastrami, brownie sundaes and frozen custard. There is live music on Fridays and Saturdays.

➕ 194 B2 ☒ 82A Lansdowne Street
☎ 617/262-2424; www.bleacherbarboston.com 🕐 Sun–Wed 11am–1am, Thu–Sat 11am–2am Ⓔ Fenway, Kenmore

City-Bar $

With its low lighting, large leather armchairs and sofas, City-Bar is a super-cool place to meet. Set in the Lenox Hotel, it serves both classic and inventive martinis, as well as rare single malt whiskies. But it is the unusual cocktails and champagne libations that pull in the younger set, who are keen to impress their dates. The American Spirit features Old Overholt rye and apple cider; the Emerald mixes kiwi puree with champagne.

➕ 195 F3 ☒ 61 Exeter Street ☎ 617/933-4800; www.citybarboston.com 🕐 Daily 4:30pm–2am Ⓔ Copley

Last Hurrah $

Beneath the Boston Omni Parker House (▶ 65), this well-known Boston watering hole was once the haunt of politicians from the nearby

State House. Nowadays, it's still a meeting place for influential young financiers at the end of the day. Apart from the cocktails, the draw here is Boston cream pie, which was invented at the hotel in 1855.

197 D2 🖂 60 School Street ☎ 617/227-8600; www.omnihotels.com ⏰ Mon–Fri 11:30am–1am, Sat 6pm –1am; Sun closed 🚇 Government Center, State Street

Sevens Ale House $

This local tavern with booths and a dartboard has been a fixture for 70 years. Regular customers come for the conviviality as much as the well-priced pitchers of ale. It is located just around the corner from the now touristy Cheers pub, on which the "Cheers" TV program was theoretically based. Beer and wine and plain food are served.

196 B3 🖂 77 Charles Street ☎ 617/523-9074; www.sevensalehouse.com ⏰ Mon–Sat 11:30am–1am, Sun noon–1am 🚇 Charles/MGH

CAMBRIDGE

🍴🍴 East Coast Grill $$

Chef Chris Schlesinger packs 'em in for his great grilled and spit-roasted entrees, oak-smoked pit BBQ, with mouth-burning sauces. Think slabs of ribs, platters of shredded pork, grilled spice-crusted mahi-mahi. But, there is also a top-class raw bar with New England's finest seafood, fruit juices and giant desserts. Friday hog roasts are a summer highlight.

194 B4 🖂 1271 Cambridge Street ☎ 617/491-6568; www.eastcoastgrill.net ⏰ Sun–Thu 5:30–10 (Fri, Sat till 10:30); Sun brunch 11–2:30 🚇 Central Square

🍴🍴🍴 Harvest $$–$$$

This has long been a showcase for the best of seasonal, modern New England cuisine, with dishes such as glazed pork tenderloin with shiitake mushrooms, fennel and sweet potato on the menu. Make sure you leave room for one of the tempting desserts. Choose

from lemon buttermilk tart with a blueberry compote and house-made cardamom ice cream, milk chocolate semifreddo, or coconut crème brulee with coconut macaroons. For a lighter meal, head for the outstanding raw bar.

194 B4 🖂 44 Brattle Street ☎ 617/868-2255; www.harvestcambridge.com ⏰ Mon–Thu 12–10 (till 11 Fri–Sat), Sun 11:30–10 🚇 Harvard Square

🍴🍴🍴 Henrietta's Table $$$

Serving breakfast, lunch, and supper at weekends, this is the perfect spot for outdoor dining on Harvard Square. This stylish bistro gives traditional New England dishes a contemporary twist, using the very best local produce: Maine rock crab cakes, chicken pot pie, peach cobbler, and a mouth-watering chocolate bread pudding sundae. Inside, expect lots of wood and fresh flowers.

194 B4 🖂 1 Bennett Street ☎ 617/661-5005 ⏰ Mon–Fri 6:30–11, 12–3, Sat–Sun 7–11, 12–3, 5:30–10 🚇 Harvard

🍴🍴🍴 Rialto $$$

At this special-occasion restaurant expect elegant Italian regional cuisine, using New England's best ingredients. Options could include orange-scented seafood brodo, whole-roasted fish and pan-roasted spiced chicken. Great value is the James Beard award-winning chef/owner Jody Adams' three-course, fixed-price menu.

194 B4 🖂 1 Bennett Street ☎ 617/661-5050 ⏰ Mon–Sat 5:30–10, Sun 5:30–9 🚇 Harvard

BARS

John Harvard's Brew House $

This is the flagship of the award-winning John Harvard's chain. They take their beers seriously here, with everything from All American Light Lager to a rich Dry Irish Stout, and seasonal microbrews.

194 B4 🖂 33 Dunster Street ☎ 617/868-3585; www.johnharvards.com ⏰ Daily 11:30am–12:30am (till 2am Fri–Sat, till midnight Sun) 🚇 Harvard Square

Where to...
Shop

DOWNTOWN

Downtown has changed in recent years, with **Macy's** (450 Washington Street, tel: 617/357-3000; www. macys.com) the sole department store. **Faneuil Hall Marketplace** (www.faneuilhallmarketplace. com) has three buildings. As well as T-shirts and souvenirs, there are more upscale shops. Try the **Boston Pewter Company** (South Market Building, tel: 617/ 523-1776; www. bostonpewtercompany.com) for pewter and New England scrimshaw, tableware and art sculptures. Select fine gemstone jewelry, fossils and minerals at **Geoclassics** (North Canopy, Quincy Market Building, tel: 617/523-6112; www.geoclassics. com). For gifts with a cultural flavor, there is the **Museum of Fine Arts**

gift shop (South Market Building, tel: 617/720-1266; www.mfa.org).

BACK BAY

Serious shoppers head for Back Bay. At the **Copley Place** shopping complex (on Huntington Avenue, between Dartmouth and Exeter streets; www.simon. com), well-known names such as **Tiffany & Co.** (tel: 617/353-0222; www.tiffany.com), **Neiman Marcus** (tel: 617/536-3660; www.neimanmarcus.com), **Louis Vuitton** (tel: 617/437-6519; www. louisvuitton.com) and **Gucci** (tel: 617/247-3000) are among the 100 stores. From here, you can take the skybridge to the **Shops at Prudential Center** (www. prudentialcenter.com). The two

department stores here are **Saks Fifth Avenue** (tel: 617/262-8500; www.saksfifthavenue.com) and **Lord & Taylor** (tel: 617/262-6000; www.lordandtaylor.com), but you will also find specialist stores.

NEWBURY STREET

Newbury Street, lined with shops, cafes and art galleries, runs from Boston Common to Massachusetts Avenue. In addition to famous names such as **Burberry** (2 Newbury Street, tel: 617/236-1000; www.burberry.com), there are the boutiques: **Serenella** (134 Newbury Street, tel: 617/262-5568; www.serenella-boston.com) stocks Italian cocktail dresses and jewelry. **Brooks Brothers** (46 Newbury Street, tel: 617/267-2600; www.brooksbrothers.com), **Cole Haan** (109 Newbury Street, tel: 617/536-7826; www.colehaan. com) and **Allen-Edmonds** (36 Newbury Street, tel: 617/247-3363; www.allenedmonds.com) rival

one another for high-quality men's shoes and clothing. **Ann Taylor** (18 Newbury Street, tel: 617/262-0763; www.anntaylor.com) is a favorite for women's clothes and accessories.

Among the art galleries are **Vose Galleries of Boston** (238 Newbury Street, tel: 617/536-6176; www. vosegalleries.com), established in 1841, for American Impressionist and Hudson River School paintings. **Judi Rotenberg** (130 Newbury Street, tel: 617/437-1518; www. judirotenberg.com) represents contemporary American artists.

CAMBRIDGE

The **Harvard Coop** (1400 Massachusetts Avenue, tel: 617/499-2000; www.thecoop.com) sells everything from books to clothes. Wander down **Brattle Street**, lined with small shops, but don't miss the **Cambridge Artists Cooperative** (59A Church Street, tel: 617/868-8434; www.cambridgeartistscoop. com), with work by local artists.

Where to...
Be Entertained

DANCE

The **Boston Ballet** (tel: 617/695-6950; www.bostonballet.org), which performs at the **Boston Opera House** (539 Washington Street, tel: 617/259-3400, www.bostonoperahouse.com), is one of America's leading companies.

THEATER

Old-style theaters include **Colonial** (106 Boylston Street, tel: 617/426-9366; www.bostoncolonialtheatre.com), **Wang Theater** (270 Tremont Street, tel: 617/482-9393; www.citicenter.org), **Huntington** (264 Huntington Avenue, tel: 617/266-0800; www.huntingtontheatre.org) and **Shubert** (265 Tremont Street, tel: 617/482-9393; www.citicenter.

org). In Cambridge, head for the **American Repertory Theatre** (Loeb Drama Center, 64 Brattle Street, tel: 617/547-8300; www.americanrepertorytheater.org). Hit shows sell out early. Call the theater, or contact **Ticketmaster** (tel: 617/931-2000; www.ticketmaster.com). For half-price tickets on the day, head for **Bostix** booths in Copley Square (open Tue–Sat 10–6, Sun 11–4) and Faneuil Hall Marketplace (open Tue–Sat 10–6, Sun 11–4) with cash (www.bostix.org).

MUSIC

The **Boston Symphony Orchestra** plays in Symphony Hall (301 Massachusetts Avenue, tel: 617/266-1492; www.bso.org), but you can hear the stars of the future at

the **New England Conservatory** (Jordan Hall, 290 Huntington Avenue, tel: 617/585-1260; www.necmusic.edu), **Berklee College of Music** (Berklee Performance Center, 136 Massachusetts Avenue, tel: 617/747-2261; www.berklee.edu) and **Longy School of Music** (1 Follen Street, Cambridge, tel: 617/876-0956; www.longy.edu). Concerts are also held in the **Isabella Stewart Gardner Museum** (► 60). For rock and pop, head to the **TD Garden** (tel: 617/624-1000; www.tdbanknorthgarden.com). The legendary **Club Passim** hosts live folk music (47 Palmer Street, tel: 617/492-7679; www.clubpassim.org) and the **Regattabar** live jazz (Charles Hotel, 1 Bennett Street, Cambridge, tel: 617/661-5000; www.regattabarjazz.com).

SPORT

Boston has three major-league teams: the **Red Sox** (baseball), the **Celtics** (basketball) and the **Bruins**

(ice hockey). For tickets for Red Sox games (► 14–17). For information on the Celtics and Bruins, call TD Garden (tel: 617/624-1000). The **New England Patriots** football team play at Foxboro, MA (tel: 508/543-1776; www.patriots.com).

WALKING TOURS

For themed tours, try **Boston by Foot** (77 North Washington Street, tel: 617/367-2345; www.bostonbyfoot.org) or a tour of the Italian North End led by chef Michele Torpor, **North End Market Tours** (tel: 617/523-6032).

Monthly magazines such as *Boston* and weekly free papers such as *The Boston Phoenix* give details of what is happening in the city. Alternatively, check out the Calendar section of the *Boston Globe* newspaper online at http://calendar.boston.com.

Cape Cod and the Islands

Getting Your Bearings

Cape Cod is one of the best and best-known beach destinations in the whole of the US. That's because it has everything. You can kick back on the porch and gaze out to sea; you can swim or walk the endless sandy beaches; you can cycle, sail, or go whale watching. Or you can explore some of the country's oldest communities, and shop for antiques, paintings and crafts. The main road, Route 6, splits the Cape (as it is always called) right up the middle. The Old King's Highway (➤ 178) is far more interesting, with its photogenic coastal villages.

Cape Cod is the kind of place people come back to year after year. Many of them rent the same cottage in the same town every summer, go to the same beach and eat at the same restaurants. And hardly two people will agree on which is the best beach, the best restaurant, even the best town. One thing is certain: you can have a great time weighing all the evidence.

White Islands Shores

Heritage Museums & Gardens

Sagamore

East Sandwich

Pocasset Forestdale

West Barnstable

Marstons Mills

North Falmouth

Osterville

West Falmouth

Falmouth

East Falmouth

Teaticket

Woods Hole

Vineyard Haven

Oak Bluffs

Martha's Vineyard

Edgartown

0   20 km

0   10 miles

Previous page:
Harvesting
cranberries

Left: Rocky
Neck Art
Colony in
Gloucester,
Cape Cod

Provincetown

Cape Cod National Seashore

Whale-watching cruises

North Truro

Wellfleet

Cape Cod Bay

Eastham

Cape Cod

Cape Cod Rail Trail

Orleans

MASSACHUSETTS

Brewster

Dennis

Barnstable

Yarmouth Port

East Harwich

West Chatham

Chatham

Centerville

Yarmouth

Dennis Port

Harwich Port

John F Kennedy Hyannis Museum

Monomoy National Wildlife Refuge

Nantucket Sound

Nantucket

Nantucket

Siasconset

To reduce your choices from the overwhelming infinite to a merely tantalizing multitude, this chapter concentrates on four areas where you might choose to spend a Cape Cod vacation. Chatham, located at the elbow of the Cape, is off the main drag and requires some finding, which means that nobody is there by accident. It still has the flavor of a small-time New England fishing village. Provincetown, at the very end of the Cape, has both great beaches and excellent art galleries, and it parties all night. It's artistic, friendly, and a good time will be had by all.

Finally, there are the islands of Martha's Vineyard and Nantucket. In general, the Vineyard is bigger, busier, and more liberal, whereas Nantucket is smaller, slower and more conservative. In season, accommodations can be tight in all of the aforementioned towns, so plan ahead. If you get shut out, the larger towns of Hyannis and South Yarmouth have many motel-style lodgings: what they lack in charm, they make up for in lower prices.

★ Don't Miss

At Your Leisure

In Four Days

If you're not quite sure where to begin your travels, this itinerary recommends a practical and enjoyable four days in Cape Cod and the Islands, taking in some of the best places to see using the Getting Your Bearings map on the previous page. For more information see main entries.

Day 1

Morning
Take the picturesque driving tour of **Historic SR 6A** (➤ 178–180). If you do nothing else en route, stop at the **9 Heritage Museums & Gardens** (➤ 87–88) in Sandwich and visit the car collection and art museum.

Afternoon
Have lunch at a clam shack anywhere along the Mid-Cape – try The Brewster Fish House (2208 Main Street, Brewster, tel: 508/896-7867) – or pack a picnic lunch and visit one of the beautiful beaches on **1 Cape Cod National Seashore** (➤ 78–80). Nauset Light Beach in Orleans, with its impressive dunes, is the most convenient to the end of the driving tour.

Evening
Find somewhere to stay in Chatham and head to Vining's Bistro (➤ 92) to enjoy your first seafood dinner on the Cape.

Day 2

Morning
Drive out to the lively resort of **2 Provincetown** (below, ➤ 81–82) at the end of the Cape, rent a bicycle and start to explore. Pack a picnic lunch and prepare to spend the first half of the day at the beach.

Afternoon
Bicycle back into town after lunch, grab a jacket or a sweatshirt and catch a **4 whale-watching cruise** (➤ 86).

Evening

Head back to your accommodations in time for dinner. Try Front Street Restaurant (➤ 93) for tempting Mediterranean-American fusion fare. Then sample the nighttime scene along Commercial Street. Stay overnight in "P-town," as the locals call it.

Day 3

Morning

Drive to Hyannis; leave the car and take the ferry (Hy-Line Cruises: www.hy-linecruises.com or the Steamship Authority: www.steamshipauthority.com) to **3** Nantucket (left, ➤ 83–85).

Afternoon

Check in on the island, then rent bicycles again or take the bus out to Madaket, at the western tip of the island, and watch the sun set.

Evening

Head to the fun, informal Arno's at 41 Main Street (tel: 508/228-7001) for lobster, shrimp, scallops and salmon.

Day 4

Morning

Rent a bicycle and pedal all the way to Great Point. It's great for fitness, for bird-watching, and allows you the freedom to pick your own private beach.

Afternoon

Back in Nantucket Town (right), have lunch at Something Natural (50 Cliff Road, tel: 508/228-0504). Then take a leisurely stroll on the cobbled streets or shop for jewelry and lightship baskets, or less expensive souvenirs, like T-shirts and hats.

Evening

Catch the last ferry back to Hyannis.

❶ Cape Cod National Seashore

For many people, Cape Cod doesn't begin until you turn the corner at Orleans onto the Outer (also called the Lower) Cape. That's because this is the beginning of the federally protected Cape Cod National Seashore. Less than a year into his term, President John F. Kennedy declared this 40-mile (64km) strip a national seashore, forever forbidding development along the sands. The National Park Service does a fine job of administering and maintaining the area, which extends from Chatham in the south all the way to the tip of Provincetown, though it cedes management to local towns at several of the beaches along the way.

Bicycling, hiking, fishing and even hunting (in some places) take place within the confines of the National Seashore, but it is the miles and miles of unspoiled beaches that attract the most visitors. Everybody has a favorite beach, and no two are exactly the same. Where you end up spreading out your towel and turning the pages of your summer beach novel will probably have more to do with where you are staying than anything else. If you're centered in Chatham, Harwich, Orleans or Brewster, you will most likely choose **Nauset Beach**, a thin finger of sand unconnected to the rest of the National Seashore, and accessible only by a single road through East Orleans. Its restrooms and changing rooms are open seasonally.

Near Eastham

If you're staying in Eastham, you can choose between two National Park Service-managed beaches: Coast Guard Beach and Nauset Light Beach. Both have restrooms, showers and changing facilities seasonally, and soft golden sands. Of the two, **Nauset Light** is easier to

Sunset at
Race Point
Beach, near
Provincetown

Above: There are fine views of the harbor and tidal flats from Captain Jack's Wharf in Provincetown

get to by car and is thus usually more crowded, the parking fee notwithstanding. If you like dunes, this is the beach to visit. Cliffs 100 feet (30m) high tower over the beach, which is reached down a long flight of wooden stairs. **Coast Guard Beach** has satellite parking (you have to take a shuttle bus from a remote lot), in season, but the beach is also accessible by an easy, pretty bike trail. This inconvenience discourages people who see easy-in, easy-out parking as a necessity.

Below: Enjoying Cape Cod National Seashore

Near Wellfleet

Wellfleet boasts several town-managed beaches, as well as Marconi Beach, named for radio inventor Guglielmo Marconi, who built his radio tower (now the historic Marconi Station

Site) just up the road. North of Wellfleet, the town of Truro manages several beaches along its eastern shore. The farthest north of these is no more than a few feet away from the Park Service's **Head of the Meadow Beach.** Although spending a day at the Head of the Meadow Beach costs a bit more than a day at the town beach, the higher parking fee gets you conveniences such as restrooms, showers and changing facilities. There are also lifeguards on duty in summer. Be warned: the ocean is cold here, even in August!

Near Provincetown

Finally, there are the Provincetown beaches, Race Point and Herring Cove. **Herring Cove** is popular with families and people with motor homes because of the snack bar (seasonal) and the long, thin parking lot that runs parallel to the sands. This is a great place to watch the sun set over Cape Cod Bay. **Race Point** may be the crown jewel of the National Seashore. It's got everything: steep dunes, soft sand, inviting surf, amenities like restrooms and showers, and a nearby visitor center to answer any questions about the local flora and fauna. There is also an 1897 Life Saving Station Museum. For many people, a favored way to spend the day is to bicycle to Race Point from Provincetown along the paved Province Lands Trail up and down through the surrounding dunes.

The waves at Herring Cove are gentle enough for children

TAKING A BREAK

Try **Moby Dick's** (Route 6, opposite Gull Pond Road, Wellfleet, tel: 508/349-9795) for lobsters, clam bakes and chowder. Open early May to mid-October 11:30–8:30.

Salt Pond Visitor Center
➕ 202 E2 ✉ US6 and Nauset Road, Eastham, MA ☎ 508/255-3421; www.nps.gov/caco ⏱ Daily 9–4:30. Extended hours in summer months; closed Dec 25 🅿 Beach parking: fee required from Memorial Day to Sep, weekends/hols; late Jun to early Sep, daily. Moderate. Pass good for any Park Service beach until midnight

Province Lands Visitor Center
➕ 202 E3 ✉ Race Point Road, Provincetown, MA ☎ 508/487-1256 ⏱ Early May–late Oct daily 9–5

CAPE COD NATIONAL SEASHORE: INSIDE INFO

Top tip On **busy summer weekends** (especially the Fourth of July and Labor Day), parking at any beach can be a nightmare. If you can, do yourself a favor and bicycle to the beach.

In more detail If you're staying in any of the towns around Hyannis, it's worth the extra few minutes' driving to go out to the National Seashore beaches. The public beaches along the Upper Cape are **often very crowded.**

② Provincetown

Ask some people about Provincetown and they'll tell you it's the gay resort town at the end of Cape Cod. However, they're only partly right. Yes, Provincetown is gay-friendly, but it's just as friendly as it is gay. Gays, lesbians, straights, couples and families love Provincetown because it is tolerant to all comers. The only people not welcome here are those who have a problem with all that tolerance. If you're not willing to live and let live, then Provincetown isn't for you. If, on the other hand, you don't care who is kissing whom, then come join in the fun.

Captain Jack's Wharf, which overlooks Provincetown harbor, is a popular place for visitors to stay

There are several Provincetowns. There's the **beach** Provincetown where most people can be found during summer days, sunning themselves on the sands, swimming in the ocean, sailing around the bay, biking along the bicycle paths or the quiet roads, or flying a kite on the beach.

Then there's the gallery Provincetown. Dozens of **art galleries** thrive here, most of them in the town's east end. Charles Hawthorne started his Cape Cod School of Art in 1899, and "P-town" has been an artist's colony ever since. Painters were not the only artists to be attracted to the area's natural beauty; Eugene O'Neill began his career as a playwright here, where the rules weren't as strict as those on Broadway. Other Provincetown alumni include John Dos Passos, Sinclair Lewis, Tennessee Williams and Robert Motherwell. The best among the current works of art are to be found at the **Provincetown Art Association and Museum** (460 Commercial Street, tel: 508/487-1750; www.paam.org), the **Rice/Polak Gallery** (430 Commercial Street, tel: 508/487-1052; www.ricepolakgallery.com) and the **Berta Walker**

Gallery (208 Bradford Street, tel: 508/487-6411; www.bertawalkergallery.com).

Finally, there is the action-packed Provincetown. Narrow-as-a-driveway **Commercial Street**, with its narrow-as-an-escalator sidewalks teems with people every summer night, and on weekends in the other seasons. Only the occasional presence of a bicyclist or a slow-moving car reminds you that this isn't

Provincetown lies at the very northern tip of Cape Cod

one giant pedestrian mall. Commercial Street is where all the action is, often continuing late into the night. Shops, too, stay open late, often keeping their doors open until around 11pm, to entice potential customers after they've had dinner. But, next morning, they may not ready for business until 10 or 11am. The strip is crowded, as people walk from one end to the other, browsing in the quirky stores, watching the performers in the clubs or on the streets, or just people-watching. There's definitely a gay singles scene going on here, but it's not dominant and you may not even notice it.

TAKING A BREAK

Right over the water, **Fanizzi's by the Sea** (539 Commercial Street, tel: 508/487-1964; www.fanizzisrestaurant.com) has marvelous views of Cape Cod Bay. Dishes range from seafood to popular Italian-American favorites. This is an excellent place for Sunday brunch.

➕ 202 E3 ℹ 307 Commercial Street, MacMillan Wharf, Provincetown, MA; tel: 508/487-3424; www.ptownchamber.com

---

PROVINCETOWN: INSIDE INFO

Top tips If you are looking for somewhere to rent a bicycle, **Arnold's Bikes** (329 Commercial Street, tel: 508/487-0844) is reliable and centrally located.

■ The **Pilgrim Monument and Provincetown Museum** (High Pole Hill Road, tel: 508/487-1310; www.pilgrim-monument.org), a 252-foot (77m) granite tower overlooking the town, commemorates the Pilgrims' landing here in 1620 (they couldn't find a source of fresh water, so continued on to Plymouth Rock). It provides an interesting diversion for a rainy day, but could never lure you from the beach on a sunny day.

Hidden gem If you can't decide between the beach and the arts, consider **Art's Sand Dune Tours** (4 Standish Street, tel: 508/487-1950, www.artsdunetours.com), which brings together the best of both worlds. These hour-long tours take you by four-wheel-drive through the Provincetown dunes of Cape Cod National Seashore. Along the way, you get to see the dune shacks where artists and writers, among them Eugene O'Neill, Jack Kerouac and Jackson Pollock, found inspiration. Tennessee Williams is said to have written *A Streetcar Named Desire* while summering in one such shack. Tours are from April to October and cost from $26 per person, $17 for children aged 6–11.

3 Nantucket

Unlike some places that are famous for what they have, Nantucket is appealing for the things it doesn't have. Traffic lights, for instance: there isn't a single one on the island. Every now and then, that makes for an infuriating intersection, especially when a ferry unloads another 30 vehicles ashore, but for the most part, the lack of traffic lights is a welcome reminder of Nantucket's lazy island pace.

There are few places as close to civilization and yet as away from it all as Nantucket. Although there is a one-hour high-speed ferry service, day-trippers are still a rarity. If you're coming to Nantucket, you're staying, and if you're staying, you'd better have reservations, because hotel rooms are hard to come by in the summer season – and expensive, even in the simplest rooms.

Most people willingly pay the inflated rates (also charged at the island's shops and restaurants) for what Nantucket does have: space. It may be the only place in New England where even in the middle of a holiday weekend, you can still find a stretch of deserted beach to call your own. Nantucket has more than 80 miles (129km) of beach, but only a few thousand rooms in hotels, inns and private homes. When you consider that hundreds of people are often crowded into the center of Nantucket Town, the remainder of the island can feel downright empty. Finding an unoccupied stretch of beach is easy – a 10-minute walk from any car park will do it.

Nantucket's cranberry harvest turns the island into an ocean of red

Island Living

A few days on Nantucket feels like an escape from it all. The cobblestoned streets in **Nantucket Town** look much the same as they did when this was the whaling capital of the world

(1800–30). Only the multitude of sport-utility vehicles on the narrow streets reminds you that you're not in the 18th century. Automobile traffic moves slowly, not only because of the rough roads, but also because of the pedestrians and bicycles.

Siasconset (pronounced *Sconset*) and **Madaket** are described by some as towns, but neither is little more than a couple of stores and a bus stop. Around the island, most houses have that gray, weathered look that comes from Cape Cod sea air spraying against cedar shingles for years on end.

A long finger of sand leads out to the lighthouse at Great Point, overlooking Nantucket Sound

Nantucket's Beaches

Nantucket's beaches also have the timeless look of summer about them. Children's Beach, Jetties Beach and Dionis Beach, all on the north (Nantucket Sound) side of the island, are popular with families for their soft sand, mild surf and plentiful facilities. Jetties even has a food stand and beach-chair rentals, as well as Fourth of July fireworks festivities.

Nantucket's south side, facing the Atlantic Ocean, has stronger surf and fewer young families along its sands. Surfside Beach is popular with teenagers and young adults, whereas Madaket (at the west end of the island) and Siasconset (on the east end) are usually quieter options. All three beaches have lifeguards and facilities – and the surf at Madaket and Siasconset can be heavy. However, although care should always be taken, it is not exceedingly dangerous.

Beyond these beaches are miles of shoreline with no names at all. Most of these are strewn along either side of the long finger of sand that leads to **Great Point**. Cycle or take a 2.5-hour Natural History Tour run by the Trustees of Reservations (tel: 508/228-6799; www.thetrustees.org) in an over-sand vehicle, across the salt marsh to see oyster catchers, ospreys and even seals and rare piping plovers – expensive but worth it.

Harvesting cranberries, a Cape specialty

Cranberry Harvest

An especially lovely time on Nantucket is October, when the **cranberry bogs** are flooded and turn into a brilliant blood-red sea as the fruits float to the top to be harvested. To see this colorful spectacle, contact the Nantucket Island Chamber of Commerce, or the Nantucket Conservation Foundation (tel: 508/228-2884, www.nantucketconservations.org), which maintains a small cranberry bog. The glory days of production, when annual harvests reached 3 million pounds (1.3 million kg) of fruit, are gone, but the tradition continues. Nantucket is rarely crowded at this time of year, so you may not even need hotel reservations.

Gray, cedar-shingle buildings in the charming village of Siasconset in southeastern Nantucket

TAKING A BREAK

At the **Even Keel Cafe** (40 Main Street, tel: 508/228-1979; www.evenkeelcafe.com), right in the heart of Nantucket Town, you can have a quick coffee or soup and a sandwich. In summer there are tables outside at the back. Alternatively, try **The Rope Walk** (1 Straight Wharf, tel: 508/228-8886; www.theropewalk.com). You can't beat the setting of this place – at the end of the pier, overlooking the water – and there is a daily raw bar for the freshest seafoood.

➕ 202 E1 ℹ️ Zero Main Street, Nantucket, MA; tel: 508/228-1700; www.nantucketchamber.org

NANTUCKET: INSIDE INFO

Top tips Leave the car in Hyannis and **travel to Nantucket by ferry**. Whether you go with Hy-Line Cruises (www.hy-linecruises.com) or the Steamship Authority (www.steamshipauthority.com), you must book early in summer.

■ The island has 12 well-maintained **bicycle paths**, covering 30-plus miles (48km). With locations at both ferry wharves, the Nantucket Bike Shop (tel: 508/228-1999; www.nantucketbikeshop.com) will rent you wheels for the day or the week.

■ For **car rental**, Hertz (tel: 800/654-3131, 508/228-9421; www.hertz.com), Nantucket Windmill (tel: 800/228-1227, 508/228-1227; www.nantucketautorental.com) and Nantucket Island Rent a Car (tel: 800/508-9972, 508/228-9989; www.nantucketislandrentacar.com) all have offices at the airport. Affordable Rentals (tel: 508/228-3501; www.affrentals.com) is downtown.

Hidden gem Sanford Farm is a nature preserve with more than 6 miles (10km) of walking trails to a deserted beach (www.nantucketconservation.org). The flat 3-mile (5km) walk from the parking lot to the beach takes about an hour. You can also reach the same beach by driving to the end of Hummock Pond Road and walking west about a half mile (0.8km).

At Your Leisure

❹ Whale-watching Cruises

There are so many humpback and finback whales feeding in the waters off Provincetown that several whale-watching cruise companies guarantee sightings (you get a free rain check if you don't see one). This doesn't ensure that you'll see a humpback breach 20 feet (6m) into the air, but you almost certainly will see whales. You might also see dolphins, seabirds and other marine life along the way.

Several companies offer cruises of varying lengths from MacMillan Pier in Provincetown. **Dolphin Fleet Whalewatch** has been in business the longest (since 1975). Its ships carry a team of researchers from the Center for Coastal Studies, who serve as guides to the whales and their habitats. As with other cruises, their boats have a well-stocked bar on board.

It can get cold, wet and rough on whale-watching cruises. Bring a rainjacket, a sweater and motion-

Every summer humpback whales come to the rich feeding grounds off Provincetown

sickness pills if you get seasick easily – and don't forget binoculars.

Dolphin Fleet Whalewatch of Provincetown

➕ 202 E3 ✉ Information and tickets: 307 Commercial Street, by MacMillan Pier departure point, Provincetown, MA ☎ 800/826-9300, 508/240-3636; www.whalewatch.com 🕐 Mid-Apr to Oct 2–10 sailings daily 💰 Expensive. Children under 5 free

❺ Cape Cod Rail Trail

What better fate for an abandoned railroad bed than to be paved over and turned into a bicycle path! The Cape Cod Rail Trail meanders for 26 miles (42km), from Route 134 in South Dennis through Harwich, Brewster, Orleans, Eastham and South Wellfleet, with a spur down to Chatham. It is one of the prettiest ways to see any or all of these Mid-Cape towns. The trail also intersects other trails that lead to town shopping areas or the beach.

Each of the towns on the Cape has bicycle rental shops, so it is fairly easy to find. **Idle Times** has four

locations near the Rail Trail, where you can rent helmets, baby seats, car racks and trailers. They have free parking at all their locations.

🚏 202 E2 ☎ 508/896-3491 for information; www.mass.gov/dcr

Idle Times Bike Shop

🚏 202 E2 ✉ Town Center Plaza, 4550 Route 6, North Eastham, MA. Summer-only locations in Orleans, Wellfleet and on Bracket Road in North Eastham ☎ 508/255-8281; www.idletimesbikes.com 🕐 Daily 9–5 (summer-only locations Memorial Day–Labor Day) 🚲 4-hour, 8-hour, 24-hour and week rental available. Rates become relatively less expensive the longer the rental period. Discounts for children's bikes

6 Chatham

Tucked away at the very bottom of the elbow of the Cape is the upscale town of Chatham. Nobody passes through Chatham on their way to somewhere else – you'd never find the town if you weren't looking for it – and that's one reason so many people love it. Chatham feels like an authentic Cape Cod town. It still supports a viable (though struggling) commercial fishing fleet, and its Main Street still has more quirky, individually owned shops than T-shirt emporiums. Every Friday night in summer, there's a free band concert in Kate Gould Park. The talent is mostly local musicians, but the crowds (often in the thousands) come from all over. Vacationers from around the Cape make a special trip for these concerts, so come early.

Chatham is also the jumping-off point for the Monomoy National Wildlife Refuge (► below).

🚏 202 E2 ℹ Main Street, Chatham, MA; tel: 800/71-5567 or 508/945-5199; www.chathaminfo.com

7 Monomoy National Wildlife Refuge

Monomoy Island is serious bird-watching territory, attracting more than 300 species of migratory birds. Harbor seals also favor the area, and this is one of the best places on the Atlantic Coast to see gray seals.

To get to the 2,750-acre (1,110ha) refuge, head for the Chatham Lighthouse and continue to Morris Island. Here, the visitor center has maps and information on the wildlife, including lists of birds. From here, the Monomoy Island Ferry (508/237-0420; www.monomoyislandferry.com) will get you to the island and back again. The service runs from mid-May until mid-October. Phone ahead to confirm sailing times.

Monomoy National Wildlife Refuge

🚏 202 E2 ✉ Wikis Way, Morris Island, Chatham, MA ☎ 508/945-0594; www.fws.gov/northeast/monomoy

8 John F. Kennedy Hyannis Museum

The Kennedy Dynasty may be fading, but John F. Kennedy still holds a special place in many hearts. "JFK" vacationed just outside Hyannis, where a small downtown museum pays tribute to the 35th President. Part of its appeal is its simplicity: some 80 photographs covering the years between 1934 and 1963, from his teenage years to his assassination. There is also a video narrated by Walter Cronkite.

🚏 202 E2 ✉ 397 Main Street, Hyannis, MA ☎ 508/790-3077; www.jfkhyannismuseum.org 🕐 Memorial Day–Oct Mon–Sat 9–5, Sun 12–5; mid-Apr to Memorial Day, Nov–Dec Mon–Sat 10–4, Sun 12–4 🎟 Inexpensive

9 Heritage Museums & Gardens

Part museum, part formal gardens and part miscellaneous collection, Heritage Museums & Gardens is full of surprises. As you wander through the 100 acres (40ha), what you see reflects the eclectic interests of founder, JK Lilly III and his family. Take the Old East Windmill; built in Orleans in 1800 to grind grain, it was taken apart, moved and re-assembled here. Then, there is the antique automobile museum housed in a replica of the round barn from Hancock Shaker Village (► 103–104). Among the interesting exhibits there's a 1913 Model T, a

1930 Duesenberg Model J and several other vehicles dating back to when cars were called horseless carriages. All are in pristine condition. In the gardens, something is almost always in bloom, be it daylilies, heather or the famous Dexter rhododendrons. Young kids will love riding the restored 1912 carousel (which is free!) and their parents will marvel at the antique wooden animals on display – not just lions and tigers and bears, but the more unusual pigs, deer, ostriches, zebras, cats and frogs.
➕ 202 D2 ✉ 67 Grove Street, Sandwich, MA ☎ 508/888-3300; www.heritagemuseumsandgardens.org ⏱ Apr–Oct daily 10–5 💲 Moderate. Half-price for children aged 6–16, children under 5 free. Free parking 🍴 Blossoms Cafe

🔟 Martha's Vineyard

Martha's Vineyard is bigger, more popular and closer to the rest of Cape Cod than its neighbor Nantucket – an advantage or a disadvantage depending on your point of view.

The primary attraction, as on Nantucket, is the beach, and in summer the population swells with folks looking to spend time by the cool ocean breezes. Tourists mainly stay on the "down-island" side of the Vineyard, where the three towns each have their own quirky character. Vineyard Haven is the year-round

Edgartown, on the eastern coast of Martha's Vineyard, is popular with visitors

ferry port, where the Black Dog Tavern (Beach Street Extension, 508/693-9223) is known as much for the T-shirts with the canine logo as for the food. Posh Edgartown has galleries, swanky shops and handsome 19th-century homes. Take a walking tour for the scoop on locals back in the days of hoop skirts and top hats. As for Oak Bluffs, with its cafes and live music venues, it's hard to believe that this village dates back to Methodist Church camp meetings. What started in 1835 with tents grew into a community of 300 small cottages, each trying to outdo its neighbors for fanciful molding and flowers galore. The Flying Horses Carousel has been delighting children here since 1884.

However, you might also want to range farther out on the island to linger on remote beaches known only by Vineyard veterans, bicycle through the seemingly out-of-place Correllus State Forest, take the even smaller ferry to the even smaller island of Chappaquiddick, or visit the picturesque fishing village of Menemsha. Whatever you do, don't leave without seeing the cliffs at Aquinnah, a stretch of marvelously colorful clay cliffs on the island's far western shore. At different times of day, the cliffs can appear red, orange, white and even blue, and erosion often turns the surrounding water a murky cinnamon color.

Getting to the Vineyard requires a ferry ride of around 45 minutes. The only year-round ferry link to the Vineyard is the Steamship Authority's 45-minute service from Woods Hole (www.steamshipauthority.com). This is also the only one that takes vehicles. Seasonal passenger ferries are from Hyannis (Hy-Line: www.hy-linecruises.com), Falmouth (Island Queen: www.islandqueen. com; Falmouth Edgartown Ferry: www.falmouthferry.com; Patriot Too: www.patriotpartyboats.com), New Bedford (SeaStreak/Martha's Vineyard: www.mvexpressferry.com), Quonset Point, RI (Martha's Vineyard Fast Ferry:

www.vineyardfastferry.com) and New York City (Seastreak: www.seastreak.com).

Alternatively, if you're not a sea-lover, you can fly year-round to Martha's Vineyard Airport with Cape Air (www.capeair.net) from Boston, Hyannis, New Bedford and Nantucket. In season, there is also a service from Providence.

➕ 202 D1 🚹 Beach Road, Vineyard Haven, MA; tel: 508/693-0085; www.mvy.com

Oak Bluffs, on Martha's Vineyard, is noted for its historic gingerbread cottages

FOR KIDS

■ The **Woods Hole Science Aquarium** (Water Street, tel: 508/495-2001; http://aquarium.nefsc.noaa.gov; open Jun–Aug Tue–Sat 11–4, Sep–May Mon–Fri 11–4), in Woods Hole at the southern end of the Cape, is a favorite with young kids. They can get their hands wet and feel what's in the ocean in the touch tanks, and watch the seals being fed at the country's oldest aquarium. Admission is free.

■ Or, head for the **Cape Cod Museum of Natural History** (869 Main Street, Brewster, tel: 508/896-3867; www.ccmnh.org; open Jun–Sep daily 9:30–4; Apr, May, Oct–Dec Wed–Sun 11–3; Feb, Mar Thu–Sun 11–3). As well as displays on the local flora and fauna, the aquarium has 65 marine creatures native to Cape Cod, ranging from eels and painted turtles to moon jellies. Learn all about whales; it's great preparation before a whale-watching trip. Admission is inexpensive.

Where to... Stay

Prices

Expect to pay for two people sharing a double room, excluding taxes
$ under $150 $$ $150–$250 $$$ over $250

SANDWICH

▽▽▽▽ Isaiah Jones Homestead $$–$$$

Romance is always in the air at this 160-year-old Victorian house, with its elegant wood paneling and fine antiques. Guests love the thoughtful details, from fluffy robes to fresh flowers and high-quality sheets. Several of the seven rooms have working fireplaces and whirlpool baths. The gardens are elegant and the Carriage House has two suites.

🚹 202 D2 ☒ 165 Main Street, Sandwich MA ☏ 800/526-1625 or 508/888-9115; www.isaiahjones.com

CHATHAM

▽▽▽▽ Captain's House Inn $$–$$$

The inn was built in 1839 by the captain of a clipper ship for his young bride-to-be. Today, it is the perfect place for visitors in search of a romantic getaway. Its grounds include an English garden, a herb garden and fountains. There are 16 rooms in the Main House, former Carriage House and Stables. Rooms are beautifully appointed.

🚹 202 E2 ☒ 369–377 Old Harbor Road, Chatham, MA ☏ 800/315-0728 or 508/945-0127; www.captainshouseinn.com

an outstanding collection of Waterford Crystal. With 16 rooms in six buildings, you can stay in the Main Inn or Converted Barn, Spa Penthouse or the cute Salt Box Cottage. At the inn's stylish Spa and Wellness Center guests can work up a sweat in the fitness facility and then enjoy a range of relaxing treatments.

🚹 202 E2 ☒ 220 Bridge Road, Eastham, MA ☏ 800/440-1281 or 508/255-0617; www.whalewalkinn.com

EASTHAM

▽▽▽▽ Penny House Inn $$–$$$

This luxury bed-and-breakfast inn is set back from the road. Its central location makes it ideal for exploring the Cape, and the beaches are just five minutes away. The 12 comfortable rooms are cozy and individually decorated, and some offer a fireplace, private balcony or luxurious two-person Jacuzzi tub. Full breakfast and afternoon tea are included, and the outdoor heated pool is open from May to September. The Day Spa offers massages and spa treatments.

🚹 202 E2 ☒ 4885 State Highway, Eastham, MA ☏ 508/255-6632; www.pennyhouseinn.com

▽▽▽▽ Whalewalk Inn & Spa $$–$$$

Built for a whaling captain more than 180 years ago, this is still an impressive place to stay, with its oriental rugs, 19th-century European country antiques and

PROVINCETOWN

▽▽▽▽ Crowne Point Historic Inn and Spa $$–$$$

A 19th-century sea captain's mansion, Crowne Point offers wrap-around porch, Victorian furnishings and hardwood floors. It oozes old-world charm, though its 40 bedrooms (all with private access off the porch) are fully equipped with TV, DVD and CD players, high-speed internet and refrigerators. The more luxurious rooms have whirlpool tubs and private decks. The bistro serves fine cuisine and there is a day spa.

⊞ 202 E3 ☒ 82 Bradford Street, Provincetown, MA ☎ 508/487-6767; www.crownepointe.com

☞☞ The Masthead $-$$$

In a quiet spot at the west end of town, this family-run motel stands right by the water, with more than 400 feet (122m) of private beach, a deck for sunbathing and even grills for barbecues. Most rooms are in apartments and cottages in the cheerful gardens, with a further eight in the motel itself. The motel is within easy walking distance of shops, restaurants and town center.

⊞ 202 E3 ☒ 31–41 Commercial Street, Provincetown, MA ☎ 800/395-5095 or 508/487-0523; www.themasthead.com

☞☞ White Wind Inn $-$$

The veranda is popular for people-watching at this 1845 mansion on Commercial Street, with its unusual stone wall, built from ship ballast.

Care has gone in to conserving the Victorian look, combining traditional furnishings with modern comforts. Of the 12 rooms, some have balconies, others fireplaces or Jacuzzis. All have WiFi, TV and refrigerators. Guests gather in the "great room," with its grand piano and cozy fire.

⊞ 202 E3 ☒ 174 Commercial Street, Provincetown, MA ☎ 508/487-1526; www.whitewindinn.com

NANTUCKET

☞☞ Carriage House $-$$

A former 19th-century carriage house, hidden behind the main street on a narrow island lane, today houses a pleasant bed-and-breakfast. The seven rooms are furnished with a few antiques and one has a canopy bed. Breakfast is usually taken on the patio. The common room, with books for guests' use, a TV and comfortable sofa, becomes the breakfast room in wet weather.

⊞ 202 E1 ☒ 5 Ray's Court, Nantucket, MA ☎ 508/228-0326; www.carriagehousenantucket.com

☞☞ Seven Sea Street Inn $-$$$

In the heart of Nantucket Town's historic district, this red oak post-and-beam inn, with its widow's walk porch (rooftop deck) was built in 1986. The owners have successfully recreated an early American atmosphere with carefully chosen reproduction furniture. Enamel gas stoves add a glow to chilly island evenings in some of the 15 bedrooms (six are in neighboring houses). There is a tasty Continental breakfast on offer, and you can expect cranberry crunch granola and muffins.

⊞ 202 E1 ☒ 7 Sea Street, Nantucket MA ☎ 508/228-3577; www.sevenseastreetinn.com

☞☞ Sherburne Inn $-$$$

This handsome building near Steamboat Wharf has been an inn

since the mid-19th century. In the eight bedrooms, the furniture includes some antiques, fine old paintings and oriental rugs; one room has a fireplace. The favorite is Room 8, with its high king-sized bed, claw-foot bath, and private balcony overlooking the old town. Continental breakfast is served.

⊞ 202 E1 ☒ 10 Gay Street, Nantucket, MA ☎ 888/577-4425 or 508/228-4425; www.sherburneinn.com

MARTHA'S VINEYARD

☞☞ Kelley House $-$$

Originally a tavern, the Kelley House has a history stretching back to 1742. Think brick fireplaces, wood paneling, and maritime memorabilia. The 43 rooms are in four historic buildings, with three suites overlooking the harbor. Amenities include an outdoor pool and the Newes from America pub.

⊞ 202 D1 ☒ 23 Kelley Street, Edgartown MA ☎ 508/627-7900; www.kelley-house.com

Where to...
Eat and Drink

Prices
Expect to pay per person for a three-course meal, excluding drinks and service

$ under $20 $$ $20–$35 $$$ over $35

SANDWICH

⌐ Seafood Sam's $

Since opening 35 years ago, Sam's has grown, with three branches (also in Falmouth, Yarmouth). This typical Cape Cod clam shack sticks to seafood, served informally and quickly. Expect lines on sunny days, when there is no better experience than eating outdoors. As for the menu, Sam's offers lobster in eight different ways, from lobster bisques to classic Cape Cod lobster dinners.

✚ 202 D2 ⊠ 6 Coast Guard Road, Sandwich, MA (on Cape Cod Canal) ☎ 508/888-4629; www.belfryinn.com ⏰ Daily 11–9

CHATHAM

⌐⌐ Vining's Bistro $–$$

Tucked away on the second floor of the mini-mall, this casual yet sophisticated cafe delivers an interestingly eclectic variety of cuisine, with innovative combinations that always deliver great taste. The wood grill and exotic spices infuse the entrees with delightful flavors. Try the salad with pear, cranberries and walnuts to start, followed by fresh seafood or spit-roasted chicken. Seafood favorites include roasted scallops, grilled fish or Portuguese cod with

sausage and saffron. There is also a fine wine list.

✚ 202 E2 ⊠ 595 Main Street, Chatham, MA ☎ 508/945-5033; viningsbistro.net ⏰ Daily 5:30–10, summer only

EASTHAM

⌐ Arnold's Lobster & Clam Bar $

For some 35 years, Arnold's has been a fixture in Eastham for families: the Cape Cod clam shack, the mini golf and the ice cream stand, offering 30 of Richardson's Dairy flavors. Innovations include a raw bar, offering the freshest selection of local oysters and clams, and a choice of cocktails. The classics pull the crowds: New England lobster clam bakes, and giant seafood rolls and onion rings.

✚ 202 E2 ⊠ Route 6, Eastham, MA ☎ 508/255-2575; www.arnoldsrestaurant.com ⏰ Mid-Jun to mid-Sep daily 11:30–8:30; mid-May to mid-Jun, mid-Sep to Columbus Day Sat–Sun 11:30–8:30

PROVINCETOWN

⌐⌐ Ciro & Sal's $$–$$$

This long-established local favorite can be found in a small alleyway off Commercial Street; you enter through the trellis on your left into the garden patio. A spacious dining room overlooks the garden, and a cozy wine cellar is decorated with Chianti bottles. The cuisine is Northern Italian with nightly specials, seafood, veal and fresh pasta dishes on the menu. Favorites include filet of sole with scallions (spring onions), mushrooms and tomatoes in a dry vermouth sauce, or marinated veal baked with eggplant (aubergine) and tomatoes in an espagnole sauce with pasta.

✚ 202 E3 ⊠ 4 Kiley Court, Provincetown, MA ☎ 508/487-6444; www.ciroandsals.com ⏰ Late Jun–Labor Day daily 5:30–10; day after Labor Day–late Jun Fri–Sun 5:30–10

⌐⌐⌐ Devon's $$–$$$

At this chic, 37-seat restaurant, the modern American/global menu features salads, such as the signature lobster cake. Entree specialties range from pork chops, with a candied ginger and peach gastrique, to grilled local scallops with a peppery butter sauce. Desserts include a Breton cake with strawberries.

+ 202 E3 ⊠ 401½ Commercial Street, Provincetown, MA ☎ 508/487-4773; www.devons.org ⏰ Jun–Sep Thu–Tue 8–1, 6–10; May, Oct Sat–Sun 8–1, 6–10

Front Street Restaurant $$–$$$

Since the early 1990s, Donna Aliperti has served Mediterranean-influenced dishes in this Victorian house. The snug atmosphere is enhanced by bare wood tables and high-backed wooden booths. Dishes include tea-smoked duck, herb-crusted rack of lamb, braised short ribs on chickpea polenta, and seared shrimp or maple-grilled salmon. The bar hops until late.

+ 202 E3 ⊠ 230 Commercial Street, Provincetown, MA ☎ 508/487-9715;
www.frontstreetrestaurant.com ⏰ Mid-May to Dec Wed–Mon 5:30–10:30; rest of year hours vary

Lobster Pot $–$$

With two dining rooms overlooking the water, it's no surprise that this is one of the most popular places in town. Seafood is really the only way to go here: you can select dishes with Asian, French and Portuguese influences, as well as a good old-fashioned Cape Cod clam bake. However, vegetarians and meat-eaters can also choose from the wide-ranging menu. Cocktails are served in the Top of the Pot bar. The atmosphere is informal and busy.

+ 202 E3 ⊠ 321 Commercial Street, Provincetown, MA ☎ 508/487-0842; www.ptownlobsterpot.com ⏰ Apr–Nov daily 11:30–10; closed Dec–Mar

The Mews $$–$$$

At the Mews there are two places to eat: the lively bar and the beachfront restaurant. Both have views of the water and an informal dress code. The menus are about the same: "Intercontinental" with filets and salads. Specials include a lobster and sweet potato stew or a spice-rubbed rack of lamb with herb polenta. The Sunday brunch is getting to be an institution with residents and visitors.

+ 202 E3 ⊠ 429 Commercial Street, Provincetown, MA ☎ 508/487-1500; www.mews.com ⏰ Daily 6–10pm, Sat–Sun 11am–2:30pm

NANTUCKET

The Boarding House $$$

The Boarding House provides relaxed sophistication. You can sit at the bar and eat a light dish, watch the world go by from the sidewalk terrace or go downstairs to the candlelit basement for a romantic meal. Chefs use only the finest natural, organic ingredients from local farms and regional purveyors. Reservations are essential.

+ 202 E1 ⊠ 12 Federal Street, Nantucket, MA ☎ 508/228-9622;
www.boardinghousenantucket.com ⏰ Daily 5:30–10, also Sat–Sun brunch 10–2. Closed Sun Oct–Apr; Mon Sep–Jun

The Brotherhood of Thieves $–$$

Named for a pamphlet in 1844 attacking supporters of slavery, the Brotherhood is one of Nantucket's favorite restaurants, serving hearty meals, with evening entertainment in summer. Sandwiches are supersized and juicy burgers come with shoestring fries. The menu is varied, including chowder, seafood casseroles, fish tacos, broiled scallops and braised lamb shank. The downstairs dining area is cozy and dark, while upstairs there are five small dining rooms, and a bar overlooking Broad Street. Outside, the new, relaxed patio and bar offers the full menu (mid-May to mid-October).

+ 202 E1 ⊠ 23 Broad Street, Nantucket, MA ☎ 508/228-2551; www.brotherhoodofthieves.com ⏰ Daily 11:30–10

Where to...
Shop

In Harwich are **Cape Cod Braided Rug Company** (4 Great Western Road, www.capecodbraidedrug.com) and the **Kemp Pottery** studio (9 Cranberry Highway, Orleans, www.kemppottery.com). For antiques, good places are **The Mews at Brewster** (2926 Route 6A, Brewster, tel: 508/896-4887) or **Mark Lawrence Fine Period Antiques** (1050 Main Street, Brewster, tel: 508/896-8381; www.fineperiodantiques.com). For more names, check out the **Cape Cod Antique Dealers Association** (www.ccada.com) and the **Cape Cod Potters** (capecodpotters.com).

In Provincetown, artists exhibit at **Provincetown Art Association and Museum** (460 Commercial Street, tel: 508/487-1750; www.paam.org). **Julie Heller Gallery** (2 Gosnold Street, tel: 508/487-2169; www.juliehellergallery.com) exhibits Karl Knaths, Ross Moffett and Harry Hensche. Contemporary work is shown at **Rice/Polak Gallery** (430 Commercial Street, tel: 508/487-1052; www.ricepolakgallery.com) and also at the **Albert Merola Gallery** (424 Commercial Street, tel: 508/487-4424; www.albertmerolagallery.com).

On Nantucket, antiques and local crafts can be found at **Sylvia Antiques and Four Winds Craft Guild** (167 Orange Street, www.sylviaantiques.com) or **Dane Gallery** (28 Centre Street, www.danegallery.com). For Nantucket lightship baskets, visit the **Golden Basket** (44 Main Street, tel: 508/228-4344; www.thegoldenbasket.com).

Where to...
Be Entertained

THEATER

Enjoy summer theater at the **Cape Playhouse** in Dennis (820 Main Street, SR 6A, tel: 508/385-3911; www.capeplayhouse.com) and the **New Provincetown Players** (238 Bradford Street, tel: 508/487-7487; www.newprovincetownplayers.org).

BICYCLING

Cape Cod has a series of designated cycle trails (▶ 86). **P&M Cycles** (29 Main Street, Buzzard's Bay, tel: 508/759-2830; www.sunsol.com/pmcycles) rents bikes for two hours, the full day or a week (closed Mondays).

In Provincetown, try **Arnold's** (329 Commercial Street, tel: 508/487-0844). The **Dennis** Chamber of Commerce (www.denischamber.com) has a downloadable Rail Trail map.

SAILING

Rent a boat or take lessons at **Flyer's Boatyard** (131A Commercial Street, Provincetown, tel: 508/487-0898; www.flyersrentals.com).

GOLF

For information on the Cape's golf courses, contact the **Cape Cod Chamber of Commerce** (5 Shoot Flying Hill Road, Centerville MA, tel: 508/362-3225; www.capecodchamber.org). The Cape Cod Welcome Center is at the junction of Route 6 and Route 132 (open Mon–Sat 10–5 in summer).

The Berkshires

Getting Your Bearings

The cool Berkshire Hills were a summer retreat for the 19th-century rich and famous. Today, everyone is welcome to enjoy the summer program of world-class culture.

In western Massachusetts, Tanglewood has been the summer home of the Boston Symphony Orchestra since 1937. What can be better on a summer evening than enjoying a concert while picnicking on the lawn? Nearby, the Jacob's Pillow Dance Festival attracts the hottest names in classical and modern dance for their open-air performances. July and August are the busiest months in what are referred to as "The Berkshires;" rooms double or triple in price and are still hard to come by.

Off-season, the cultural scene doesn't die, it just moves indoors. A major boost was the opening of MASS MoCA in 1999. In North Adams, old factory buildings were transformed into the country's largest venue for contemporary art, boosting the local economy. With the nearby Sterling and Francine Clark Art Institute and the Williams College Museum of Art, the northern end of the Berkshires is a destination in its own right. But, the Berkshire Hills are just as lovely in fall. Hike part of the Appalachian Trail, or just hunt for antiques in Sheffield and Great Barrington.

★ Don't Miss

Previous page: Hikers take a rest by Benedict Pond, Beartown State Forest

In Two Days

If you're not quite sure where to begin your travels, this itinerary recommends a practical and enjoyable two days in the Berkshires, taking in some of the best places to see using the Getting Your Bearings map on the opposite page. For more information see the main entries.

Day 1

Morning
Enjoy a leisurely breakfast, then drive down US 7, the antiques corridor of the Berkshires. Sheffield is the unofficial antiques capital, but equally interesting furniture, collectibles and other assorted treasures can be found in Great Barrington.

Afternoon
Have a snack lunch at the historic Red Lion Inn in Stockbridge (➤ 107), then cruise over to the **4 Norman Rockwell Museum** (➤ 103). If the museum itself doesn't appeal, just walk around the picturesque town that inspired the artist's (above) many *Saturday Evening Post* covers.

Evening
Get yourself to Lenox in time for an early dinner at Gateways Inn (51 Walker Street, tel: 413/637-2532) before heading off for an evening of top-flight classical music at **1 Tanglewood** (➤ 98–99).

Day 2

Morning
Make an early start for a walk on the **2 Appalachian Trail** (➤ 100–101). This famous walking trail runs through two conservation areas that are within easy reach by car: Beartown State Forest (right) and October Mountain State Forest. Choose from the trails, long or short. Whatever you decide, expect beautiful scenery and stunning vistas.

Afternoon
Grab a quick lunch at one of the cafes in the Jacob's Pillow Grounds. Then catch a matinee performance at **3 Jacob's Pillow** (➤ 102), which is to dance what Tanglewood is to music. Tickets for top performers sell out, so order them in advance.

Evening
After the performance at the Pillow, you can treat yourself to a fine dinner at the Red Lion in Stockbridge (➤ 107) or, if you have the stamina, drive up to Williamstown for a performance of the **8 Williamstown Theatre Festival** (➤ 105).

1 Tanglewood

A blanket big enough for two spread out on a rolling green lawn. A picnic basket filled to the flaps with freshly baked bread, delicious cheeses, inventive salads and gourmet pasta dishes. A bottle of fine wine to be sipped on a moonlit night. What could be more perfect? Music, you say? Okay. How about the Boston Symphony Orchestra?

Smaller concerts are held at the Seiji Ozawa Hall

If it sounds too good to be true, then it must be Tanglewood, the nation's premier summer music festival, and the main reason the Berkshire Hills are what they are today. In the era before air-conditioning, the Boston Symphony Orchestra decided that its urban home was too hot for concerts in July and August, and took up summer residence in the Berkshires, where the temperature and humidity were more bearable, especially at night. The location, 2 hours from Boston and 3 hours from New York, immediately appealed to wealthy patrons of the arts in these two cities, who continue to come here in droves each summer. The top names in classical music find Tanglewood almost as enticing as the audiences do.

Pianist Garrick Ohlsson is one of the world-renowned musicians to have wowed audiences at Tanglewood

Picnicking on the lawn is, without doubt, the romantic way to go, but those who prefer an actual seat will have to plan ahead. You will pay more for a reserved seat in the 5,000-seat Koussevitzky Music Shed (designed in 1938 by noted architect Eliel Saarinen and later named for the BSO's erstwhile music director, Serge Koussevitsky), but you have a good view of the stage, and are under cover in case of bad weather. If you're content to sit on the lawn, you can wait

The Boston Symphony Orchestra performing at Tanglewood

until the day and see how the weather turns out before assembling your picnic.

Tanglewood's schedule is usually announced in the winter and subscription holders get the first chance at the best seats. But good seats are available when public booking opens in early spring (dates vary, check the website), and even if you wait until June, you're likely to find seats for all but the most popular weekend performances.

Try to attend a midweek concert, when the site is a lot less crowded. You'll have plenty of elbow room and fewer sport-utility vehicles hogging space in the parking lot. And if you prefer a seat in the Shed, you can often get tickets to midweek concerts a few days before (sometimes even the day of) the show.

TAKING A BREAK

You can get gourmet picnic fixings at various delicatessens in town. Try **Haven Cafe & Bakery** (8 Franklin Street, Lenox, tel: 413/637-8948, www.haven.berkshireculinary.com).

➕ 200 A1   ✉ West Street, Lenox, MA. From Lenox, take Route 183 1.4 miles (2.3km) west. Mailing address: Symphony Hall, 301 Massachusetts Avenue, Boston, MA   ☎ Box office and general information: 617/266-1200 or Ticketmaster 800/347-0808; www.bso.org   💵 Tickets range from around $18 for seats on the lawn to $115 for the best seats in the Koussevitzky Music Shed. Lawn tickets for children under 17 are free. Children under 5 are not permitted in the Koussevitsky Music Shed or Seiji Ozawa Hall during concerts   🕐 Mid-Jun to first weekend in Sep daily evenings (also Sat–Sun afternoons)

TANGLEWOOD: INSIDE INFO

In more detail Nowadays, Tanglewood offers far more than Boston Symphony Orchestra concerts. This **wide-ranging festival of culture** includes chamber music, opera and recitals; there are open rehearsals, talks and panel discussions; contemporary music and dance are also on the program. Lawn seats, where you take your chances with the weather, are priced around $17.

■ Smaller concerts are held in the 1,180-seat **Seiji Ozawa Hall,** where seats inside usually range from $33 to $51.

■ Several times a month, Tanglewood stages **opera** in a venue known simply as "the Theatre." It, too, has attracted the top names, from Jessye Norman to Kiri Te Kanawa. Prices range from around $65 to $100. Note there are no lawn seats for opera performances.

2 **The Appalachian Trail**

The Appalachian Trail is arguably the finest hiking trail in the United States. Built by volunteers from 1921 to 1937 and designated a National Scenic Trail in 1968, it snakes 2,174 miles (3,498km) from Maine all the way down to Georgia. Each year, hundreds of hardy souls set out to hike the trail from one end to the other – a journey of five to six months – and quite a few of them finish the trek.

However, not everybody need go to such extremes. The trail meanders through the Berkshires, so you can make a pleasant day hike of it. Although at times along its length the Appalachian Trail scales heights of 5,000 to 6,000 feet (1,520m to 1,830m), the highest summits in the Berkshires are no more than 3,500 feet (1,065m).

Beartown State Forest

The best place to catch up with the Appalachian Trail is at **Beartown State Forest**. Leave Great Barrington on US 7/ SR 23, continuing on SR 23 east for a little over 5 miles (8km). Turn left on Blue Hill Road; there are signs for the park entrance, on Benedict Pond Road. Here you will find a placid lake where you can swim, fish or take an hour-long stroll around the circumference of its shores. Follow the Loop Trail around the pond; on the eastern side, you come to the intersection with the Appalachian Trail (marked by white blazes on the trees). In the course of your day hike, you may cross paths with one or more hikers taking aim at the trail's entire length.

October Mountain State Forest

Another Appalachian Trail crossroads lies in **October Mountain State Forest** (from Interstate 90 take Route 20 into Lee, then turn right on Center Street and follow signs to the main entrance). Ask at the park headquarters how to get to the Appalachian Trail, or see which of the dozen other trails in the park best fits your ability. The Appalachian Trail is linear: remember, how far you go is how far you have to come back.

The trail wends through pastureland (below) on its way across New England

THE APPALACHIAN TRAIL: INSIDE INFO

Top tip Bring **insect repellent** to combat the gnats and mosquitoes. **Deep Woods Off** is particularly effective, as are **Avon's Skin So Soft** lotions and oils. Powdered garlic capsules are also reportedly effective.

In more detail There are several **websites** that have detailed information about the history of the Appalachian Trail. They also provide online maps, tips on hiking some, or all, of it and, most importantly of all, safety suggestions. See www.nps.gov/appa or www.appalachiantrail.org.

The 1.5-mile (2.4km) loop around Benedict Pond is a shorter, less hilly option to the Appalachian Trail itself

TAKING A BREAK

Before you set out on your day hike, make your way to **Guido's Fresh Marketplace** in Great Barrington (760 Main Street, tel: 413/528-9255), where you can buy a picnic lunch.

🔷 200 A1
Beartown State Forest
✉ 69 Blue Hill Road, Monterey, MA ☎ 413/528-0904;
www.mass.gov/dcr/parks/western 🕐 Daily dawn–dusk 💷 Inexpensive

October Mountain State Forest
✉ 256 Woodland Road, Lee, MA ☎ 413/243-1778;
www.mass.gov/dcr/parks/western 🕐 Daily dawn–dusk 💷 Free

3 Jacob's Pillow Dance Festival

What began as dance pioneer Ted Shawn's attempt to legitimize dance as an honorable career for men has resulted in the country's premier summer venue for dance. All the biggest names in American dance have performed here – Twyla Tharp, Mark Morris, Merce Cunningham and the Dance Theater of Harlem – and the festival also hosts international companies as well.

At the end of the festival's first summer in 1933, the crowds were so big that Shawn had to turn people away. By 1942, the first permanent theater had been built, and despite wartime rationing, the crowds climbed the hill on foot and on horseback to see performances in ballet, folk and modern dance.

Today, the audiences arrive via station wagons and sport-utility vehicles rather than horses, and the quality of the performers has kept pace. The festival is a hot ticket, especially on summer weekends. If you want to see a popular show, get your seats as far in advance as possible. The summer schedule is first announced in January and tickets go on sale in April. You can order them over the phone, by mail or on the internet.

Dancers on the Pillow's outdoor Inside/Out stage give free performances during the Festival

If the performances alone don't sate your appetite, consider the free pre- and post-performance discussions, as well as many special events, including lectures, free exhibits and tours.

The Pillow Café (tel: 413/243-2455) offers dining under a tent, but reservations are a must. Pillow Pub, which serves sandwiches and salads and has a snack bar for tea, coffee and cookies, is another option. You can make up a picnic from the selection of snacks on offer at the pub or bring your own and sit at the picnic tables on the grounds. Alternatively, ask at your inn or bed-and-breakfast if they'll make up a picnic for you (some places pride themselves on their gourmet picnic baskets).

➕ 200 A1 ✉ 358 George Carter Road, Becket, MA. From Route 7, take Route 20 east approximately 8.3 miles (13.3km). Turn left onto George Carter Road. Travel half a mile (1km) and make a right at the entrance to Jacob's Pillow ☎ Box office: Mar–Aug 413/243-0745; information the rest of the year 413/243-9919; www.jacobspillow.org 🕐 Season: Mid-Jun to Aug. Evening performances usually start at 8 or 8:15pm. Afternoon performances on weekends start at 2 or 2:15. Check the website or phone ahead

At Your Leisure

4 Norman Rockwell Museum

If, while strolling along Stockbridge's Main Street, you feel like you've walked into a painting, it's because you have. The artist Norman Rockwell, of *Saturday Evening Post* fame, called Stockbridge home from 1953 until his death in 1978, and if he were to return today, there is little he wouldn't recognize.

The largest collection of Rockwell's work is housed in this museum just outside of Stockbridge. Some people love Rockwell's visions of the common events of people's lives, such as visits to the doctor, sibling rivalry and rain disrupting a baseball game. Others dismiss Rockwell's Americana as too sentimental to be considered serious art.

From time to time, the museum collects all 323 of Rockwell's *Saturday Evening Post* covers (dating from 1916 to 1963) in a single exhibit. Other draws are Rockwell's studio itself (relocated here, along the banks of the Housatonic River). His "Four Freedoms" series was intended to create support for World War II, while several portraits done in the 1960s and 1970s reveal a political side few knew about.

✛ 200 A1 ✉ Route 183, Stockbridge, MA ☎ 413/298-4100; www.nrm.org 🕐 Museum: May–Oct daily 10–5; Nov–Apr Mon–Fri 10–4, Sat–Sun 10–5. Studio: May–Nov daily 10:30–4:45 💲 Moderate. Children under 18 free

5 The Mount

The Mount was the home of Pulitzer Prize-winning author Edith Wharton, best known for *The Age of Innocence*. Wharton fans may wish to tour the white Classical Revival mansion, which she designed. She was no dilettante when it came to home design. Following the publication of her best-selling novel, *The House of Mirth*, she wrote: "Decidedly, I'm a better landscape gardener than novelist, and this place, every line of which is my own work, far surpasses *The House of Mirth*." It is one of only a handful of National Historic Landmarks designed by a woman.

The Mount was the original home of Shakespeare & Co., which now has its own 30-acre (12ha) premises just a short walk from the center of Lenox. For more than 30 years, the company has followed its ideal: to train, to educate and to entertain. These specialists in the works of the Bard also present some thoroughly modern plays, attracting theatergoers from the end of May through to mid-September to its three performance venues.

✛ 200 A1
The Mount
✉ 2 Plunkett Street, Lenox, MA ☎ 413/551-5100; www.edithwharton.org 🕐 May–Oct daily 10–5 💲 Expensive

Shakespeare & Co.
✉ 70 Kemble Street, Lenox, MA
☎ Box office: May–early Sep 413/637-3353; information the rest of the year 413/637-1199; www.shakespeare.org

6 Hancock Shaker Village

Ask any high-school student what he or she remembers about the Shakers and the invariable one-word answer is: celibacy. This community,

Inside the impressive Round Stone Barn, built in the 1820s

The laundry and machine shop in Hancock Shaker Village dates from 1790

so named for its fervor during religious rites, led an ascetic life, believing that spirituality could be attained by performing routine tasks to perfection. Shaker communities prospered from 1774 to the mid-19th century, gaining a reputation for their craftsmanship and ingenuity, and the simple, ordered lifestyle attracted followers until about 1960.

The Shaker community in Hancock was one of the most important, and when the religious movement died out it became an outdoor museum of Shaker life in America. Some 20 buildings are located on more than 750 acres (303ha) here, with a full range of special events, programs and even Shaker meals available.

The most impressive building on the property is the Round Stone Barn dating from around 1826 and designed so that one person standing in the middle could feed more than 50 cows easily, and milk them nearly as easily. The original Brick Dwelling, built in a swift 10 weeks in 1830 by 100 Shaker men and women, is also of interest. Shaker Sisters staffed the huge communal kitchen downstairs.

Upstairs, dormitory-style "retiring rooms" housed men on one side of the building and women on the other (with separate entrances). The sexes came together only to participate in meetings and worship.

Visitors may go inside the Barn, the Brick Dwelling and all the other buildings in the village. Bringing it all to life are the regular demonstrations of crafts, from woodworking, weaving and spinning to broom and box making, and sometimes blacksmithing. Follow the one-mile Farm and Forest Trail loop to see the crops and meadows.

🚩 200 A1 ✉ PO Box 927, Route 20, MA (near the intersection of routes 20 and 41) ☎ 800/817-1137 or 413/443-0188; www.hancockshakervillage.org 🕐 Memorial Day weekend–Oct daily 10–5; Apr, May 10–4; closed rest of year. Self-guided tours with map of the village 💷 Expensive. Children 12 years and under: free

7 Sterling and Francine Clark Art Institute

The northern Berkshires is home to a trio of important art collections. Forming a cultural triangle are MASS MoCA (► 105) and, in

Williamstown, Williams College's own art museum plus nearby, the Sterling and Francine Clark Art Institute. "The Clark" features some of the greatest painters in history. From England come Constable, Turner and Gainsborough. From France, the great Impressionists are represented by Claude Monet *(Spring in Giverny)*, Pierre-Auguste Renoir *(Onions)*, Claude Monet *(The Cliffs at Etretat)*, and Edgar Degas *(Dancers in the Classroom)*. There are also outstanding works by American artists like Winslow Homer, Mary Cassatt and John Singer Sargent. As well as the permanent collection, the Clark curates major special exhibitions. The main museum has changed little since opening in 1955. The galleries are small, with windows looking out over the meadows and a pond – making it more like a grand home than a museum. The institute has expanded, moving into new fields, such as photography. A recent addition is the avant-garde Stone Hill Center, whose outdoor terrace cafe is a lovely spot in summer and the early days of fall. Otherwise, have lunch indoors in either the Courtyard Cafe or the Clark Cafe.

🗺 200 A2 ✉ 225 South Street, Williamstown, MA ☎ 413/458-2303; www.clarkart.edu 🕐 Jul–Aug daily 10–5; Sep–Jun Tue–Sun 💲 Moderate

🖳 Williamstown Theatre Festival

Every summer, the college town of Williamstown hosts a theater festival, with different productions of classic and new plays, readings and workshops in several different venues. The festival, which was begun in 1955 to draw tourists to this sleepy part of the northern Berkshires, has become a model for summer theaters around the country and its productions regularly attract many top-name Broadway and Hollywood actors and directors. Many festival productions have later gone on to Broadway.

🗺 200 A2 ✉ 1000 Main Street, Route 2, PO Box 517, Williamstown, MA. From Lenox

Adams Memorial Theatre, Williamstown

take Route 7 north to Williamstown. In town, continue east on Route 2; the Adams Memorial Theatre is on the left ☎ 24-hour information: 413/597-3399. Box office (summer only): 413/597-3400; www.wtfestival.org 🕐 Season: late Jun–late Aug. Main Stage performances: Tue–Fri 8pm, Sat 8:30pm. Matinees Thu 3pm, Sat 4pm, Sun 2pm 💲 Main Stage production tickets: $30 to $55 depending on date and seat location

🖳 MASS MoCA

A sparkling example of recycling an old industrial site, MASS MoCA is the largest center for contemporary arts in the United States. Find it in North Adams, where vast 19th-century factory buildings were stripped out to create 19 galleries. With 110,000 square feet (10,000sq m) of open, flexible space, they can display even the largest art installations. As well as being visually provocative, this complex blurs the usual distinctions between artistic disciplines, so music, dance, film, theater, and more are regularly featured. An ongoing exhibit (until 2033) is *Sol LeWitt: A Wall Drawing Retrospective* featuring 105 of the late New Englander's large-scale wall drawings. If you ever thought modern art – in all its guises – was not for you, try to spend some time here. Informal and welcoming, this complex could just change your mind.

🗺 200 A2 ✉ 87 Marshall Street, North Adams, MA ☎ 413/662-2111; www.massmoca.org 🕐 Jul–Sep daily 10–6; Oct–Jun Wed–Mon 11–5 💲 Moderate

Where to... Stay

Prices
Expect to pay for two people sharing a double room, excluding taxes
$ under $150 $$ $150–$250 $$$ over $250

STOCKBRIDGE

▽▽▽ Inn at Stockbridge $$–$$$

The inn, once a millionaire's summer home, is separated from Stockbridge by the Massachusetts Pike. The owners have renovated the modern Georgian-style building throughout and added a cottage at the rear, with four themed bedrooms. The modern Barn offers four luxury suites. The breakfast buffet is served in the dining room.
✚ 200 A1 ⊠ 30 East Street, Stockbridge, MA ☎ 888/466-7865, 413/298-3337; www.stockbridgeinn.com

LENOX

▽▽▽ Brook Farm Inn $–$$$

This converted 19th-century farmhouse stands in a residential area just off the Old Stockbridge Road. The two rooms at the front are the most attractive, with canopy beds and antique furnishings. All 15 rooms have their own bathrooms. The owners put out a new "poem of the day" to inspire their guests each morning, and at 4pm they serve tea in the poetry library.
✚ 202 A1 ⊠ 15 Hawthorne Street, Lenox, MA ☎ 800/285-7638, 413/637-3013; www.brookfarm.com

▽▽▽ The Kemble Inn $$–$$$

On a hill facing the Berkshire Mountains, this luxurious bed-and-breakfast inn retains the elegance of a bygone era. Completely restored in 2007, the foyer, dining room and library look much as they did in 1881, and the music room boasts a Steinway piano, modern American art and European primitive paintings. The 14 romantic bedrooms are named for American authors associated with the Berkshires. A full, gourmet breakfast is served.
✚ 200 A1 ⊠ 2 Kemble Street, Lenox, MA ☎ 800/353-4113, 413/637-4113; www.kembleinn.com

▽▽▽ The Summer White House $$

A classic Berkshire "Cottage," or summer home, dating from 1885, the Summer White House is themed on things presidential. With its porches, gables and large windows, the house feels spacious and airy. The bedrooms are named for First Ladies: Eleanor Roosevelt, Edith Wilson and Abigail Adams, who was the first President's wife to live in the newly built White House in Washington DC. Downstairs, the library has a grand piano, antiques and paintings. Close to the shops and restaurants of Lenox and only a mile (1.5km) from Tanglewood.
✚ 200 A1 ⊠ 17 Main Street, Lenox, MA ☎ 413/637-4489; www.thesummerwhitehouse.com

WILLIAMSTOWN

▽▽▽ 1896 House $–$$$

With its 17 acres (7ha) of grounds either side of US 7, including a duck pond, a brook and bridges, this old inn on the outskirts of Williamstown is a terrific retreat. There is also a tavern restaurant and two upscale "motels" situated in the grounds. There are six luxury suites in a variety of period styles.
✚ 200 A2 ⊠ 910 Cold Spring Road (Rt 7), Williamstown, MA ☎ 888/999-1896, 413/458-1896; www.1896house.com

Where to...
Eat and Drink

Prices
Expect to pay per person for a three-course meal, excluding drinks and service

$ under $20 $$ $20–$35 $$$ over $35

GREAT BARRINGTON

🍷 Barrington Brewery & Restaurant $–$$

This popular microbrewery offers handcrafted brews made on-site. In the informal, wood-floored restaurant, you can enjoy your choice of the tasty pub food on offer, ranging from burgers and sandwiches to steaks and seafood. There is also a good selection of fresh salads.

🏢 200 A1 🖂 420 Stockbridge Road, Great Barrington, MA ☎ 413/528-8282; www.barringtonbrewery.net ⓒ Mon–Thu 11:30–9:30, Fri–Sat 11:30–10, Sun 11:30–9

STOCKBRIDGE

🍷 Red Lion Inn $$$

The historic Red Lion offers both formal dining and quick snacks. In the dining room, take time over sweet pea and shiitake risotto or seared scallops with wild onion hash. Order a local brew and a sandwich in the flower-filled courtyard, or the pub downstairs. Drinks are served all day on the front porch.

🏢 200 A1 🖂 30 Main Street, Stockbridge, MA ☎ 413/298-5545; www.redlioninn.com ⓒ Daily 7am–9:30pm (also Fri–Sat 9:30–10pm)

LENOX

🍷 Bistro Zinc $$–$$$

Inside this popular modern French bistro you'll find wood floors, large windows, a long bar and closely spaced, small tables. There are nightly specials and an extensive, seasonally changing menu, with appetizers like crispy duck wontons, and entrees such as Scottish salmon with gnocchi, steak *frites* or roasted free-range chicken. If you still have room for dessert, try the crème brûlée.

🏢 200 A1 🖂 56 Church Street, Lenox, MA ☎ 413/637-8800; www.bistrozinc.com ⓒ Daily 11:30–3, 5:30–10

🍷 Church Street Cafe $$$

A strong local following has built up for the "eclectic American" cooking served here and whether you wear shorts or a suit and tie, you are made welcome. Signature dishes include sautéed Maine crab cakes, pan-roasted chicken with pumpkin flan, and rustic beef stew served with caramelized fall vegetables. Take time over the excellent wine list. If you are budget-conscious, try the less expensive lunchtime menu. Reservations are recommended.

🏢 200 A1 🖂 65 Church Street, Lenox, MA ☎ 413/637-2745; www.churchstreetcafe.biz ⓒ Daily 11:30–2, 5:30–9; closed Jan–Apr; Nov, May Sun–Mon

WILLIAMSTOWN

🍷 Hobson's Choice $–$$

Expect a country feel at this eatery, with a beamed ceiling and agricultural implements on the walls. The chef-owner is known for his straightforward all-American dishes, particularly steaks and seafood. Pasta and vegetarian dishes also available, along with traditional desserts: death by chocolate, mud pie, apple strudel and Grand Marnier fudge parfait.

🏢 200 A2 🖂 159 Water Street, Williamstown, MA ☎ 413/458-9101; www.hobsonsrestaurant.com ⓒ Daily 5–9:30

Where to...
Shop

ANTIQUES

The villages along US 7 are known for their antiques shops. Expect everything from folk art to painted furniture and quilts.

In Great Barrington, **Great Barrington Antiques Center** (964 S. Main Street, tel: 413/644-8848; www.greatbarringtonantiquescenter. com) and **Berkshire Art Gallery** (80 Railroad Street, tel: 413/528-2690; www.berkshireartgallery.com) are worth exploring. Lenox, Sheffield, Stockbridge and Williamstown are also good hunting grounds.

CRAFTS

Collectors of glass should check out **An American Craftsman Gallery**

(36 Main Street, tel: 413/298-0175; www.anamericancraftsman.com), a few doors down from the Red Lion Inn. Try **Hancock Shaker Village** (▶ 103–104) for crafted wood items, **MASS MoCA** (▶ 105) for a large selection of gifts and books, and the **Sterling and Francine Clark Art Institute** (▶ 104) for art books, posters and other art-related material.

OUTLET SHOPS

Catch a bargain or two at **Prime Outlets at Lee** (US 20 East; www.primeoutlets.com). The center offers savings of up to 65 percent at 60 designer outlet stores, including COACH Factory, Cole Haan, Michael Kors, Nike Factory Store and Under Armour.

Where to...
Be Entertained

HIKING AND BICYCLING

For hiking and bicycling maps and information contact the Department of Conservation and Recreation (www.mass.gov/dcr).

At **Bartholomew's Cobble**, a nature reserve near Ashley Falls, there are marked trails. At **Monument Mountain**, high above Great Barrington, trails lead to fine views of Devils Pulpit. On a clear day, you can see five states from the top of **Mount Greylock**, which at 3,491 feet (1,063m) is the highest point in Massachusetts. For more energetic hikes or whitewater trips, sign up with a specialist outfitter such as **Berkshire Outfitters** (www.berkshireoutfitters.com) in Adams or **Zoar Outdoor** (tel: 800/ 532-7483; www.zoaroutdoor.com).

HISTORIC HOMES

Sculptor Daniel Chester French's vacation home is **Chesterwood** (4 Williamsville Road, off SR 183, Stockbridge, tel: 413/298-3579; www.chesterwood.org), and **Naumkeag** (Prospect Hill Road, Stockbridge, tel: 413/298-3239; www.thetrustees.org) is a 44-room "summer cottage" with a garden.

FALL FOLIAGE

Although the displays in Vermont and New Hampshire are better known, the Berkshires are equally impressive. The Mohawk Trail (www.mohawktrail.com), SR 2 between North Adams and Greenfield, is popular with leaf-peepers in October.

Vermont

Getting Your Bearings

There is something special about Vermont. Maybe it's the fact that the entire state has only one city with more than 20,000 people. Maybe it's the law banning billboards from marring the beautiful Green Mountain landscape. Maybe it's the cheese from the hundreds of dairies and creameries. Whatever it is, it's wonderful, and while you may not be able to put your finger on exactly what makes Vermont so special, you will notice it almost as soon as you cross the state border.

Woodstock and Manchester are two of the state's top resort destinations. Manchester, in southwestern Vermont, boasts some of the state's finest inns and some of the best fishing in the northeastern United States. Woodstock is in central Vermont, at the center of countless different kinds of outdoor activities. The driving tour on pages 181–183 shows a scenic route between the two areas. The tour, indeed all of Vermont, is at its most gorgeous during fall foliage season, but that's also when rates are highest at lodgings throughout the state.

Summer is the time when all of Vermont's wares are on display. The state has only two limited-access highways, but hundreds of byways, dirt roads and hiking trails. This is the place to trade your briefcase for a backpack, your cell phone for a fishing pole, and your laptop for a trail map; you might travel via horseback or bicycle from one inn to another, or you might choose to spend all day fishing for trout in one of the gin-clear streams.

Vermont has more to offer than natural beauty and outdoor activities. Burlington may feel more "town" than "city," when compared to Boston and New York, but it has a buzzing nightlife. Festivals across the state celebrate everything from maple sugar and jam to Mozart and jazz. Since locals enjoy theater, movies and eating out, all that is on offer – just not in every community.

Top: Laid back and leisured: life in Vermont

Bottom: A horse farm near Roxbury, Vermont

Previous page: Fall foliage

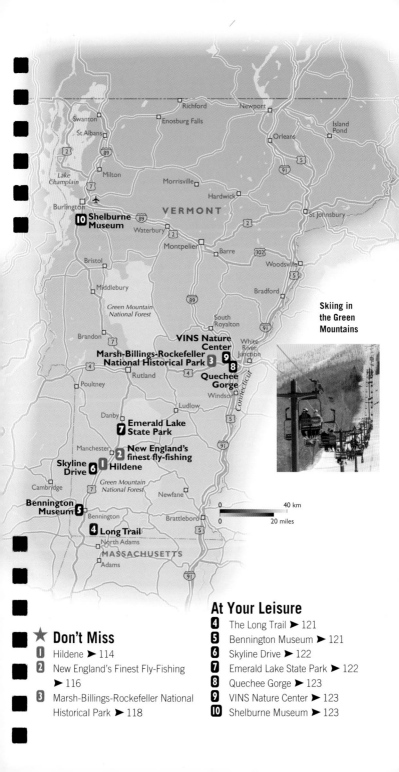

Skiing in
the Green
Mountains

★ Don't Miss

At Your Leisure

In Four Days

If you're not quite sure where to begin your travels, this itinerary recommends a practical and enjoyable four days in Vermont, taking in some of the best places to see using the Getting Your Bearings map on the previous page. For more information see the main entries.

Day 1

Morning
Make your way from your base in Manchester to **1 Hildene** (► 114–115), the historic home of Robert Todd Lincoln (left). In winter, you can ski cross-country on the grounds. In summer, the lawns and gardens are glorious.

Afternoon
Have lunch at the Perfect Wife (► 128) in Manchester center, then stroll down Main Street toward the outlet stores. Learn to fly-fish at **Orvis** headquarters (► 116), or drive out to **7 Emerald Lake State Park** (► 122) for the afternoon. If you're feeling energetic, you could hike part of the **4 Long Trail** (► 121), one of New England's prettiest hiking paths.

Evening
Have dinner at one of the fine inns or at Bistro Henry in Manchester center (► 127). Nightlife here is pretty tame, but the clear Vermont air and rural countryside make for great stargazing from your hotel porch or balcony.

Day 2

Morning
Head north to the Woodstock area (right), following the first half of the **Vermont driving tour** (► 181–183). The route takes you through some of Vermont's finest scenery, passing the ski resorts of Okemo and Stratton.

Afternoon
Stop for lunch in Weston at the Bryant House Restaurant (tel: 802/824-6287; www.vermontcountrystore.com), just a few steps from the Vermont Country Store. If you arrive in Woodstock early enough, visit the **9 VINS Nature Center** (► 123), with its magnificent birds of prey, or visit the Kedron Valley Stables (► 130).

Evening
Settle in at your Woodstock accommodations, then head to Osteria Pane e Salute (61 Central Street, tel: 802/457-4882; www.osteriapaneesalute.com), for authentic Italian dishes.

Day 3

Morning
Spend the day at the **3** **Marsh-Billings-Rockefeller National Historical Park** (➤ 118–120). Start by hiking to the top of **Mount Tom** (➤ 118) for a commanding view of the entire Woodstock area.

Afternoon
Visit **Billings Farm and Museum** (➤ 118–119), a working dairy farm where you can watch cows being milked, and introduce yourself to week-old calves and pet sheep. Across the street is the historic mansion that was home to both Marsh and Billings, as well as Mary and Laurance Rockefeller.

Evening
Drive east along US 4 to the nearby town of Quechee. If there's still daylight, check out **8** **Quechee Gorge** (above, ➤ 123). Or watch glassblowers at work at the Simon Pearce Studio. Dine at the Simon Pearce Restaurant (➤ 128), overlooking a waterfall on the Ottauquechee River.

Day 4

Drive north on I-89 to Burlington. To the south is Shelburne, home of the **10** **Shelburne Museum** (below, ➤ 123–124), a veritable cornucopia of art and architecture from all over New England and New York. It's almost like the region's attic. Break the journey in Montpelier and sample the work of student chefs from the New England Culinary Institute at Main Street Grill and Bar (118 Main Street, tel: 802/223-3188; www.necidining.com).

FOLK ART

❶ Hildene

Vermont isn't usually known for its historic homes – most of the state's pleasures are to be found outdoors, not in. The exception that proves the rule is Hildene, a majestic 24-room Georgian Revival mansion overlooking hundreds of acres of the choicest land in Manchester.

A Summer Home

Hildene was built in 1905 as a summer home for Robert Todd Lincoln, the only son of President Abraham Lincoln to survive to adulthood. He loved Vermont and was a frequent visitor for more than 40 years before building his estate here.

The house is impressive by any definition, but compared to the extravagant "cottages" built around the same time in Newport by the Astors and Vanderbilts, it is on a much more human scale. What is extraordinary, however, is the 1908 **Aeolian organ**, with 1,000 pipes. The house was remodeled to house the organ, with the pipes concealed in cabinets on the staircase landing and columns for air from the bellows in the cellar. When the organ is played, music suffuses the air, permeating every corner of the house. Lincoln summered here until his death in 1926; his descendants lived here until 1975.

Robert Todd Lincoln, son of Abraham Lincoln, built Hildene as a summer home

Rooms at Hildene, such as the library (right), are authentically furnished, and feature much Lincoln memorabilia

What to See

Start your visit with a video presentation at the Welcome Center, then go on to the house. Listen to the organ, see the common rooms, a few bedrooms and the servants' quarters. Best of all, is the famous **stove pipe hat** worn by President Abraham Lincoln – one of only three still in existence. Behind the home are the luxurious **formal gardens**, laid out in a grid formation in imitation of a stained-glass window. Mid-June is the time to see the spectacular array of some 1,000 peony blossoms. There is much to see at other times. Thanks to restoration work, the **Cutting and Kitchen Gardens** now reflect the fruits and flowers grown here a century ago. Beyond, are 420 acres (170ha) of meadows and farmland, where animals are reared using traditional techniques such as rotational grazing. However, the barn that houses the goats for the cheese-making operation has up-to-date solar power!

TAKING A BREAK

The **Marsh Tavern**, within the historic Equinox resort (➤ 125), is a special place for a casual meal.

🏁 200 A2 📧 SR 7A, Manchester, VT ☎ 802/362-1788; www.hildene.org 🕐 Daily 9:30–4:30; closed major hols 💵 Moderate. Guided tours at noon Jun to mid-Oct; self-guided the rest of the year

---

HILDENE: INSIDE INFO

Top tips Entry just to Hildene's **trails, lawns and gardens** costs about half the full admission price. In summer, the gardens are a popular site for evening weddings (don't worry – festivities start after the last tour leaves).

■ In winter, the grounds are ideal for **cross-country skiing**, with more than 9 miles (14km) of trails for skiers of all abilities. In the Welcome Center you can rent skis or escape the cold for a cup of hot chocolate.

② New England's Finest Fly-Fishing

The Manchester area is a hot spot for fishing aficionados of all ability levels, not only because of its multitude of lakes, rivers and streams, but also because of its outfitters and instructors. There is even a museum devoted to fly-fishing.

Getting Started

The flagship store of **Orvis**, in Manchester Village, is the place for fishing enthusiasts. There is a pond inside the store, part of the outdoor pond behind the showroom that is stocked with trout, making it the perfect place to show beginners how to cast a fly rod and identify feeding patterns. Even rank amateurs should make Orvis their first stop. From mid-April through mid-October, the store runs short fly-fishing courses that can teach even the most inexperienced angler to land the big ones. The classes are not cheap, but the fee does include all equipment, lunches and fishing licenses.

Once you have stocked up on the latest gear, you can wade hip deep into Manchester's Batten Kill River for trout, drive north to Lake St. Catherine for bass and pike or go west to the Harriman Reservoir for lake trout.

The clear streams near Manchester are perfect for those seeking solitude

American Museum of Fly Fishing

Fly-fishing fanatics will delight in the **American Museum of Fly Fishing**. It has every imaginable piece of lore about fly-fishing, as well as a collection ranging from over 1,000 rods to 20,000 flies, including one tied way back in 1789.

Learn to cast a line or stock up on the latest fishing gear: Orvis in Manchester

TAKING A BREAK

For the makings of a glamorous picnic, try the **Gourmet Deli & Cafe** (4961 Main Street, tel: 802/362-1254) in Manchester Center.

Orvis
➕ 200 A2 ✉ SR 7A, Manchester, VT ☎ 802/362-3750; www.orvis.com
🕐 Mon–Fri 10–6, Sat 9–6, Sun 10–5. Two-day fly-fishing classes mid-Apr to mid-Oct 💰 $470 for two-day classes, including all equipment plus lunches, a fishing license and access to fishing on the Batten Kill River before and after class

American Museum of Fly Fishing
➕ 200 A2 ✉ SR 7A in Manchester Village, two blocks south of the Equinox Hotel ☎ 802/362-3300; www.amff.com 🕐 Tue–Sat 10–4 💰 Inexpensive for adults, discounts for children

Vermont Fish and Wildlife Department
➕ 200 B4 ✉ 103 South Main Street, Waterbury, VT ☎ 802/241-3700; www.vtfishandwildlife.com

---

MANCHESTER: INSIDE INFO

Top tip Anglers love the **Charles Orvis Inn**. Now part of the Equinox Resort (► 125), rooms are named for fly patterns, such as Royal Coachman.

Hidden gems Deep in the southern section of the Green Mountain National Forest (www.fs.fed.us), **Somerset Reservoir** is harder to get to than most fishing holes in southern Vermont. But the unspoiled wilderness surrounding it makes it worth the trouble it takes to get there. A dirt road that's closed in winter is the only route that goes near it. Be prepared to share the solitude with other anglers. To get there from Manchester, take US 7 or SR 7A south to East Arlington. Turn left onto the Kelly Stand Road (see the signs for Kansas) and follow it about 10 miles (16km) to the Grout Pond parking area. You'll have to walk about a mile (1.5km) from here. The southern end of the reservoir requires a lot more driving. Take US 7 south to Bennington, turn left onto SR 9 east. About 2 miles (3.5km) past Searsburg, turn left onto Somerset Road and follow it 9 miles (14km) to the end.

3 Marsh-Billings-Rockefeller National Historical Park

People around Woodstock will tell you that Marsh-Billings-Rockefeller is a national park. If that suggests towering redwoods, deep canyons, buffalo roaming and log cabins you are in for a surprise. Although smaller than more famous parks, its scenic 555 acres (225ha) are an impressive and educational place, with plenty to do and see.

Marsh-Billings-Rockefeller is actually classified as a National Historical Park. It is still protected by the federal government, still has plenty of unspoiled forest, and still enjoys prompt maintenance and has lots of helpful rangers to answer questions.

Mount Tom Forest

Frederick Billings (Billings, Montana, is named for him) planted thousands of trees and built a 20-mile (32km) network of carriage roads and hiking trails on what used to be farmland here in the 1870s. It remains today one of the country's best examples of managed forests. Trails starting at Faulkner Park in town lead to a small lake known to locals as "the Pogue." Other paths ascend gently up the slopes of **Mount Tom** to its peak, where the reward is a panoramic view of the entire town below, including, in the right weather, several covered bridges over the Ottauquechee River. In winter, the carriage trails become groomed cross-country skiing trails (operated by a private company, the Woodstock Inn and Resort's Nordic Center).

The parlor in the Marsh-Billings-Rockefeller Mansion is lavishly furnished with period furniture

Billings Farm and Museum

Although not part of the National Park system, this working farm is an important part of the history of the extensive estate. Kids will love the **working farm**, and they might even take an interest in the museum portion of the property, which displays the self-sufficient lifestyle of the 19th-century hillfarms that shaped Vermont's landscape. In the dairy barn, they can

View of Woodstock, looking east from the South Peak of Mount Tom

watch the herd of Jersey cows being milked, or they can go next door to pet day-old calves. They can visit chickens in the chicken coop, sheep in the pasture and horses in the barn.

The **Billings Farm House** won't appeal as much to kids, but their parents might like to tour the ahead-of-its-time 1890 abode. It had indoor plumbing, running water, and a multitude of rooms for a simple farm house. Most interesting is the basement creamery, where the fresh milk was used to make butter and cream.

Marsh-Billings-Rockefeller Mansion

The third part of the park is the residential complex, built for the family of George Perkins Marsh in 1805. Marsh, a noted writer and conservationist, grew up in this home, but sold it to Frederick Billings in 1869. The Billings family renovated the mansion twice before finally selling it to Mary F. and Laurance S. Rockefeller in 1954.

The interiors are lavishly furnished with period furniture, Tiffany windows and Asian ceramics. The **art collection** is upward of 400 paintings; highlights include works by artists such as Albert Bierstadt (who portrayed the American West) and Thomas Cole (of the Hudson River School).

In 1992, the Rockefellers donated the forest land and the mansion to the US government, which turned it into a National Historical Park.

MARSH-BILLINGS-ROCKEFELLER NATIONAL HISTORICAL PARK: INSIDE INFO

Hidden gem The **Prosper Road entrance** to Mount Tom Forest is well known to locals. The hiking trails from this end of the park are a little longer and a little more interesting than the switchbacks that go up the front side of the mountain from Faulkner Park. From the center of Woodstock, take SR 12 north across the Iron Bridge over the Ottauquechee River and turn right to stay on SR 12. Bear left at the first fork (don't go to Billings Farm) and left again at the next fork. Look for signs for Prosper Road on your left. Turn left onto Prosper Road and continue up the hill for about a half mile (0.8km). After the cemetery, there is a small parking lot on the left. Trails begin here.

In more detail The **Woodstock Inn and Resort's Nordic Center** (▶ 126) maintains cross-country skiing trails in Mount Tom Forest in winter. If you want to ski the forest, you need to get a pass from them. They can also provide trail maps and rental skis. The center is located on SR 106, just south of town.

Admission to Mount Tom Forest is free; mountain bikes, snowmobiles and other motorized vehicles are prohibited in the forest. A discounted combination ticket is available for Billings Farm and Museum and for the Marsh-Billings-Rockefeller Mansion.

At Billings Farm you can watch cows being milked

TAKING A BREAK

For lunch, stock up on locally produced fruits, cheeses and freshly baked bread at **Woodstock Farmers' Market** (1 mile (1.6km) west of Woodstock on Route 4, tel: 802/457-3658; www.woodstockfarmersmarket.org).

➕ 200 B3 ✉ 54 Elm Street, Woodstock, VT ☎ 802/457-3368 🕐 Late May–Oct daily 10–5 🎫 Guided tours of Marsh-Billings-Rockefeller Mansion and gardens: inexpensive. Tours of Mount Tom Forest: free

Billings Farm and Museum
➕ 200 B3 ✉ PO Box 489, SR 12 and River Road, Woodstock, VT ☎ 802/457-2355; www.billingsfarm.org 🕐 May–Oct daily 10–5; Nov–Feb Sat–Sun 10–3:30 🎫 Moderate. Reduced price admission for children aged 3–15 and adults aged over 62

At Your Leisure

🄴 The Long Trail

This 270-mile (435km) trail is the oldest long-distance hiking trail in the United States, predating even the Maine-to-Georgia Appalachian Trail that overlaps some of the same territory. Carved between 1910 and 1930 by the Green Mountain Club, the Long Trail runs the length of Vermont from Massachusetts to Canada. The Appalachian Trail joins the Long Trail for its first 100 miles (160km) in southern Vermont, making this portion more traveled and more populated. The trails diverge at Sherburne Pass (near Killington), but the beauty of the Long Trail is so great that it has lured away many a hiker who had intended to follow the Appalachian all the way to Maine.

Along the way are some 70 huts, lean-tos and other primitive campsites. You can also enjoy a day hike almost anywhere on the length of the path. Near Manchester, the best way to access the trail is by taking Route 11 approximately 6 miles (10km) east of Manchester Center. Take the turnoff on the left side to the trailhead. From there, you can continue to hike north to Bromley Mountain, south to Stratton Mountain, 40 miles (64km) south to Massachusetts, or 230 miles (370km) north to Canada.

Whichever way you decide to go, wear comfortable shoes, bring plenty of water and insect repellent, and don't forget your camera. In addition to rugged mountain peaks and pristine ponds peeking through the thick green hardwood forests, you you might see deer, raccoons and, if you're lucky, a rare peregrine falcon. The Green Mountain Club publishes the *Long Trail Guide*, which has detailed maps and descriptions.

✚ 200 A2

The Green Mountain Club
✉ 4711 Waterbury-Stowe Road, Waterbury Center, VT ☎ 802/244-7037; www.greenmountainclub.org

🄵 Bennington Museum

This rates as a hidden gem, with its eclectic collection. Don't miss the Bennington Flag, allegedly flown at the Battle of Bennington on August 16, 1777. Labeled as one of America's oldest flags, with 13 white and red stripes, it has the numerals 76 emblazoned in the corner. Then there is locally made pottery and furniture, as well as a 1924 Wasp touring car. The highlight has to be the paintings by American folk artist Grandma Moses. A farmer's wife, who lived nearby, she only took up painting seriously in her seventies, carrying on for 30 years. Her naïve scenes of Vermont country life a century ago hang in galleries around the world – but the world's largest public collection is right here!

✚ 200 A2 ✉ 75 Main Street, Bennington, VT ☎ 802/447-1571; www.benningtonmuseum.org 🕐 Sep–Oct daily 10–5; Feb–Aug, Nov, Dec Thu–Tue 10–5 ⑲ Inexpensive

Hiking is popular in Vermont. The Long Trail, which runs the length of the state, is suitable for day trips and longer hikes

OFF THE BEATEN TRACK

At **Grafton** you can see what a Vermont village might have looked like in the 1800s. The foundation that sponsored the town's preservation even buried the power lines. Check out the cheese-making process at Grafton Village Cheese Company (www.graftonvillagecheese.com) or simply sample some of its excellent wares. If you're here in winter, you can strap on boards or snowshoes at the Grafton Ponds Outdoor Center (www.graftonponds.com).

❻ Skyline Drive

If you want to see the views from atop one of the Green Mountains, but you don't want to spend all day hiking just to get there, get behind the wheel and head up to Skyline Drive. The entrance is on SR 7A just south of Manchester. There is a fee but you'll quickly make it to the 3,848-foot (1,173m) summit of Mount Equinox. The road to the top is about 5 miles (8km) long, and the views are stunning, though as you would expect from somewhere with a paved road, you won't have the place entirely to yourself.

🔲 200 A2 ✉ 1A St. Bruno Drive, Arlington, VT ☎ 802/362-1114 🕓 May–Oct Mon–Wed 9–5, Thu–Sun 9–dusk, closes 35 min before sunset 💰 Moderate charge for car and driver, additional fee per passenger

❼ Emerald Lake State Park

The lake at this 430-acre (174ha) park, 8 miles (13km) north of Manchester, isn't quite the color of emeralds, but the park is a gem nonetheless. Motors are prohibited on the lake, making it a quiet spot for swimming, fishing and boating, and there are excellent camping facilities. For those who want to get away from car campers, several hiking trails meander through the hills above the lake.

🔲 200 A3 ✉ US 7, East Dorset, VT ☎ 802/362-1655; www.vtstateparks.com 🕓 Late-May to mid-Oct daily 10–9 💰 Inexpensive

Views from the Skyline Drive are stunning

8 Quechee Gorge

Don't believe the hype: Quechee Gorge is not the Grand Canyon of the east, though it is still impressive. The 165-foot (50m) gorge was carved thousands of years ago by the glacial erosion of the Ottauquechee River. A pleasant half-mile (0.8km) walking trail takes you from the side of the road down to water level, where there's even a refreshing swimming hole. You can also get a fine view of the gorge from the bridge that spans the chasm.

Quechee State Park
➕ 200 B3 ✉ US 4, Quechee, VT. Park in the Quechee Gorge Gifts parking lot on the north side of the road ☎ 802/295-2990; www.vtstateparks.com

9 VINS Nature Center

Raptors large and small are the star attractions at VINS, the 47-acre (19ha) nature center of the Vermont Institute of Natural Science. Watch these predators demonstrate their flying and hunting skills and learn how they are rehabilitated here. Residents include eagles (bald and golden), owls (great horned, snowy and northern saw-whet) as well as red-tailed hawks and peregrine falcons. There are songbirds, too, such as rose-breasted grosbeaks and cedar waxwings. Ask about the new audio tour.
➕ 200 B3 ✉ US 4, near Quechee Gorge, VT ☎ 802/359-5000; www.vinsweb.org
🕐 May–Oct daily 9–5:30; Nov–Apr daily 10–4
💵 Moderate. Discounts for children. Ask about special tours

10 Shelburne Museum

Though the museum is 95 miles (153km) from Manchester (a good 2-hour drive), its unique collection makes it well worth the trip, especially on a cool or rainy day. Founded in 1947 by Electra Havemeyer Webb, Shelburne is known as "New England's Smithsonian" for good reason. In addition to paintings and other arts, it has one of the finest collections of American folk art and architecture in the USA.

Among the museum's 150,000 exhibits are decoys, quilts, weather vanes and other Americana. These compete for space with more traditional museum fare like paintings and prints by artists as diverse as Rembrandt, Andrew

Above left: Quechee Gorge was carved by glacial erosion
Below: The Shelburne Museum houses a fine collection of folk art and architecture

AN ANTIQUES CORRIDOR

If you're an antiques hound, head for **SR 30**, from Brattleboro to Townshend. There are dozens of antiques shops along this 18-mile (29km) strip. On a Sunday, just north of the town, from May through October, the Original Newfane Flea Market starts at 6am, with 150 to 200 dealers setting out their wares.

Wyeth, Grandma Moses, Monet, Winslow Homer and Degas.

The collection is distributed among 39 buildings on the museum's 45-acre (18ha) site, many of which are attractions in their own right. There's an 1890 railroad station, a schoolhouse, a 1901 Vermont round barn, a lighthouse, a jail and an 18th-century general store. Perhaps the most curious piece is the steamboat, *Ticonderoga*, a designated National Historic Landmark, "moored" nowhere near water.

🚆 200 A4 ✉ US 7, Shelburne, VT ☎ 802/985-3346; www.shelburnemuseum.org 🕓 Mid-May–Oct daily 10–5. For special programs check website 💵 Expensive. Discounts for children aged 5–18, children aged under 5 free

MAPLE SYRUP

Want to know how maple syrup gets from the depths of the forest to the top of your pancakes? Vermont is the perfect place to find out: the state makes more maple syrup than any other in the country, producing 500,000 US gallons (about 2 million liters) each year. Dozens of sugarhouses are open to the public.

Sugaring is weather-dependent. Temperatures have to be above freezing during the day, and below freezing at night to stimulate movement of maple sap from the roots to the budding leaves of the trees. In Vermont, that happens from late February to early April. Sugarers tap small spouts into the trees to siphon off sap, then at the sugarhouse they use wood-fired furnaces to turn the sap into syrup. It's an expensive, time-consuming process, especially when you consider that you need 40 US gallons (151 liters) of sap to make a single gallon (3.8 liters) of maple syrup.

In the Manchester area, you can visit a sugarhouse at Merck Forest and Farmland Center, and at Woodstock, Kedron Sugar Makers and Sugarbush Farm (▶ 129). The Vermont Maple Sugar Maker's Association has a complete list of sugarhouses.

Merck Forest and Farmland Center
✉ Off SR 315, near Manchester, VT ☎ 802/394-7836; www.merckforest.org

Kedron Sugar Makers
✉ 6102 Kendall Road, South Woodstock, VT ☎ 802/457-1480; www.kedron.com

Sugarbush Farm
✉ At US 4 in Taftsville, leave main road, cross Red Covered Bridge, go up hill, make a left on Hillside Road ☎ 800/281-1757 or 802/457-1757; www.sugarbushfarm.com

Maple Sugar Maker's Association
✉ 491 East Barnard Road, South Royalton, VT ☎ 802/763-7435; www.vermontmaple.org

Where to...
Stay

Prices
Expect to pay for two people sharing a double room, excluding taxes
$ under $150　　**$$** $150-$250　　**$$$** over $250

MANCHESTER

⚒⚒ The Chalet Motel $

Accommodations can be costly in Vermont's summer, fall and winter, but the Chalet Motel offers affordable, family-oriented lodging in the heart of the Green Mountains. The 43 rooms are large and comfortable, with all the latest modern facilities. Some have kings, others queen beds, and there are convertible couches. All the rooms have color TVs, refrigerators, coffee-making facilities and telephones. To keep children and parents happy, there is a heated outdoor pool, as well as a game room. The Chalet Motel is close to attractions, from designer outlet shopping to historic Hildene, and golf at Manchester Country Club.

✠ 200 A2 ⊠ Routes 11/30, Manchester Center, VT ☎ 800/343-9900 or 802/362-1622; www.thechaletmotel.com

⚒⚒⚒ The Equinox Resort and Spa $$$

Behind the long-pillared porch, this rambling 1769 hotel has the luxurious add-ons of a first-class resort: concierges, a sumptuous spa and a challenging 18-hole golf course. Guests can enjoy hands-on instruction in the art of falconry, followed by a hawk walk along the resort's scenic trails, or take a 2-day fly-fishing trip on the Batten Kill River to learn the latest techniques. Thanks to tasteful renovations, there is a more contemporary look, from the Great Room to the guest rooms, with their custom-made beds. For dining, choose from the new Chop House (steaks), the new Falcon Bar (wine and local cheeses), as well as the popular Marsh Tavern (New England fare).

✠ 200 A2 ⊠ Historic SR 7A. Manchester Village, VT ☎ 800/362-4747 or 802/362-4700; www.equinoxresort.com

⚒⚒⚒ Manchester View $-$$$

Established in the 1950s, this classic New England country inn has been consistently highly rated. Rooms range from standard through to luxury suites. There are also some specialty rooms, such as the delightful Robert Frost Room housed in a converted barn, which combines turn-of-the-20th-century fittings with up-to-the-minute facilities such as modems and DVD players. All the rooms are now non-smoking, and there's a pool and complimentary access for guests to golf and tennis close by at the Manchester Country Club.

✠ 200 A2 ⊠ Route 7A. Manchester Center, VT. ☎ 800/548-4141 or 802/362-2739; www.manchesterview.com

DORSET

⚒⚒ Inn at Westview Farm $-$$

The informal 10-bedroom inn stands on the edge of town. Although there are some attractive antiques, decoration and furnishings are stylish rather than folksy. In the small restaurant, imaginative dishes range from herb-crusted venison to grilled saffron shrimp. Save room for the special warm chocolate cake or buttermilk panna cotta.

✠ 200 A2 ⊠ 2928 SR 30, Dorset, VT ☎ 800/769-4903 or 802/867-5715; www.innatwestviewfarm.com

WOODSTOCK

◇ Braeside Motel $

Set on a peaceful hillside, this 12-room motel is a mile (1.6km) northeast of Woodstock. Close by is the Marsh-Billings-Rockefeller National Historical Park and the Billings Farm and Museum. All rooms have their own private entrance, TV, refrigerators and air-conditioning. But the windows do open, so you can enjoy the fresh Vermont air. Free WiFi is available.

⊞ 200 B3 ⊠ 432 Woodstock Road, Woodstock, VT ☎ 802/457-1366; www.braesidemotel.com

◇◇◇ Jackson House Inn $$-$$$

With its white picket fence and wrap-around porch, this 120-year-old Victorian inn, set in 3.5 acres (1.5ha) of gardens, has 15 eclectically decorated rooms. The award-winning restaurant, in its cathedral-ceiling dining room, has an open hearth fireplace and fine views of the garden. Breakfasts are an event: fresh smoked salmon and shallots in scrambled eggs, fresh baked scones, fruit compote with peach schnapps, Santa Fe omelets. At sunset, guests are invited to enjoy a glass of wine in the library.

⊞ 200 B3 ⊠ 114–3 Senior Lane, Woodstock, VT ☎ 800/448-1890 or 802/457-2065; www.jacksonhouse.com

◇◇◇ The Shire Riverview Motel $-$$

This attractive colonial motel is within easy walking distance of Woodstock's shops and restaurants and the Village Green. The motel's 42 guestrooms are bright and comfortable, furnished in New England style, and most have views of the Ottauquechee River. There is an attractive outdoor sitting area with rocking chairs lacing the river where you can relax in the fresh Vermont air.

⊞ 200 B3 ⊠ 46 Pleasant Street, Woodstock, VT ☎ 802/457-2211; www.shiremotel.com

◇◇◇ The Woodstocker Bed-and-Breakfast $-$$$

In the heart of the village, with Mount Tom on the doorstep, the bright yellow Woodstocker is popular with hikers, cross-country skiers and couples looking for a relaxing break. The British owners have a catalog of "innkeeper of the year" awards for this relaxed nine-room gem, with its library, wood-burning stove, and a 24-hour, self-service food station. Breakfast is a generous buffet, backed with waffles, pancakes and egg dishes.

⊞ 200 B3 ⊠ 61 River Street, Woodstock, VT ☎ 802/457-3896; www.woodstockervt.com

◇◇◇ Woodstock Inn and Resort $$-$$$

With standards of comfort and cuisine that would grace a city hotel, this is no cozy village inn. Everything is on a large scale, from the grand piano in the lounge to the 142 bedrooms. Most guests come for the sports facilities, which include tennis courts, a golf course, squash and spa facilities. In winter, guests have free access to the hotel's ski touring center (Sunday to Thursday). The elegant dining room has an excellent New England menu.

⊞ 200 B3 ⊠ 14 The Green, Woodstock, VT ☎ 800/448-7900 or 802/457-1100; www.woodstockinn.com

QUECHEE

◇ The Quechee Inn at Marshland Farm $-$$

Within walking distance of the Quechee Gorge, this 18th-century farmhouse overlooking the Ottauquechee River has been transformed into a comfortable inn. Of the 25 bedrooms, those in the old house with river views have the most atmosphere, with wide pine-plank floors and country decor. Guests come here to get away from it all and hike or cross-country ski along the 11 miles (18km) of trails. Breakfast is a generous buffet with eggs, bacon, pancakes, muffins and

Where to...
Eat and Drink

Prices

Expect to pay per person for a three-course meal, excluding drinks and service
$ under $20 $$ $20–$35 $$$ over $35

MANCHESTER

☜☜☜ Bistro Henry $$$

Although the food at Bistro Henry is described as Mediterranean, there are some interesting variations – Maine crab cakes, game in season, lobster bisque, seasonal seafood. Main courses might be Moroccan chicken with couscous or braised lamb shank with garlic mashed potatoes and Merlot gravy. Leave room for the rich desserts, which are superb.

✚ 200 A2 ⊠ SR 11/30, Manchester Center, VT ☎ 802/362-4982; www.bistrohenry.com ✆ Tue–Sun 5–9

☜☜☜ Chantecleer $$$

In a former dairy barn with a stone fireplace, Michel Baumann's restaurant is grander than most country eateries. Dishes combine European and American tradition: whole Dover sole with capers and lemon, rack of lamb, escargot with hazelnut butter, fresh fish and game. Elaborate desserts include Basel torte and crème brûlée.

✚ 200 A2 ⊠ SR 7A North, East Dorset, VT, 3.5 miles (5.5km) north of Manchester ☎ 802/362-1616; www.chantecleerrestaurant.com ✆ Summer Wed–Mon 6–9:30; winter Wed–Sun. Closed 3 weeks Nov, Apr to mid-May

WARREN

☜☜☜ Pitcher Inn $$$

Nine of the bedrooms at this beautiful, luxurious inn are in the main house; two more are in the converted barn next door. Much love and care has been put into the decoration of the public rooms and bedrooms, with original art works and antiques, all with a Vermont theme. A favorite is the School Room, complete with slate chalkboard and chalk, school desk and globe. Some rooms also have wood-burning fireplaces to complete the experience. The chef works with local produce preparing Vermont-raised lamb, quail and rabbit, as well as organic heirloom tomatoes, local free-range eggs and artisan cheeses. If you're looking for somewhere to celebrate that special occasion, this is the place to choose.

✚ 200 B4 ⊠ 275 Main Street, Warren, VT ☎ 802/496-6350; www.pitcherinn.com

VERGENNES

☜☜☜ Strong House Inn $–$$$

Well-placed for attractions such as Shelburne Museum, the Vermont Teddy Bear Factory and Lake Champlain, this is a destination in its own right, with its lovely white-painted wooden buildings dating back to 1834. Rooms, some of which have working fireplaces, are furnished in a historic Victorian style, with all the comforts of today, such as high-speed internet. It's also popular for rug hooking and quilting retreats.

✚ 200 A4 ⊠ 94 West Main Street, Vergennes, VT ☎ 802/877-3337; www.stronghouseinn.com

fruit. Dinner (for which there is an additional charge) is more elegant. Dishes include duck, salmon and beef, and there is always a vegetarian option.

✚ 200 B3 ⊠ 1119 Quechee Main Street, Quechee, VT ☎ 800/235-3133 or 802/295-3133; www.quecheeinn.com

Garlic John's $$

This chef-owned Italian restaurant has long been a favorite dinner spot with locals who return for typical Italian dishes: hot and cold antipasti, veal piccata, sole Florentine, swordfish Provençal, roasted garlic and spinach ravioli. There are usually pasta specials, as well as popular desserts, such as tiramisu and cheesecake. Choose from a straightforward list of Italian wines.

✚ 200 A2 ⊠ SR11/30, Manchester Center, VT ☎ 802/362-9843 ⑥ Sun–Thu 4–9, Fri–Sat 4–10

Mistral's at Toll Gate $$$

The favorite tables in this romantic riverside restaurant are by the windows, with a view of the lovely creek. The exquisitely prepared classic French cuisine changes with the seasons, and includes dishes like chateaubriand béarnaise and salmon cannelloni stuffed with lobster. The wine list is extensive and has received accolades for

its excellence. Reservations are recommended.

✚ 200 A2 ⊠ 10 Toll Gate Road, Manchester, VT ☎ 802/362-1779 ⑥ Thu–Mon 6–9

The Perfect Wife $$–$$$

Chef Amy Chamberlain has created a fine-dining experience with an atmosphere to match. There is seating in the cobblestone-walled dining room or in the greenhouse garden room. The American cuisine is creative, incorporates fresh ingredients and blends refreshing flavors with a freestyle flair. Dishes include chipotle (smoked chili pepper) Caesar salad, turkey schnitzel and rack of lamb with Cabernet-mint demi glace. Have your wine with dinner, and save room for the homemade desserts. Then relax in the tavern upstairs.

✚ 200 A2 ⊠ 2594 Depot Street, Route 11/30, Manchester Center, VT ☎ 802/362-2817; www.perfectwife.com ⑥ Jun–Aug Mon–Sat 5–10; Sep–May Tue–Sat 5–10; closed most public hols

WOODSTOCK

Bentley's $$

A Woodstock landmark for 30 years, with Victorian sofas and antique lamps, this is strictly informal: maple mustard chicken, meat loaf, baby back ribs, steaks and salads. There is dancing on Saturday nights.

✚ 200 B3 ⊠ 3 Elm Street, Woodstock, VT ☎ 802/457-3232; www.bentleysrestaurant.com ⑥ Daily 11:30–9:30, Sun brunch from 11am

Mountain Creamery $

A good, old-fashioned soda fountain, complete with delicious fruit pies, pastries and homemade ice cream, the Creamery is popular with families traveling with children. It also offers favorites such as grilled-cheese sandwiches and tuna melts for lunch. Nostalgia galore is the theme here.

✚ 200 B3 ⊠ 33 Central Street, Woodstock, VT ☎ 802/457-1715 ⑥ Daily 7am–3pm (later in summer)

The Prince and the Pauper $$–$$$

Dress up for a meal here. Cocktails are served from 5pm, dinner from 6pm. The menu has European classics, such as veal with a mushroom sauce, and modern American dishes like seared tuna with Cajun spicing.

✚ 200 B3 ⊠ 24 Elm Street, Woodstock, VT ☎ 802/457-1818; www.princeandpauper.com ⑥ Sun–Thu 6–9, Fri–Sat 6–9:30

QUECHEE

Simon Pearce Restaurant $$$

Set in a converted mill, this place is as stylish as Pearce's creations (▶ 129). Dishes such as cod crusted with horseradish, and roast duckling with mango chutney are full-flavored. Breads are home-made; the wine list is excellent.

✚ 200 B3 ⊠ The Mill, Quechee, VT ☎ 802/295-1470; www.simonpearce.com ⑥ Mon–Sat 11:30–2:45, 6–9, Sun 11–2:45, 6–9

Where to...
Shop

GENERAL STORES

These country shops once satisfied every need in rural communities. Some have survived to fuel nostalgia. Most famous is the **Vermont Country Store** (SR 100, tel: 802/824-3184; www.vermontcountrystore.com) in Weston. There is also a branch in Rockingham (SR 103, tel: 802/463-2224). Several less commercial stores are used by locals more than visitors, but call ahead for directions to save time negotiating the back roads. Try **JJ Hapgood Store** (off SR 11 in Peru, tel: 802/824-5911), which enjoyed 15 minutes of fame in the 1987 Diane Keaton movie *Baby Boom*; and the **Taftsville Country Store** (tel: 802/457-1135; www.taftsville.com) in Taftsville.

TRADITIONAL PRODUCE

You can buy cheese and maple syrup at country stores, but it is more fun to go to farms where they are made. Finding your way can be difficult, so phone ahead for directions and opening times.

Cabot Creamery (Cabot Village, CR 215, off US 2, tel: 800/837-4261; www.cabotcheese.com) has built a worldwide reputation over 90 years, and its award-winning New England mature cheddar is particularly toothsome. Daily tours are available. **Sugarbush Farm** (off Hillside Road, Woodstock, tel: 802/457-1757; www.sugarbushfarm.com) sells a dozen varieties of hand-waxed cheese, plus maple syrup from its own sugarhouse. Other picturesque outlets include: the **Sugar Shack** at Arlington (tel: 802/375-6747), **Dwight Miller Orchards**, East Dummerston (tel: 802/254-9635; www.vtfarmorg.com) and the **Richardson Farm** near Woodstock (tel: 802/436-7017). For more information on where to go to buy maple syrup products visit www.vermontmaple.org.

CRAFTS

Vermont has an abundance of skilled craftspeople. The **Northeast Kingdom Artisans Guild** cooperative features crafts and fine art by more than 100 artisans (430 Railroad Street, St. Johnsbury; www.nekartisansguild.com). In Middlebury, **Frog Hollow Vermont State Craft Center** (85 Church Street, www.froghollow.org) showcases the work of more than 250 Vermont craftspeople. One of the state's best-known craftsmen, **Simon Pearce**, works at the **Mill in Quechee** (US 4, Quechee, www.simonpearce.com). Here, world-class potters and glassblowers work in the converted riverside mill, which doubles as a showroom for almost everything from handsome furniture to elegant glasses. You can see how teddy bears are "born" at the **Vermont Teddy Bear Company** in Shelburne (US 7, www.vermontteddybear.com).

OUTLET SHOPPING

The **Manchester Designer Outlets** (www.manchesterdesigneroutlets.com) in Manchester Center sell a wide selection of big-name, designer labels at low prices. Advertisements insist that discounts can be as much as 70 percent. The attractive village, with 30 factory stores, plus restaurants, is geared for browsing, and the unhurried pace makes a welcome change to city malls. Footwear, handbags, accessories, books, cards and CDs, as well as jewelry and furniture are heavily discounted.

Where to...
Be Entertained

HIKING AND BICYCLING

Three companies put together self-guiding hiking tours in the area, tailored to time and ability: **Country Inns Along the Trail** (tel: 802/247-3300; www.inntoinn.com) in Brandon; **Vermont Inn-to-Inn Walking** (tel: 802/228-8799; www.vermontinntoinnwalking.com); and **Country Walkers** (tel: 802/244-1387; www.countrywalkers.com) in Waterbury. Several companies provide bicycle tours, taking your luggage from inn to inn. Try **VBT Bicycling Vacations** (tel: 802/453-4811; www.vbt.com) or **POMG Bike Tours of Vermont** (tel: 802/434-2270; www.pomgbike.com). Contact **Bike Vermont** (tel: 802/457-3553; www.bikevt.com) for weekend and multiday tours.

SKIING

The area comes into its own in winter, attracting 5 million skiers to 20 resort areas. Skiers head for **Killington** (www.killington.com), where there are miles of trails for every type of skier. Families love **Okemo** (www.okemo.com) for its warm welcome and organization, while **Stratton** (www.stratton.com) is packed with New Yorkers. Farther north, picturesque **Stowe** challenges the best skiers with its "Front Four" twisting double-diamond runs. The excellent **Stowe Mountain Resort Ski and Snowboard School** (www.stowe.com) is renowned.

Vermont has many cross-country skiing centers. For around 50 miles (80km) of groomed trails and real solitude, try to get a room at **Blueberry Hill Inn** in Goshen (www.blueberryhillinn.com), deep in Green Mountain National Forest.

WATER SPORTS

Fishing, canoeing and sailing are readily available along the shores of **Lake Champlain**.

BattenKill Canoe (6328 Route 7A, Arlington, tel: 800/421-5268; www.battenkill.com) provides easy 2-hour paddles on the Batten Kill River or trips from inn to inn.

FISHING

Visitors aged 15 and over need a license, available from any Town Clerk's office, some commercial outlets and fish and game wardens. The Vermont Fish and Wildlife Department issues a *Fish & Wildlife Guide* (www.vtfishandwildlife.com). **The Battenkill Angler** (www.battenkillangler.com) is a full-service outfitter dedicated to fly-fishing apparel. The **Hawk Inn**

and Mountain Resort (www.hawkresort.com) near Ludlow offers an extensive fly-fishing program on the Black River.

HORSEBACK RIDING

At **Kedron Valley Stables** (Route 106, South Woodstock, tel: 800/225-6301; www.kedron.com) you can have a riding lesson, go on a trail ride, or ride from inn to inn. **Pond Hill Ranch** (1683 Pond Hill Ranch Road, tel: 802/468-2449; www.pondhillranch.com) in Castleton offers 1-hour trail rides in the Green Mountains (April through October), and lessons all year. Longer trail rides by appointment.

GOLF

There are some 67 well-maintained courses. Green fees are low and tee times plentiful. Contact **Vermont Golf Association** (www.vtga.org) for details.

Rhode Island and Southeastern Connecticut

Getting Your Bearings

Rhode Island is America's smallest state geographically, but because most of the state is coastline, it offers an endless number of waterside attractions. It's not called the Ocean State for nothing.

Many of the major attractions are in the upscale town of Newport, which bills itself as "America's first resort." Founded in 1639, this was the cradle of America's religious freedom, but grew rich thanks to skilled ship's captains and traders. The real transformation came in the late 19th century, when a million dollars really meant something. The Vanderbilts, Astors and the rest of America's millionaires flocked here for the yachting regattas, lawn tennis and society parties. They built indescribably opulent mansions, calling them "summer cottages." Today, tours of these extravagant homes draw millions of visitors each year.

Newport is at its best, and its most crowded, in the summer months (especially weekends), when the weather is warm, the beaches are inviting and the world-famous festivals are in full swing. An hour or so away, in Southeastern Connecticut, the nation's third smallest state, are the contrasting attractions of Mystic Seaport and two of the largest casinos in the world.

Marble House, one of Newport's grand mansions

Narragansett Bay

Fort Adams 🀫 **State Park/Museum of Yachting**

Previous page: Rhode Islanders' love of the sea, ships and sailing inspired its epithet, the Ocean State

Watch the sun set over Newport harbor and live the life of leisure, at least for a few days

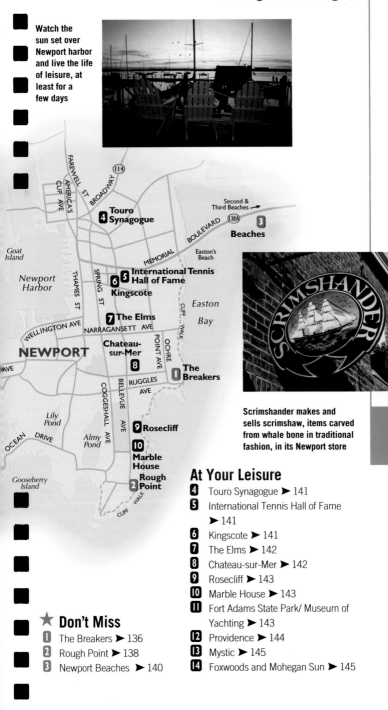

Scrimshander makes and sells scrimshaw, items carved from whale bone in traditional fashion, in its Newport store

At Your Leisure

★ Don't Miss

In Three Days

If you're not quite sure where to begin your travels, this itinerary
recommends a practical and enjoyable three days in Rhode Island
and Southeastern Connecticut, taking in some of the best places to
see using the Getting Your Bearings map on the previous page.
For more information see the main entries.

Day 1

Morning
Make your way to **❶ The Breakers** (above, ➤ 136–137), Newport's most
magnificent mansion. The tour is unforgettable, but gets crowded later in
the day. Spend the rest of the morning following the **Cliff Walk** (➤ 184–
186) to get an overview of the luxurious mansions on Bellevue Avenue
and the stunning ocean view that initially attracted their super-rich owners
to Newport.

Afternoon
If the weather's great, put together a picnic lunch and squander the rest of
the day at one of Newport's **❸ beaches** (➤ 140). If it's cold or rainy, stop
for lunch at the Brick Alley Restaurant (➤ 147), then tour the interior of
one of the mansions, perhaps the **❼ Elms** (➤ 142) or **❽ Chateau-sur-Mer**
(➤ 142).

Evening
Head to Lower Thames Street in the early evening so you can catch a little
shopping there before stores close. Choose a spot for dinner beforehand
– the long wait for tables at the award-winning Commodore's Room at the
Black Pearl (➤ 147) is definitely worth it. Bars and clubs along this same
stretch provide post-dining entertainment.

Day 2

Morning

Start at **6 Kingscote** (➤ 141–142), Newport's first "summer cottage." This home started the seaside town's boom in popularity with the rich and famous. Then stroll across to the nearby **5 International Tennis Hall of Fame** and Museum (right, ➤ 144), with the oldest grass courts in the world.

Afternoon

Have lunch at the lively Red Parrot (➤ 147) at the heart of Newport's waterfront, then drive over to **11 Fort Adams State Park** (below, ➤ 143), where you can lie on the beach or play frisbee on the large lawns. Alternatively, visit the **11 Museum of Yachting** (➤ 143).

Evening

Walk around the Washington Square historic district and the waterfront to see where colonial-era ships came and went, bringing Newport the riches that made it famous. Dine at the White Horse Tavern (➤ 147), America's oldest surviving restaurant, or the Brick Alley Restaurant (➤ 147).

Day 3

Morning

Head west across Rhode Island and follow US 1 along the Connecticut coast to the town of Mystic. Tour the **13 Mystic Aquarium** (➤ 145).

Afternoon

Take a side trip to Noank and the famous lobster shack, Abbott's Lobster in the Rough (➤ 147), then visit **13 Mystic Seaport** (➤ 145), a re-creation of a 19th-century whaling village, complete with a museum and period shops. It is also still a working shipyard.

Evening

Head to one of the nearby **14 casinos** (➤ 145), for a night of entertainment. Alternatively, enjoy the food and the stunning views over Long Island Sound at the Flood Tide Restaurant (at the intersection of US 1 and SR 27, ➤ 147).

1 The Breakers

This massive stone palace occupies an acre of land and is surrounded by 10 acres (4ha) of lawns and gardens. It was built between 1893 and 1895 by Richard Morris Hunt for Cornelius Vanderbilt II, grandson of Commodore Cornelius Vanderbilt I, the richest man in American history. Money was no object, and Cornelius thought nothing of spending the family fortune on every conceivable luxury.

Opulence oozes from every corner, with scores of crystal chandeliers hanging from gold-encrusted ceilings, red alabaster columns framing 12-foot (3.5m) windows, and miles of oriental rugs. There was even hot and cold running and fresh sea water in each of the 23 bathrooms. You can't help but try to add up the cost of everything in the **dining room** alone, and your jaw will drop at the sight of the marble-sheathed great hall, which measures 50 feet (15m) in every direction.

Above: Cornelius Vanderbilt II

Top: When The Breakers was commissioned no expense was spared

Left: The vast great hall was designed for sumptuous entertaining

The **Music Room**, one of two rooms that were custom-made in Paris, dismantled, then shipped to Newport for reassembly, is so immense that it makes the grand piano within it look like a spinet. Red velvet and gold leaf compete for space on the walls, the moldings, the curtains, the furniture and even the finely decorated ceiling.

The Breakers took some 2,000 workmen around two years to build, and constant concerns over the intricate details demanded by the Vanderbilts were believed to have sent its architect (who did not live to see its completion) to an early grave.

The addition of audiotours in several languages enhances the experience. Listen to first-person reminiscences of life in the house, including the stories of servants and their children.

The mansion's dining room: the pillars are made from pure alabaster

TAKING A BREAK

Head over to the waterfront for a casual meal of clams at **Flo's Clam Shack** (4 Wave Avenue, Middletown, tel: 401/847-8141). Place your order at the window, and then enjoy your plate meal or clam roll with a beautiful water view of Easton Bay.

✚ 202 C2 ✉ 44 Ochre Point Avenue near Bellevue Avenue, Newport, RI
☎ 401/847-1000; www.NewportMansions.org ⏰ Early Apr to mid-Oct daily 9–5; mid-Oct to Dec 9–4; Jan to early Apr 10–4 💵 Expensive. Discounts available for tours of more than one mansion; call 401/847-1000 for details, or check the web at www.NewportMansions.org

THE BREAKERS: INSIDE INFO

Top tips This is the most popular of all the mansions and it can get crowded quickly. To **avoid the crowds,** go early in the morning.
■ The Preservation Society of Newport County, which runs The Breakers, operates 10 mansions in all and offers **discounts** on visits to more than one house. It offers tours of Chateau-sur-Mer, Chepstow, The Elms, Green Animals, Hunter House, Isaac Bell House, Kingscote, Marble House and Rosecliff (➤ 141–143 for information on other mansions). Not every house is open all year, and Chepstow is open for tours by reservation only.

Hidden gem The **Breakers Stable and Carriage House,** on Coggeshall Avenue, was also designed by Richard Morris Hunt. More than a dozen different horse-drawn vehicles are on display here, including Alfred Gwynne Vanderbilt's famous *Venture*. Admission is free with a ticket stub from any Preservation Society mansion.

2 Rough Point

For most visitors to Newport, the mansions are top of the must-see list. However, for anyone interested in architecture, the city offers far more than just the stately homes of the fabulously wealthy. Walking round the historic district is like stepping into a catalog of building design from colonial times to the early 20th century. Nowhere else in the country has such an impressive collection in such a compact area. Nowadays, conservation is deemed a "good thing," but it wasn't always so. One of the important figures who worked to preserve the city's heritage was the heiress, Doris Duke, whose home was Rough Point.

Dog Lover

To find out more about the remarkable Doris Duke, take a tour of Rough Point. Way out at the end of Bellevue Avenue, this house is as exquisitely furnished as its neighbors; the difference is that this actually feels like a home – albeit one with Louis XVI chairs, 16th-century tapestries, Ming vases and paintings by Renoir and van Dyck. In the **ballroom**, for example, stands the grand piano that was played by Doris Duke to entertain her friends at the small parties she gave. In the **Solarium**, with its panorama over gardens to the Atlantic Ocean, the sofas and chairs are chocolate brown, a sensible color when dogs are allowed to climb up onto the furniture!

The stately Rough Point, viewed from the Cliff Walk

Room With a View

Surrounded by 10 acres (4ha) that were landscaped by Frederick Law Olmsted (designer of New York's Central Park), the house was built in the late 1880s for Frederick Vanderbilt. What you see today, however, reflects the Dukes, who

Stained-glass
heraldry
complements
the aristocratic
ambience of
the interior

extended the mansion to its present 49 rooms. In the **Yellow Room**, Mrs Duke chose the rock crystal chandeliers because the light flattered ladies' complexions. Doris had less formal taste; after her mother's death in 1962, she moved the dining-room table from center-stage to a position by the window, with its glorious views.

Behind the Scenes

The tour takes in the **kitchen and pantry**, with their copper pans and humidor for cigars, and there is also a small gallery space, with changing exhibitions.

Doris Duke died in 1993, but you can still feel her presence in this mansion, from the full-length portrait of her as a child to the sofa cushion embroidered with the words, "Familiarity Breeds." Her influence also remains in the city: the Newport Restoration Foundation, which she established in 1968, now owns some 80 historic buildings across the city.

TAKING A BREAK

Annie's (176 Bellevue Avenue, tel: 401/849-6731), a welcoming diner serving breakfast and lunch, is a great place to take time out from sightseeing.

🖪 202 C2 ✉ 680 Bellevue Avenue, Newport, RI ☎ 401/847-8344;
www.newportrestoration.org 🕐 Early May–early Nov Tue–Sat 9:45–3:45.
Guided tours 3 times per hour 💰 Expensive. Children under 13 free

❸ Newport Beaches

Newport's long beaches are what originally attracted the former owners of the lavish estates, and they continue to draw those of more modest means to the area today.

Easton's Beach, also known as First Beach because it's the first in the line of the three beaches, is one of Newport's most popular, on Memorial Boulevard just below the entrance to the Cliff Walk. Lockers, bathhouses, restrooms, a snack bar and a carousel are open from Memorial Day to Labor Day.

There's a small bay beach at **Fort Adams State Park** (➤ 143) that's good for swimming, as well as areas for boating, sailing and fishing. Admission to the park is free. Where Narragansett Bay meets the Atlantic, **Brenton Point State Park** has gentle waves and conditions conducive to fishing and kite-flying.

Newport's two other great swimming beaches are actually in the neighboring city of Middletown, where many of the more affordable accommodations are also located. **Sachuest Beach**, or Second Beach, is on Sachuest Point Road, about 2 miles (3km) east of Easton's Beach. It's popular with those who favor sand dunes, which is apparently a lot of people – the parking lot holds 1,000 cars, and on sunny August weekends it fills up quickly.

Just on the other side of Sachuest Point is **Third Beach**. Part of this beach is private, but the public part is great for families and also has some small sailboats. A plus for solitude-seekers: this is usually the least crowded beach.

🞣 202 C2 🞤 Although Newport's beaches, toilets and showers are free, there is a charge for parking your car between Memorial Day weekend and Labor Day. The charges vary from beach to beach, from weekdays to weekends. Off season, parking is free. See www.GoNewport.com

Gooseberry Beach (top right), Sachuest Beach (center right) and Easton's Beach (right) are among Newport's most popular

At Your Leisure

❹ Touro Synagogue

The oldest extant synagogue in the United States dates to 1763, some 100 years after the first Jews emigrated here from Portugal. George Washington visited the synagogue in 1790 and promised the congregation that the new nation would cherish religious freedom by giving "bigotry no sanction; to persecution no assistance." It is said that Thomas Jefferson, who visited with Washington, was so inspired by the building's portico that he used the design for his own estate, Monticello, in Virginia.

The interior follows the graceful lines of 18th-century architecture. Of particular note are the 500-year-old Torah, which accompanied the first Jews to Newport from Portugal, and the trapdoor by the central pulpit, a reminder of the days when freedom of worship was not guaranteed.

The new Loeb Visitors Center celebrates America's first amendment rights and its history of religious tolerance and freedom.

➕ 202 C2 ✉ 72 Touro Street (at Spring Street), Newport, RI ☎ 401/847-4794; www.tourosynagogue.org ⏰ Tours operate Jul–early Sep, Sun–Wed and Fri 9:30–4:30; Sep–Oct and Jun Sun–Fri 11–2:30; closed Jewish hols 💲 Free; donations accepted

❺ International Tennis Hall of Fame

The first US National Lawn Tennis Championships (forerunner of the US Tennis Open) were played on the grass court here in 1881, when this building was better known as "The Casino." It was built only a year earlier as a social club by architect Stanford White of McKim, Mead and White. In fact, it was Mr White's first commission.

The Tennis Hall of Fame was founded in 1954, and all the greats of men's and women's tennis are now enshrined here, from Bill Tilden and Helen Wills Moody to Bjorn Borg and Evonne Goolagong, Steffi Graf and Pete Sampras. The exhibits on the history of the game are what you might imagine, but the interactive displays where you can test your own abilities are better than expected.

Every July, the Hall of Fame plays host to the Campbell's Hall of Fame Tennis Championship, the only tournament in the United States still played on grass. You, too, can play on any of the complex's 13 grass courts (the only public lawn tennis courts in the US), just by calling ahead and reserving a court any time from May through September.

➕ 202 C2 ✉ Newport Casino Lawn Tennis Club, 194 Bellevue Avenue, Newport, RI ☎ 800/457-1144 or 401/849-3990; www.tennisfame.com ⏰ Daily 9:30–5 💲 Moderate. Children under 16 free; discounts for students and seniors

❻ Kingscote

Although this Gothic Revival house gets fewer mentions than the more glittering mansions nearby, this is arguably the most important. In the early 19th century, Southern plantation owners sailed north to avoid the heat of summer. In 1839, architect Richard Upjohn was commissioned to design a summer cottage on a country road on the edge of town. With its Gothic arches and windows, towers and angled roofs, the romantic, medieval-style house triggered Newport's "cottage

International Tennis Hall of Fame

The lavish entrance foyer at Edward J. Berwind's mansion, The Elms

boom." Although later enlarged by architect Stanford White, Kingscote remained in the same family from 1864 to 1972, when it was given to the Preservation Society. That's why it still looks as if you could move in tomorrow – and feel at home.
➕ 202 C2 ✉ 253 Bellevue Avenue, Newport, RI ☎ 401/847-1000; www.NewportMansions.org 🕐 May to mid-Oct daily 10–5 💲 Expensive. Discounts available for tours of more than one mansion; call or check website for details

🕖 The Elms

Now a National Historic Landmark, The Elms was built in 1901 for coal magnate Edward J. Berwind in the style of an 18th-century French chateau. The guided Rooftop and Behind-the-Scenes tour (advance reservations required) looks at the service parts of the mansion, including the basement, the laundry room, the wine cellar and even the steam room, where the full-time staff kept operations humming through the social engagements and blowout parties enjoyed by Newport's elite. You also see the showpiece rooms.
➕ 202 C2 ✉ 367 Bellevue Avenue, Newport, RI ☎ 401/847-1000; www.NewportMansions.org 🕐 Apr to mid-Oct daily 10–5; mid-Oct to Jan 2 daily 10–4 🎧 Audiotour moderate; special tour moderate

🕗 Chateau-sur-Mer

This granite Victorian mansion, built in 1852 for the wealthy merchant William Shepard Wetmore, was the biggest house in town until the Vanderbilts moved in. Wetmore's son, George Peabody Wetmore, held his inaugural ball here in 1889 upon becoming governor of Rhode Island. Despite its name, Chateau-sur-Mer is significantly more removed from the sea than the other mansions – you can't even see the ocean from the Cliff Walk.
➕ 202 C2 ✉ 474 Bellevue Avenue, Newport, RI (between Shepard and Leroy) ☎ 401/847-1000; www.NewportMansions.org 🕐 Apr to mid-Oct daily 10–5; mid-Oct to mid-Nov daily 10–4

FOR KIDS
Green Animals Topiary Garden contains 80 sculpted trees and hedges, including 21 in the shape of animals. There's a giraffe, a donkey, a lion and an elephant, not to mention a policeman and a sailboat. The estate is 10 miles (16km) north of Newport in Portsmouth, but the tour is on the Newport Preservation Society combination ticket.

9 Rosecliff

With a ceiling painted with clouds and blue sky, the ballroom at Rosecliff is Newport's largest. The floor-to-ceiling windows are filled with panoramic views of the terrace, landscaped gardens and the ocean. So magnificent is the 1902 mansion that scenes for *High Society*, *The Great Gatsby*, *True Lies* and *Amistad* were shot here. The exterior is covered in white terracotta tiles. The interior was a regular backdrop for extravagant parties in the 1900s.

🖪 202 C2 ✉ 548 Bellevue Avenue, Newport, RI ☎ 401/847-1000; www.NewportMansions.org 🕓 Apr to mid-Nov daily 10–5 💲 Expensive. Discounts available for tours of more than one mansion; call or check website for details

10 Marble House

The 1892 home of Mrs William K. (Alva) Vanderbilt, constructed entirely of marble on the outside, drips with gold inside. The dining room chairs, made of solid bronze, are so heavy that two footmen were required to seat each dinner guest. The mansion is identifiable from the Cliff Walk – just look for the Chinese Tea House, which hosted rallies for women's rights to vote.

🖪 202 C2 ✉ 596 Bellevue Avenue, Newport, RI ☎ 401/847-1000; www.NewportMansions.org 🕓 Apr to mid-Oct daily 10–5; mid-Oct to Jan 2 10–4

11 Fort Adams State Park/ Museum of Yachting

Accessible from downtown Newport by water taxi (Oldport Marine, Sayers Wharf) or by ferry (Bowen's Landing), this park boasts great views and a variety of sports activities. Each August, crowds come for the Newport Folk Festival and Jazz Festival (www.GoNewport.com). Within the park is Historic Fort Adams (tours) and the Museum of Yachting, good for sailors and the history of the America's Cup races.

🖪 202 C2 ☎ Park: 401/847-2400. Museum: 401/847-1018; www.moy.org 🕓 Park: dawn–dusk, year round (staffed only from Memorial Day to Labor Day). Fort: Memorial Day–Columbus Day daily 10–4. Museum: Memorial Day to Oct 1 Wed–Mon 10–5:30 💲 Park: free. Fort: tour inexpensive. Museum: inexpensive

---

OFF THE BEATEN TRACK

Watch students of all ages learning how to restore and build wooden boats at the **International Yacht Restoration School** on Newport's historic waterfront. Undergoing long-term restoration is the *Coronet*, an 1885 schooner and one of America's most historic yachts (449 Thames Street, Newport; www.iyrs.org; free).

Marble House was designed by architect Richard Morris Hunt

⓬ Providence

Rhode Island's capital city has blossomed, thanks to energetic downtown renewal: waterside parks, restaurants, shops and art galleries. One example is the stunning new Chace Center exhibition space (20 North Main Street, www.risdmuseum.org), part of the Rhode Island School of Design.

The city spans both sides of the Providence River. In summer, this is the backdrop to WaterFire (www.waterfire.org), a unique combination of music and a hundred bonfires. To the east of the river, much of the 17th- and 18th-century part of town survives. To the west is Federal Hill, synonymous with the Italian restaurant scene.

Dominating everything is the Rhode Island State House (tours, www.rilin.state.ri.us), which boasts one of the world's largest self-supporting marble domes (and is not a little reminiscent of St. Peter's in Rome).

The east side is home to two of the best universities in the country within shouting distance of each other in the fashionable, wealthy College Hill neighborhood. Brown University, built in 1764 and a member of the elite Ivy League, is the larger of the two. For many years, its University Hall was the only building on campus, and during the Revolutionary War, it served as a barracks for French and American soldiers. The Rhode Island School of Design (RISD), just down the road, is one of the top art and design schools in America. The collection of art at its museum spans the last millennium, with works from around the globe, as well as special exhibitions by RISD faculty. The most popular galleries are those where works of European masters like Monet, Cézanne, Matisse, Manet and Rodin hang. The American wing features the works of Gilbert Stuart and John Singer Sargent.

From RISD, you can walk south along narrow Benefit Street, where stately old colonial homes rub shoulders with lovingly restored Victorian houses. Turn left at Power

The bonfires of WaterFire, an innovative and powerful installation by sculptor Barnaby Evans, light the Providence River

The wooden whaleship *Charles W. Morgan* on display at Mystic Seaport

Street to see John Brown House, ironically home to an 18th-century slave trader and revolutionary, not the abolitionist of the same name. The collection of china, glassware and colonial furniture contained within the house is museum quality.

🞧 202 C2 🏠 One Sabin Street, Providence, RI; tel 800/233-1636 or 401/751-1177; www.goprovidence.com

🔢 Mystic

Mystic Seaport is America's leading maritime museum. Combining museum, working shipyard and 19th-century village, it brings to life Mystic's days as the center of the whaling industry. It has more than 500 vessels, and you can board three of them, including the 1841 wooden whaleship *Charles W. Morgan*.

In the village, you can look around the shops and businesses that typically supported the whaling industry, including a ship's chandlery and craftsmens' shops. Kids will be interested in the one-room schoolhouse and the Children's Museum, where they can take part in the same games played by whaling-era kids.

At nearby **Mystic Aquarium**, kids will clamor loudest to see the

Atlantic bottlenose dolphins, seals and penguins. Also on site is the Institute for Exploration, specializing in deep-sea discoveries, underwater wrecks and their treasures. The focus of the exhibition is a display about the ill-fated *Titanic*.

🞧 202 B1

Mystic Seaport

✉ 75 Greenmanville Avenue, Mystic, CT
☎ 888/973-2767 or 860/572-0711; www.mysticseaport.org 🕙 Apr–Oct daily 9–5; Nov–Mar 10–4 💰 Expensive; second day free. Combination ticket with Mystic Aquarium

Mystic Aquarium

✉ 55 Coogan Boulevard, Mystic, CT
☎ 860/572-5955 ; www.mysticaquarium.org
🕙 Apr–Oct daily 9–6; Nov and Mar 9–5; Dec–Feb 10–5 💰 Expensive. Tickets valid for 3 consecutive days. Combination ticket with Mystic Seaport

🔢 Foxwoods and Mohegan Sun

Two of the biggest draws in New England, **Foxwoods** and **Mohegan Sun**, are also two of the biggest casinos in the US, complete with large and luxurious spa hotels. Built on Native American reservations some 20 years ago, a mere 10 miles (16km) apart, the two separate resorts offer all sorts of gambling, such as slot machines, table games and high-stakes bingo. However, crowds also come from New York and Boston to attend star-studded live concerts and major sporting events, enjoy fine dining, shopping and nightclubs, and to play the championship golf courses. Don't miss Mashantucket Pequot Museum where graphic exhibits bring to life the story of Native Americans.

🞧 202 B2

Foxwoods Resort Casino

✉ 350 Trolley Line Boulevard, Mashantucket, CT ☎ 800/885-3000 or 860/312-3000; www.foxwoods.com

Mohegan Sun

✉ 1 Mohegan Sun Boulevard, Uncasville, CT
☎ 888/226-7711 or 860/862-8000; www.mohegansun.com

Where to...
Stay

Prices

Expect to pay for two people sharing a double room, excluding taxes

$ under $150 $$ $150–$250 $$$ over $250

NEWPORT

Abigail Stoneman Inn $$$

A luxurious grand house, this inn has only five rooms: three suites and two staterooms, all with fireplaces, whirlpool baths, king-size beds and marble bathrooms. Champlin Mason, architect for grand mansions, designed this 1866 gem in the heart of the historic district. High tea, with scones and cakes, is something to shout about.

🛈 202 C2 ⬚ 102 Touro Street, Newport, RI ☎ 800/845-1811 or 401/847-1811; www.abigailstonemaninn.com

Burbank Rose $–$$

This small B&B is a pleasant get-away in this popular destination. Rooms have air-conditioning, cable TV and wireless internet. Some rooms share a sitting room. Some rooms have a kitchenette, with a refrigerator stocked with breakfast items. For other rooms, a Continental breakfast is served. The Burbank Rose is only a mile from the fabled Newport mansions and the beach, within walking distance of the shops and the harbor. There is parking nearby.

🛈 202 C2 ⬚ 111 Memorial Boulevard W, Newport, RI ☎ 401/849-9457; www.burbankrose.com

Newport Marriott Hotel $–$$$

The 319-room modern hotel on Newport's harborfront is spacious and only minutes from all the city's main attractions. Among the hotel's wide range of amenities are an indoor swimming pool, fitness center, hot tub, whirlpool and, overlooking the water, Fathoms Restaurant, specializing in seafood.

🛈 202 C2 ⬚ 25 America's Cup Avenue, Newport, RI ☎ 401/849-1000; www.newportmarriott.com

The Old Beach Inn $–$$

Close to the Cliff Walk, the mansions and beaches, this elegant inn was built in 1879. Named for garden flowers, the six romantic guest rooms have secondary themes, such as music in the Lily Room. The Continental breakfast includes freshly baked pastries; on Sundays a hot entree is served.

🛈 202 C2 ⬚ 19 Old Beach Road, Newport, RI ☎ 888/303-5033 or 401/849-3479; www.oldbeachinn.com

MYSTIC

The Adams House $–$$

In the country, yet minutes from downtown Mystic, this is a six-bedroom, 1750s Colonial home surrounded by flower gardens. All have private baths. The separate Garden Cottage is ideal for families or friends. Breakfast is generous, with homemade entrees, as well as pastries and fresh fruit.

🛈 202 B1 ⬚ 382 Cow Hill Road, Mystic, CT ☎ 860/572-9551; www.adamshouseofmystic.com

Steamboat Inn $–$$$

Within walking distance of the town's most popular attractions, this attractive inn is a good central choice. The 11 guestrooms are cheerful, light and relaxing, and all but one of them have views of the Mystic River and the motor yacht moored outside.

🛈 202 B1 ⬚ 73 Steamboat Wharf, Mystic, CT ☎ 860/536-8300; www.steamboatinnmystic.com

Where to...
Eat and Drink

Prices

Expect to pay per person for a three-course meal, excluding drinks and service

$ under $20 $$ $20–$35 $$$ over $35

NEWPORT

🍷🍷 Brick Alley Restaurant $–$$

Its simple menus have ensured Brick Alley's popularity for more than 25 years. Load up your plate at the salad bar, then choose from pizza and pasta or steaks and ribs. Alternatively, try the daily fresh fish special. The Sunday brunches are always busy, so reservations are essential.

➕ 202 C2 ⊠ 140 Thames Street, Newport, RI ☎ 401/849-6334; www.brickalley.com 🕐 Mon–Fri 11:30–10, Sat 11:30–10:30, Sun 10:30–10

🍷🍷 Commodore's Room at the Black Pearl $$$

Overlooking bobbing boats, this is a Newport landmark for seafood. Whether you choose lobster, steak, lamb or veal, the recipes are classic, the service attentive. At the cheaper, informal tavern, with its outdoor patio, the same culinary care is paid to everything from sandwiches and salads to baked cod and lobster.

➕ 202 C2 ⊠ 30 Bannister's Wharf, Newport, RI ☎ 401/846-5264; www.blackpearlnewport.com 🕐 Mon–Sat 11:30–2, 5:30–9, Sun 12–3, 5:30–9; closed early Jan–early Feb

🍷 The Red Parrot $$

The popular watering hole serves steaks, chicken, chops and seafood, all with a Caribbean twist. The list of exotic cocktails is impressive.

➕ 202 C2 ⊠ 348 Thames Street, Newport, RI ☎ 401/847-3800; www.redparrotrestaurant.com 🕐 Daily 11:30–10 (Fri–Sat till 11)

🍷🍷 White Horse Tavern $$–$$$

Known for its local seafood, the tavern was first licensed to sell liquor in 1687 – patrons have included pirates, state legislators and director Steven Spielberg and his film crew during the shooting of *Amistad*. There is a champagne brunch on Sundays. Dinner is expensive but lunch, Sunday brunch and drinks are not if you want to soak up the atmosphere.

➕ 202 C2 ⊠ 26 Marlborough Street, Newport, RI ☎ 401/849-3600; www.whitehorsetavern.us 🕐 Thu–Sat 11:30–2:30, Sun brunch 12–3, Mon–Sun 5:30–9

MYSTIC

🍷 Abbott's Lobster in the Rough $–$$

This archetypal lobster shack in the picturesque village of Noank also serves excellent clams, mussels and crab. You can also order chicken, grilled cheese sandwiches or a fresh vegetable platter. Simple, but fun.

➕ 202 B1 ⊠ 117 Pearl Street, Noank, CT ☎ 860/536-7719; www.abbotts-lobster.com 🕐 Memorial Day–Labor Day daily 12–9; Labor Day–Columbus Day 12–7; May Sat–Sun 12–7

🍷🍷 Flood Tide $$–$$$

Part of the Inn at Mystic, the restaurant uses organic ingredients as much as possible. Imaginative dishes include wild king salmon with *prosciutto*, and grilled tuna steak with sesame sticky rice. Desserts are equally as good.

➕ 202 B1 ⊠ Junction US 1 and SR 27, Mystic, CT ☎ 860/536-8140; www.innatmystic.com 🕐 Daily 4–5 (tea), 5:30–9 (Sat–Sun till 9:30)

Where to...
Shop

NEWPORT

Rhode Island has a long history of furniture-making, and **antiques** shops abound in Newport. **Ball and Claw** (29 America's Cup Avenue, tel: 401/848-5600; www.theballandclaw.com) sells furniture by Jeffrey Greene. At **Thames Glass** (688 Thames Street, tel: 401/846-0576; www.thamesglass.com), glassblower Matthew Buechner fashions vases and witty fish. Silversmith **JH Breakell** (128 Spring Street, tel: 401/849-0195; www.breakell.com) creates pins and bracelets. **Newport Scrimshanders'** (14 Bowen's Wharf, tel: 800/635-5234 or 401/849-5680; www.scrimshanders.com) Brian Kiracofe carves bone just as sailors once did.

MYSTIC

The **Courtyard Gallery** (12 Water Street; www.courtyardgallerymystic.com) focuses on art, **Toy Soldier** on toys (27 Coogan Boulevard; www.toysoldiermystic.com).

PROVIDENCE

For a modern mall, head over to **Providence Place**, with more than 170 stores. Showcasing the skills of RISD alumni and faculty is **risd/works** (20 North Main Street; www.risdworks.com), while **OOP!** (220 Westminster Street; www.oopstuff.com) features works by local and national artisans, including everything from wedding jewelry, ceramics and clothing to wall art, furniture and gifts.

Where to...
Be Entertained

SAILING

A big thrill is cruising aboard an America's Cup yacht. Out on the water, under sail, see the Newport the millionaires saw. Details of cruises from the **Newport Visitor Information Center** (23 America's Cup Avenue; www.gonewport.com).

HORSEBACK RIDING

Newport Equestrian Academy (tel: 401/848-5440; www.newportequestrian.com) arranges beach rides.

FESTIVALS

Newport hosts a wide range of festivals from the **Great Chowder Cook Off** (June) to the **Black Ships Festival** (July), which commemorates the state's cultural links with Japan.

In July, set in the grandeur of Newport's gilded mansions, the **Newport Music Festival** attracts international artists for a special 17-day classical music marathon, offering 65 high-class chamber music concerts. Then in August, more international artists hit town for the legendary **Newport Folk Festival** and the world-famous **Newport Jazz Festival**. Both are held on the grounds of Fort Adams State Park.

Other highlights include the **Campbell's Hall of Fame Tennis Championships**, played in July on the grass courts at the International Tennis Hall of Fame (▶ 141).

Coastal Maine to the White Mountains

Getting Your Bearings

Maine has statewide air-conditioning. When the rest of New England reaches its boiling point in July and August, the traffic swells up I-95 like mercury in a thermometer. Everyone is in search of cool nights, a wealth of outdoor activities and, if they're lucky, a glimpse of a moose. Don't worry about Maine becoming uncontrollably crowded in summer. It is bigger than all the other New England states combined, so there is more than enough solitude to go around.

In everybody's rush to get to the coolest place in the northeast, New Hampshire often gets overlooked. On your way from Boston to Maine, you pass through the Granite State for little more than half an hour, but New Hampshire rises to the same heights that Maine does: Mount Washington, the tallest peak in the northeast, is in the New Hampshire portion of the White Mountains. New Hampshire also boasts a midsize city, Portsmouth, that's as attractive as anything in all of New England.

Maine has more than 3,000 miles (4,830km) of coastline, but only some 30 miles (48km) of beaches. The main stretch of sand is from Portland, the state's largest city, southward through the seaside communities collectively known as the Kennebunks. It continues into New Hampshire, whose shoreline totals all of 18 miles (29km), but offers all the fun of the fair. Since these beaches all are within an easy drive of Boston, they can be crowded in high summer.

North of Portland – a growing tourist destination with enough indoor attractions to fill a rainy day – the coast turns rocky. Although this makes for poor sunbathing, it does make for stunning snapshots. The northeast coast is simply picturesque, as are the handful of towns sprinkled along the way – Camden, Castine, Blue Hill, Belfast, Port Clyde. Each has its own charms that can be experienced only by walking or bicycling through the uncrowded streets. The most dramatic scenery is to be found in and around Acadia National Park, near Bar Harbor.

Finally, there are the White Mountains, which stretch across the top third of New Hampshire and poke into Maine's interior. This is the land of blue lakes and blueberries, of wild rivers and wild moose. There's no gorgeous rocky coast here, but there are thousands of miles of wilderness to explore. The most celebrated terrain can be found within the confines of Maine's extremely remote Baxter State Park, but an away-from-it-all experience is easily within the reach of anybody with a picnic lunch, a bottle of water, and the gumption to get off the road and into the woods.

Previous page: Portsmouth Harbor

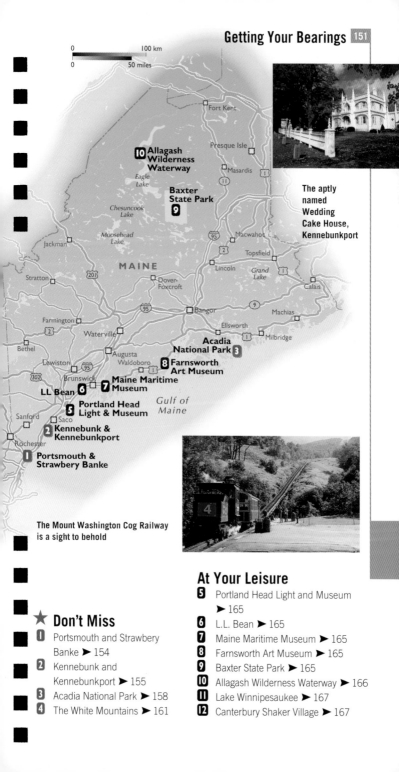

The aptly
named
Wedding
Cake House,
Kennebunkport

The Mount Washington Cog Railway
is a sight to behold

In Six Days

If you're not quite sure where to begin your travels, this itinerary recommends a practical and enjoyable six days in Coastal Maine and the White Mountains, taking in some of the best places to see using the Getting Your Bearings map on the previous page. For more information see the main entries.

Day 1

Drive north from Boston, stopping in **1 Portsmouth** (➤ 154) for lunch. Spend the afternoon looking around the town and visit historic **1 Strawbery Banke** (➤ 154). Continue north to the **2 Kennebunks** (➤ 155–157), arriving in time for dinner. Overnight in Kennebunkport.

Day 2

Spend the day at one of the beaches in Kennebunkport. A favorite is **Goose Rocks Beach** – long, wide and just north of town. If it's not beach weather, visit the **Seashore Trolley Museum** or just wander around the stores and galleries of Kennebunkport and Kennebunk lower village. Have dinner at the sophisticated White Barn Inn (➤ 169).

Day 3

Stop in Portland for a quick visit to the **5 Portland Head Light and Museum** (below, ➤ 165), then continue up the coast to Freeport to visit **6 L.L. Bean's** (➤ 165) flagship store, as well as Freeport's hundreds of other outlet and regular stores. Don't spend too much time here, however. You still want to get to Bar Harbor tonight so you can have a full day to explore Acadia National Park.

Day 4

You can easily spend all day at 3 **Acadia National Park** (➤ 158–160). Hike the waymarked trail around Jordan Pond, rent a bicycle and cruise along the carriage trails, paddle a sea kayak into Somes Sound, or just sit on a rock and soak up the superb scenery. After your day of activities, you may like to have dinner at Abel's Lobster Pound (tel: 207/276-5827).

Day 5

Head west through Maine to the 4 **White Mountains** (left, ➤ 161–164). Take SR 3 west to Augusta, go north on SR 27, then US 2 west to Gorham, New Hampshire. Along the way, you'll pass through almost every kind of scenery New England has to offer: rocky coast, tidal flats, rolling farmland, rural villages and White Mountain National Forest. Ascend **Mount Washington,** or, especially in October when the foliage is at its most colorful, drive across the **Kancamagus Highway.**

Get out of the car and hike one of the countless trails, or just stop and have a picnic lunch. You can spend the night at one of the White Mountain towns, or continue south to 11 **Lake Winnipesaukee** (right, ➤ 167).

Day 6

Spend the day on the lake, boating, fishing, swimming or just sunning yourself. On your way back to Boston, stop at 12 **Canterbury Shaker Village** (➤ 167), for a glimpse of life in a Shaker community.

❶ Portsmouth and Strawbery Banke

Back in 1630 when English settlers landed at the mouth of the Piscataqua River, they called the spot Strawbery Banke, for the plentiful wild strawberries growing there. You may think that the title is misspelled, but 400 years ago, spelling had yet to be standardized. Less than 25 years later, the name was changed to Portsmouth; but the original moniker lives on, thanks to this outdoor museum, one of the largest in the US.

A bastion against urban sprawl: the lovely New Hampshire town of Portsmouth

What looks like a New England village is actually an assembly of 18th- and 19th-century buildings saved from the city's mid-20th-century expansion. There are simple homes, a mansion, workshops, a store – even a privy, though this is a reconstruction, one of the few on this 10-acre (4ha) site. Stories are everywhere. In the **Shapley-Drisco House**, furnishings from the 1790s contrast with those from the 1950s. Enter the **Pitt Tavern** and you follow the footsteps of George Washington and John Hancock. The **Shapiro House** tells how a family of 20th-century Russian immigrants coped with life in a new country. Watch demonstrations of pottery and coopering; see how gardening techniques have changed.

However, there is more to Portsmouth than Strawbery Banke. The city is a harmonious mix of old and new. Many of the handsome homes dating back two centuries and more are open to the public. Shopping, cafes and live music every night: you'll wish you could spend more time here.

✚ 201 E2
🛈 500 Market Street, Portsmouth, NH; tel: 603/436-3988; www.portsmouthchamber.org

Strawbery Banke
✉ Street, Portsmouth, NH ☎ 603/433-1100; www.strawberybanke.org
🕐 May–Oct daily 10–5; Nov–Apr Sat–Sun 10–2. Guided tours on the hour
🎟 Moderate; entry for 2 consecutive days. Discounts for children aged 5–17, children under 5 free

2 Kennebunk and Kennebunkport

The Kennebunks (as Kennebunk and Kennebunkport are collectively known), on opposite sides of the Kennebunk River, are among the most charming villages on the Maine coast. Of the two, Kennebunkport is the more precious, with hardly a store or gas station open past 10pm. Kennebunk is equally sleepy, though a few essential services cater to those who don't rise and set with the sun.

The population here doubles in summer, and nearly triples on summer holiday weekends, when it's risky to venture to a restaurant without a reservation and downright impossible to find a hotel room. The flood of tourists strangles traffic negotiating the two-lane bridge across the river, but it also provides the stores with enough business to keep them afloat through the cold Maine winters. As with most resort towns, many stores cater purely to a tourist clientele, but there is also a good selection of crafts, clothing, pottery and art.

Kennebunkport on the Kennebunk River is one of Maine's most idyllic towns

Best Beaches

The excellent **beaches**, with calm waters and long expanses of soft white sand, are the reason people come to the Kennebunks. The water is usually too cold for swimming

except for the heartiest souls on the hottest days, but it makes for a bracing dip between sunbathing sessions.

Which beach to choose? Well, that depends on what you fancy. In Kennebunk, **Gooch's Beach**, parallel to Beach Avenue, is popular, with calm surf and lots of room. Everyone comes here on the Fourth of July to watch the fireworks display. **Mother's Beach,** located west of Gooch's Beach, is smaller and a bit more remote, but offers a playground. Both have lifeguards and restrooms in season and are off SR 9 and SR 35. Connecting these and other beaches in Kennebunk is a sidewalk, perfect for strolling, rollerblading or jogging. Since some of the beaches are up to half a mile (1km) from the shops, be sure to pack a lunch, carry a chaise, and bring plenty of water, because you can't get any of these things on the beach. As for getting to the beach, in high summer the easiest way is to take the Shoreline Explorer service (www.shorelineexplorer.com). This runs along the coast from York up to the Kennebunks; each section has its own fare, own timetable – even its own name, such as the Shoreline Trolley and Kennebunk Shuttle.

Above: Wedding Cake House is among Kennebunkport's many historic buildings

Top: Kennebunkport's attractive harbor

North of Kennebunkport, **Goose Rocks Beach** is in a residential neighborhood east of Cape Porpoise, just off SR 9. Low dunes back the two crescent-shaped beaches. At high-tide, this 3-mile (5km) ribbon of sand easily accommodates the relatively few folks who make the 10-minute drive out here. At low tide, it becomes a tidal flat where you can walk in ankle-deep ocean. To get there, take SR 9 out of town; this starts out as School Street, then becomes Mills Road. At Dyke Road turn right; at the fork in the road, turn left.

Seashore Trolley Museum

On rainy days, the most popular attraction (besides heading an hour south to outlet shops in Kittery, or an hour north to L.L. Bean in Freeport) is the **Seashore Trolley Museum** in Kennebunkport. Kids love to ride the working trolley back through time: the historical dioramas and real-life displays

re-create an era when trains, trams and trolleys, rather than cars, took people everywhere.

TAKING A BREAK

For the real Maine experience, try the informal, no-nonsense **Nunan's Lobster Hut** (SR9, Cape Porpoise, tel: 207/967-4362), 2 miles (3km) from Kennebunkport. It's well worth the short drive.

Above:
Along the
waterfront at
Kennebunkport

➕ 201 F3
ℹ️ 17 Western Avenue, Kennebunk, ME; tel: 800/982-4421 or 207/967-0857; www.visitthekennebunks.com

Seashore Trolley Museum
➕ 201 F3 ✉️ 195 Log Cabin Road, Kennebunkport, ME ☎ 207/967-2712; www.trolleymuseum.org ⏰ Late May to mid-Oct daily 10–5; early May and late Oct Sat–Sun 10–5 💲 Inexpensive. Discounts for children aged 6–16

THE KENNEBUNKS: INSIDE INFO

Top tip If you must drive to the beach, you will have to pay to park.
Beach passes must be bought ahead of time, though many hotels and inns provide them for their guests or have them for guests to buy. Otherwise, in Kennebunk, buy them at the Town Hall (1 Summer Street); in Kennebunkport from the Town Offices (6 Elm Street) or the police station (101 Main Street). Warning: the sticker does not entitle you to a space, so get to the car park early. Ogunquit has an ordinary pay-on-entry parking lot.

In more depth The town of Ogunquit, about 10 miles (16km) south, is also attractive, with a 3-mile-long (5km) beach, plus a great restaurant scene and art galleries. Ogunquit is popular with gay travelers, though neither the town nor the travelers advertise this.

3 Acadia National Park

Acadia was the first national park east of the Mississippi River when it was established in 1919 and is still the only one in the northeast quarter of the country. Even though at 40,000 acres (16,195ha) it's one of the smallest parks in the system, Acadia is one of the most popular, drawing more than 2 million visitors annually.

If this sounds crowded, take solace in the fact that the vast majority of visitors do little more than drive the park loop road. This means that there are 39,999 other acres (16,193ha) for you to explore by bicycle, canoe, kayak or on foot.

Acadia's Carriage Trails
John D. Rockefeller, who purchased pristine land at the beginning of the 19th century, carved out a 45-mile (72km) network of carriage trails and linked them with 16 hand-cut stone bridges. Hiking and horseback riding are popular carriage-trail pursuits but, as the multitude of bicycle rental shops in the nearby town of Bar Harbor, the gateway to the park, will testify, bicycling is the preferred way to explore.

Beautiful Jordan Pond, in Acadia National Park

Acadian landscapes: long stretches of rocky coast

Hiking Trails

Hiking in Acadia is a treat, since many of the trails were cut by the same stonemasons who built the carriage roads: in other words, carved, rather than just hacked out of the mountains. There are more than 125 miles (200km) of hiking trails in addition to the carriage trails, and most get no more than a few visitors per day. The 3.3-mile (5km) loop around Jordan Pond is the most popular, though many people turn around when they see they will have to scramble across a section of low, jagged boulders. (It's inconvenient, but not difficult.) Check in at the Hulls Cove Visitor Center for a list and map of the park's hiking trails.

The Maine coast is home to a variety of sealife, including Northern starfish

Somes Sound

Sea kayakers of all abilities will love the waters in and around Acadia, from the bathtub-still Somes Sound, a fjord-like bay, to the stronger surf of the open ocean. Outfitters in Bar Harbor and other towns on the island run trips, which range from a few hours to a full-day voyage to an offshore island.

Cadillac Mountain

Even the less active are able to take in the beauty of Acadia with a drive to the top of Cadillac Mountain (1,530 feet/466m), a beautiful spot for watching the dawn of a new day. If the thought of a 4:30am start doesn't appeal, you can come later in the day. It's almost as exhilarating at sunset.

Mount Desert Island

Mount Desert Island (pronounced *dessert*) is the lobster claw-shaped island on which most of the park sits (two areas in other nearby peninsulas are also under federal protection). Bar Harbor, the major town, offers excellent restaurants and shops.

TAKING A BREAK

Jordan Pond House (Park Loop Road, tel: 207/276-3316) is an institution; stop here for a light lunch, afternoon tea, delicious home-made ice cream selection or, most famously, fresh popovers.

➕ 199 D1/E2 ✉ Park Headquarters, 2 miles (3.2km) west of Bar Harbor on SR 233, Bar Harbor, ME ☎ 207/288-3338; www.nps.gov/acad/home.htm 🕐 Hulls Cove Visitor Center, just north of Bar Harbor near Hulls Cove Inlet and just off SR 3: Jul–Aug daily 8–6; mid-Apr to Jun and Oct 8–4:30; Sep 8–5. Visitor Center at Park Headquarters: mid-Apr to Oct Mon–Fri 8–4:30; Nov to mid-Apr daily 8–4:30 💵 7-day car pass: May to late Jun, moderate; late Jun to mid-Oct, expensive

Crashing waves at Thunder Hole, a cleft in the rocky cliffs on the east coast of Mount Desert Island

ACADIA NATIONAL PARK: INSIDE INFO

Top tip In the peak season (July and August), bicycle rentals sometimes sell out. To avoid disappointment, call Bar Harbor Bicycle Shop (tel: 207/288-3886; www.barharborbike.com) and **reserve a bicycle** in advance.

In more detail There are several other tiny towns on Mount Desert Island. The largest of them are **Northeast Harbor**, on the eastern lobe, and **Southwest Harbor**, on the western lobe. Each is home to a few restaurants, hotels and shops of a slightly more charming variety than those found in Bar Harbor.

4 The White Mountains

The White Mountains aren't so much an attraction as an entire region, covering 768,000 acres (310,000ha). Yet there isn't a town of more than 10,000 people to be found anywhere in this mountainous area. Still, you don't come here for the towns. The lure of the White Mountains is the trails for hiking, country roads for biking and rivers for canoeing. Sounds like too much exertion? You can take a driving tour of the same scenery, ride up the side of the Northeast's highest mountain in a railway car or visit the house where Robert Frost wrote many of his poems.

Mount Washington

The first stop on any visit to the White Mountains should be **Mount Washington**, at 6,288 feet (1,917m) the tallest mountain in the Northeast. Around New Hampshire you'll often see bumper stickers proudly proclaiming "This Car Climbed Mount Washington." If you can't resist the temptation of a slow, narrow, white-knuckle drive to the top of a mountain, by all means join this lusty club. But you might want to consider some better ways to get to the summit.

The Swift River courses across the prettiest part of the White Mountains

The first is hiking. Get a copy of the Appalachian Mountain Club's *White Mountain Guide*, available from any local bookstore or online (www.outdoors.org). Although the hike is very strenuous, it is the unpredictable weather that poses

the greatest threat. Allow 6 hours to get up, and 3 to 4 for the return journey, plus some time to enjoy the views from the peak.

If, on the other hand, you read that with alarm, you may prefer to use the **Mount Washington Cog Railway**, which operates from May to November. This 3-mile (4.8km) track, laid in 1869, remains a marvelous engineering accomplishment. The steepest part of the climb, Jacob's Ladder, angles upward at an exciting 37 percent grade. The leisurely ride takes about 3 hours round trip.

Finally, there is a van tour up the 8-mile (13km) **Mount Washington Auto Road**, which you can pick up in Great Glen on Route 16. The road is only open when weather permits, and not at all between the end of October and mid-May. SnowCoach tours operate December through March. The 1-hour trip in an all-wheel drive vehicle takes up to nine passengers through the snow to just above the tree line, with

the option to return by cross-country ski, telemark ski or snowshoe. Remember that the top of Mount Washington has worse weather than almost any place in North America. The average temperature is just below freezing, and the winds, which once reached a record 231mph (370kph), are fierce even in summer.

Kancamagus Highway

The Kancamagus Highway, which parallels the Swift River from Conway to Lincoln, is a less inclement excursion. It's designated a National Scenic Byway and with good reason. On weekends in fall foliage season, this out-of-the-way road is often choked with motorists tootling through the corridor of ocher and vermilion leaves. The most popular stop on the 26.5-mile (43km) route is **Sabbaday Falls**, just about halfway along, though there are dozens of other worthwhile places where you can pull over and have a look around at covered bridges, or start off on a day hike through the mountains.

The Kancamagus Highway is wide enough to be a favorite with bicyclists, and steep in only a few portions. Those who

prefer mountain biking should head to Great Glen Trails
(www.greatglentrails.com), near the entrance to the Mount
Washington Auto Road. You can also rent bikes and
helmets here.

Franconia Notch State Park

Hikers gravitate toward the town of Franconia Notch State
Park. A notch is a mountain pass, and Franconia Notch is
barely wide enough to squeeze an 18-wheeler through. That
leaves plenty of unspoiled wilderness in which to hike, bike,
swim or just enjoy a warm afternoon. Dozens of hiking trails
lace the state park, including the home stretch of the Georgia-
to-Maine Appalachian Trail. Were it not for the helpful park
rangers, you would never be able to distinguish the state park
from the surrounding national forest.

The lure of the White Mountains is their quiet beauty

For centuries, there were two memorable sights. The
first was the **Old Man of the Mountain**, a natural granite

formation that resembled the profile of a human head. Sadly,
in 2003, the rock tumbled down. Although the idea of a
fake replacement has been ruled out, you can peer through
special telescopes at the viewing area to see what the profile
once looked like. A symbol of New Hampshire's rugged
individualism, the Old Man still features on road signs, license
plates and the New Hampshire quarter.

The second landmark is the **Flume**, a 90-foot-deep (27m)
gorge through which Flume Brook cascades. You can walk
the 3 miles (5km) of well-maintained trails, bridges and
boardwalks that crisscross the area.

In the nearby town of Franconia is the literary highlight
of the White Mountains, **Frost Place**. Robert Frost spent
19 summers here from 1921 to 1940, and wrote as many as
half of his poems in this house. The simple 1859 farmhouse
contains several signed first editions.

North Conway

If the White Mountains can be said to have a commercial
center, it must be North Conway. The outlet shops along the

town's major intersection cause traffic jams on gray Saturdays. The surrounding area is much prettier, however, as evidenced by the existence of the **Conway Scenic Railroad**, which takes passengers on rides through the Mount Washington Valley. Trips vary in length from 1 to 5 hours, priced accordingly.

TAKING A BREAK

For maple syrup treats, stop at **Polly's Pancake Parlor** at Sugar Hill, on a working maple syrup farm (tel: 800/432-8972 or 603/823-5575).

White Mountains Tourist Office
➕ 201 D4 ✉ PO Box 10, North Woodstock, NH. Visitor Center at Exit 32 off I-93 in North Woodstock ☎ 800/346-3687 or 603/745-8720; www.visitwhitemountains.com

Frost Place
✉ Ridge Road, Franconia ☎ 603/823-5510; www.frostplace.org 🕐 Jul to mid-Oct Wed–Mon 1–5; late May–Jun Sat–Sun 1–5 💲 Inexpensive

Franconia Notch State Park
✉ Franconia Notch Parkway, Franconia ☎ 603/745-8391; www.franconianotchstatepark.com 🕐 Mid-May to late Oct 💲 Inexpensive

Mount Washington Cog Railway
☎ 800/922-8825 or 603/278-5404; www.thecog.com 🕐 May–Nov; call for times 💲 Expensive

Mount Washington Auto Road
☎ 603/466-3988; www.mountwashington.org

Mount Washington SnowCoach
☎ 603/466-2333 💲 Expensive

Conway Scenic Railroad
✉ Route 16, North Conway ☎ 800/232-5251 or 603/356-5251; www.conwayscenic.com 🕐 Mid-Apr to mid-Oct, Dec; weekends off-season; call for times 💲 Moderate to expensive

Visitors enjoy the spectacle of Sabbaday Falls on the Swift River

THE WHITE MOUNTAINS: INSIDE INFO

Top tip Avoid the busy roads that **form a rectangular route** around the White Mountains. From Glen, north of North Conway, head west into the mountains on SR 302. In Bartlett, Attitash is a ski resort in winter, a playground in summer, with a Mountain Coaster ride, Alpine Slide and more (www.attitash.com). Drive through Hart's Location to Crawford Notch, the main passage through the center of the White Mountains. Park and enjoy the wild and wonderful views. Finish with tea at the century-old Mount Washington Resort.

Hidden gem The town of **Jackson**, nestled in its own corner of the White Mountains, is much more picturesque than North Conway, its more commercial neighbor. With some 200 miles (320km) of cross-country skiing trails, the area is an especially fine place to visit in winter.

At Your Leisure

5 Portland Head Light and Museum

This was one of the first lighthouses in the country, and it is still one of the most picturesque. It was a working lighthouse as recently as 1989, when it went fully automated. The former keeper's quarters have been converted into an excellent museum, and the surrounding Fort Williams Park is a fine place for a picnic overlooking Casco Bay.

🚩 198 A1 ✉ 1000 Shore Road, ME (US 1 North to Oak Hill, then right on SR 207, and left on SR 77. Turn right onto Shore Road) ☎ 207/799-2661; www.portlandheadlight.com 🕐 Memorial Day to mid-Oct daily 10–4; mid-Apr to Memorial Day and mid-Oct to mid-Dec Sat–Sun 10–4 💲 Inexpensive. Children aged under 6 free

6 L.L. Bean

L.L. Bean's vast flagship store in Freeport, Maine, is the catalog come to life, with helpful salesfolk who really know their boots from their boats. Best of all, the store is open 24 hours a day, seven days a week. There are outdoor concerts on summer weekends.

🚩 198 A1 ✉ 95 Main Street, Freeport, ME ☎ 877/755-2326 (toll free US and Canada); www.llbean.com

7 Maine Maritime Museum

With paintings, models and photographs, Maine's extensive seafaring and maritime history is showcased in exhibits covering boatbuilding, shipping, fishing and cruising. History is fun here, with plenty for children to enjoy; interactive exhibits range from the Tugboat Pilothouse to a Pirate Play Ship. One whole building is devoted to Maine lobstering: Who would have guessed that the industry dates back to the 1820s? For another exhibit, you enter through a bank vault door. This emphasizes that carrying cargo made money for the ship's owners. Summer brings hands-on activities and river cruises on the Kennebec River.

🚩 198 B1 ✉ 243 Washington Street, Bath, ME (Past Bath Iron Works) ☎ 207/443-1316; www.mainemaritimemuseum.org 🕐 Daily 9:30–5 💲 Moderate. Discounts for families, seniors and children aged 4–16

8 Farnsworth Art Museum

This excellent small museum in Rockland is like a beginner's guide to American art. The top-quality collection boasts works by artists who painted in New England in general and Maine in particular: George Inness, Winslow Homer, George Bellows and John Marin. Works by more contemporary artists with Maine connections include Louise Nevelson and Robert Indiana. But it is the Wyeth Center that pulls in the art lovers. What was a church is now a gallery devoted to three generations of one artistic family: the Wyeths. NC Wyeth was a respected illustrator and painter, his son, the late Andrew Wyeth, is one of America's most acclaimed painters, and his son is Jamie Wyeth. Andrew's best-known work is *Christina's World* (1948), painted at the Olson farm in Cushing, ME, a property owned by the museum (10 miles/16km away).

🚩 198 C1 ✉ 16 Museum Street, Rockland, ME ☎ 207/596-6457; www.farnsworthmuseum.org 🕐 Mid-May to Nov daily 10–5 (Wed and first Fri of month Jun–Oct until 8); Nov to mid-May Wed–Sun 10–5 💲 Moderate

9 Baxter State Park

Baxter State Park is a hikers' and outdoor enthusiast's paradise. The reward for venturing so far afield, of course, is solitude and wilderness unmarked by roads for automobiles – miles and miles of wilderness, more than 20,000 acres (8,098ha) in all. Maine's highest mountain, Mount

Baxter State Park's untamed landscapes reward visitors in search of solitude and wilderness

Katahdin (5,267 feet/1,605m), is the terminus of the Appalachian Trail, and one of its most challenging ascents. You can hike other trails among the 200 miles (322km) offered here or canoe the several ponds and lakes. Out of the park you can go whitewater rafting down the west branch of the Penobscot River. Several outfitters offer packages.

Baxter is truly away from it all. The terrain is as untamed as it was when Governor Percival Baxter deeded the land to the state in 1931 and decreed that it be "forever left in its natural wild state." Reservations are required for all lodging options, from your own tent to simple cabins and bunkhouses (call far in advance).

➕ 198 C4　✉ 64 Balsam Drive, Millinocket, ME　☎ 207/723-5140; www.baxterstateparkauthority.com
🅿 Moderate. Camping permits inexpensive; bunkhouses also available

🔟 Allagash Wilderness Waterway

Canoeists, take note: the Allagash Wilderness Waterway is one of the best trips in the country. The Allagash is designated a National Wild and Scenic River and development is forbidden for 500 feet (150m) on either side of the 92-mile (148km) corridor between Chamberlain Bridge and Allagash. The trip takes 7 to 10 days, with campsites along the route. Several outfitters in the town of Greenville offer guided tours of the waterway, as well as equipment packages.

➕ 198 C5　✉ Office at 106 Hogan Road, Bangor, ME　☎ 207/941-4014; www.maine.gov/doc/parks　🅿 Inexpensive

The Allagash Wilderness Waterway

OFF THE BEATEN TRACK

Hanover, on the Connecticut River in New Hampshire near the Vermont border, is the home of Dartmouth College, a founding member of the Ivy League, with a well-respected business school. Hanover is truly a college town – almost every business here caters to undergraduates or faculty – and it's also one of the prettiest villages in New England. Come here in summer when it's serene and free of boisterous college students, or the second weekend in February when Winter Carnival's skiing races, snow sculptures, and free-flowing beer bring everybody out of hibernation. For information, call the Hanover Chamber of Commerce (tel: 603/643-3115; www.hanoverchamber.com) or Dartmouth College (tel: 603/646-1110; www.dartmouth.edu) for Winter Carnival details.

FOR KIDS
The **Portland Sea Dogs** are an affiliate of the Boston Red Sox, and play their home games in Hadlock Field, an old-style ballpark with more seats than you'd expect for a minor-league team. Players are young and raw, with names you've never heard of, but the games are usually competitive, the stands are close to the field, and the emphasis is on family fun. The season runs from mid-April through the first weekend in September. Tickets are hard to come by, so call ahead (tel: 800/936-DOGS or 207/879-9500; www.portlandseadogs.com).

⓫ Lake Winnipesaukee

The paucity of ocean beaches goes somewhat unnoticed in New Hampshire, largely because of the abundance of sandy lake beaches in the center of the state where you can cool your toes on hot summer days. The biggest, and consequently the most popular, is Lake Winnipesaukee, just northeast of Laconia. Several communities around the lake have access to the water, but most people opt to stay around Weirs Beach because of its sandy shores, its boardwalk, its child-friendly amusements, and its proximity to I-93 and the towns of Meredith and Laconia. Those in search of a quieter lakeside stay should head over to Wolfeboro, on the eastern shore of the lake.

Lakes Region Association
➕ 201 D3 ✉ PO Box 737, Route 3, Exit 20, Tilton, NH ☎ 800/605-2537 or 603/286-8008; www.lakesregion.org

⓬ Canterbury Shaker Village

If you missed the Hancock Shaker Village (▶ 103–104) in Massachusetts or want to learn more about the lives of the Shakers, then visit this outpost a half hour north of Concord. More than two dozen original buildings remain from the days when this was a working 19th-century Shaker village. To get a feel for how the community lived in those days, follow the self-guided tour or, even better, join one of the guided tours, to go into buildings that are normally closed. For lunch, sit at a long communal table in the restaurant, Greenwood's at Canterbury Shaker Village. You can eat here, even if you do not want to enter the village.

➕ 201 D3 ✉ 288 Shaker Road, Canterbury, NH ☎ 603/783-9511; www.shakers.org
🕙 Mid-May to Oct daily 10–5; Check for pre-Christmas programs on early Dec weekends
💲 Expensive. Reductions for seniors, children aged 6–17; children under 6 free

The white clapboard Canterbury United Community Church in the village of Canterbury

Where to... Stay

Prices

Expect to pay for two people sharing a double room, excluding taxes

$ under $150 $$ $150–$250 $$$ over $250

PORTSMOUTH

♥♥♥ Martin Hill Inn $–$$

This 19th-century inn, decorated with antique mahogany furniture and delicate oriental porcelain, captures the essence of Portsmouth, one of New England's oldest communities. Bedrooms are themed, from formal colonial to country Victorian; all have queen-size beds and air-conditioning. Strawbery Banke and the downtown attractions are only a 15-minute stroll away.

✚ 201 E2 ⊠ 404 Islington Street, Portsmouth, NH ☎ 603/436-2287; www.martinhillinn.com

KENNEBUNKPORT

♥♥♥ Captain Lord Mansion $$–$$$

The popular inn (with conference facilities and 20 bedrooms) would be unrecognizable to its first owner, shipbuilder and merchant Nathaniel Lord. Some elements of Lord's 19th-century home remain, including the impressive four-story staircase. There are four quiet rooms in a separate house behind the main inn.

✚ 201 F3 ⊠ 6 Pleasant Street, Kennebunkport, ME ☎ 800/522-3141 or 207/967-3141; www.captainlord.com

♥♥♥ White Barn Inn $$$

This luxury inn may be housed in a converted barn, but there is absolutely nothing rustic about the setting: galleries of antiques, a piano bar and plain, polished wood floors. By contrast, some of the bedrooms are quite plain, though the nine suites are as luxurious as any in North America. The inn's restaurant is renowned for its excellent cuisine.

✚ 201 F3 ⊠ 37 Beach Avenue, Kennebunk Beach, ME ☎ 207/967-2321; www.whitebarninn.com

BAR HARBOR

♥♥♥ Bar Harbor Inn and Spa $$–$$$

This large oceanfront complex is near the shops and restaurants of Bar Harbor. Many guestrooms in the Main Inn and Oceanfront Lodge have views of the bay, while the less expensive rooms in the Newport Building have views of the expansive grounds. The Reading Room restaurant is one of the most romantic in Bar Harbor.

✚ 199 E2 ⊠ Newport Drive, Bar Harbor, ME ☎ 800/248-3351 or 207/288-3351; www.barharborinn.com

♥♥♥ Manor House Inn $–$$

Hidden behind tall hedges and set back from the street, Manor House is typically Victorian, with deep gables and wraparound porch. Its interior is equally authentic, with oriental rugs, polished wood floors and antique desks. Even the beds in each of the 18 rooms exude character, with tall, carved head- and footboards.

✚ 199 E2 ⊠ 106 West Street, Bar Harbor, ME ☎ 800/437-0088 or 207/288-3759; www.barharbormanorhouse.com

♥♥♥ Mira Monte Inn and Suites $–$$

The owners of this 19th-century inn have created a family atmosphere. The library, furnished with large overstuffed chairs, is a favorite room. The simply furnished

Where to...
Eat and Drink

Prices
Expect to pay per person for a three-course meal, excluding drinks and service
$ under $20 $$ $20–$35 $$$ over $35

PORTSMOUTH

⚑⚑⚑ Blue Mermaid Island Grill
$–$$$

A casual restaurant in the historic area known as The Hill, this is a local favorite. The food has Caribbean influences, with wood-grilled seafood and spicy entrees like plantain-encrusted grouper with mango, grilled banana and sweet potato hash, or grilled beef fillet with horseradish, *chipotle* (smoked jalapeno chili) mashed potatoes and green beans. Locally brewed draft beer; tropical coolers and margaritas are available from the bar downstairs, where there is live entertainment some weekends.

🔒 201 E2 ✉ 409 The Hill, Portsmouth, ME
📞 603/427-2583; www.bluemermaid.com
🕐 Mon–Thu 11:30–9, Fri–Sat 11:30–10, Sun 10–9

KENNEBUNKPORT

⚑⚑⚑⚑ The White Barn Inn $$$

One of New England's finest restaurants is housed in a restored 1820s barn. Crisp linen and candles on the tables combine with the rustic, wood-beamed interior to create the perfect setting for a romantic meal. The seasonal,

---

and resort lies close to White Mountain National Forest, Echo Lake State Park and North Conway. Ledges Dining Room serves New England cuisine, the Tullamore Tavern offers cocktails, beer and wine, and the temperature-controlled outdoor swimming pool and whirlpool spa are popular in every season.

🔒 201 D4 ✉ 2660 West Side Road, North Conway, NH 📞 800/533-6301; www.whitemountainhotel.com

HART'S LOCATION

⚑⚑⚑ Notchland Inn $$–$$$

This 1860s granite mansion is set in beautiful grounds near Crawford Notch. In this getaway, the 13 rooms and three cottages are tastefully decorated. Dinner is a feature, with a deliberately leisurely five-course meal served at a single sitting Wednesday to Sunday.

🔒 201 D3 ✉ US 302, Hart's Location, NH
📞 603/374-6131 or 800/866-6131; www.notchland.com

---

bedrooms have spectacular views; Mira Monte means "look at the mountains." Acadia National Park and Cadillac Mountain fill the windows.

🔒 199 E2 ✉ 69 Mount Desert Street, Bar Harbor, ME 📞 800/553-5109 or 207/288-4263; www.miramonte.com

WHITE MOUNTAINS

⚑⚑⚑⚑ Inn at Thorn Hill & Spa $$–$$$

This handsome 19th-century inn is close to Mount Washington and is popular with skiers in winter. Bedrooms are Victorian-style in the main inn, but more rustic in the carriage house. The lounge and restaurant complete the picture.

🔒 201 E4 ✉ 42 Thorn Hill Road, Jackson, NH 📞 800/289-8990 or 603/383-4242; www.innatthornhill.com

⚑⚑⚑ White Mountain Hotel and Resort $–$$$

At the base of White Horse Ledge, this contemporary country hotel

fixed-price menu, featuring classic New England cuisine, changes weekly. Desserts are irresistible. Reservations are essential. Jackets are required for men.

+ 201 F3 ⊠ 37 Beach Avenue, Kennebunk Beach, ME ☎ 207/967-2321; www.whitebarninn.com ⊙ Mon–Thu 6–9:30, Fri–Sun 5:30–9:30

PORTLAND

Fore Street $$$

This is one of New England's best-known restaurants, run by Sam Hayward, one of the region's best-known chefs. Reservations are essential to watch your meal prepared before you, either on a spit over an open hearth, or in the apple wood-fired oven. This informal place has a passion for food that radiates from the open kitchen. As well as excellent desserts, Hayward is proud of this cheese board. There is also a separate bar.

+ 198 A1 ⊠ 288 Fore Street, Portland, ME ☎ 207/775-2717; www.forestreet.biz ⊙ Sun–Thu 5:30–10, Fri–Sat 5:30–10:30 (Oct–May Sun 5:30–9:30)

BAR HARBOR

Lompoc Café $-$$

You may choose to eat at tables inside the cafe or sit outside and enjoy watching the action on the bocce court (Italian bowling). From the local brewery, which is out of town, the Lompoc serves a range of seasonal ales, including an unusual but appealing blueberry brew. Expect bistro food, such as stuffed mushrooms and chicken baked with garlicky cheese.

+ 199 E2 ⊠ 36 Rodick Street, Bar Harbor, ME ☎ 207/288-9392; www.lompoccafe.com ⊙ Mid-May to Oct daily 11:30–9:30

ROCKLAND

Cafe Miranda $-$$

A chef and staff with a sense of humor make a visit to this clapboard side-street restaurant a must. Lobster bibs are banned on the wide-ranging menu that has a definite Italian slant, but also includes outrageous titles such as Dave's Fairgrounds Delite, Nascar Paté and 50mph Tomatoes. Desserts include a fabulous chocolate-covered caramel walnut torte, and home-made ice creams.

+ 198 C1 ⊠ 15 Oak Street, Rockland, ME ☎ 207/594-2034; www.cafemiranda.com ⊙ Daily 5–9:30

WHITE MOUNTAINS

1785 Inn $$-$$$

Beams, an old brick oven and a stone fireplace in the dining room are testimony to the inn's long history. The menu mixes tradition with invention. Entrees such as rack of lamb are always popular, and for dessert how about trying coffee mousse in a crunchy walnut pastry shell?

+ 201 E4 ⊠ SR 16, North Conway, NH ☎ 800/421-1785 or 603/356-9025; www.the1785inn.com ⊙ Daily 5–9 (also Fri–Sat 9–10pm)

Thompson House Eatery $-$$

In a 200-year-old brick farmhouse, expect imaginative, modern dishes: crab cakes on a toasted croissant; warm blueberry and strawberry cobbler with ginger ice cream. Many ingredients are from the chef's organic garden.

+ 201 E4 ⊠ 193 Main Street, Jackson, NH ☎ 603/383-9341; www.thompsonhouseeatery.com ⊙ Thu–Mon 11:30–3, 5:30–10, Wed 5:30–10

WOLFEBORO

Cider Press $-$$

After 30 years, this family restaurant in a renovated barn is a fixture. Food is hearty: soups, steaks, scallops and ribs. Desserts include Boston cream pie, carrot cake and New York cheesecake. A variety of cider-based drinks adds to the fun.

+ 201 D3 ⊠ 30 Middleton Road, Wolfeboro, NH ☎ 603/569-2028; www.theciderpress.net ⊙ Summer Tue–Sun 5–8 (Sat till 9); winter hours vary

Where to...
Shop

MAINE

Shopping is changing Maine's image. The state known for its rugged outdoors is transforming its post-industrial towns into retail outlets, thanks to its imaginative craftspeople and its bargain-priced factory outlet stores.

Outlet Stores

Millions of shoppers a year flock to **Kittery Outlets**, a 90-minute drive north of Boston, with over 120 brand-name factory outlets in 13 malls (exit 3 off I-95, tel: 207/439-4367; www.thekitteryoutlets.com). Farther north (about 2.5 hours from Boston) is **Freeport**, best known as the home of L.L. Bean, open 24/7. But the attractive town has expanded, with 170 stores

and designer outlets attracting 4 million visitors a year (tel: 800/865-1994 or 207/865-1212; www.freeportusa.com).

Crafts

At the other end of the shopping spectrum are the collectibles created by the potters and painters, jewelers and quilters who continue the craft traditions of old. See their work at the **Old Port** historic district of Portland, or out at **Deer Isle Village** and **Stonington**.

Unusual, but easily accessed is the **Center For Maine Craft** (West Gardiner Service Plaza, SR 126, off Exit 103 from I-95 South, www.mainecrafts.org). Works range from hip, contemporary jewelry and ceramics to paintings and glass.

NEW HAMPSHIRE

With so much to do out of doors in New Hampshire, it is no surprise that this is a good place to buy the clothes, as well as the equipment, for hiking, biking and camping. Shopping in New Hampshire is boosted by its lack of sales tax.

Outlet Stores

There are 50 name-brand and designer stores at the **Tanger Outlet Center** (www.tangeroutlet.com) in Tilton. Up in North Conway, **White Mountain Outlets** boasts all the top names, including Liz Claiborne, L.L. Bean and Polo Ralph Lauren. This is also home to the **Chuck Roast Mountainwear** outlet (Route 16, tel: 603/356-5589; www.chuckroast.com), famous for its lifetime guarantees on rugged jackets, hats, mitts and vests.

Antiques and Crafts

The **League of New Hampshire Craftsmen** (www.nhcrafts.org)

has seven stores across the state, in North Conway, Center Sandwich, Meredith, Hanover, Littleton, Wolfeboro Falls and Concord. Pieces are juried, and you can buy smaller articles such as fragrant soaps, candles and brightly colored quilts. Some 75 years ago, **Sandwich Home Industries** of Center Sandwich (junction of SRs 109/113, tel: 603/284-6831; www.nhcrafts.org) was the inspiration for the League of New Hampshire Craftsmen when local women started up a cooperative, making souvenirs and household items using local materials. You can watch artisans working on pewter at Hillsborough Center, where the artists at **Gibson Pewter** (18 East Washington Road, tel: 603/464-3410; www.gibsonpewter.com) make bowls and tankards in all styles. Known as **Antique Alley**, Route 4 between Portsmouth and Concord is dotted with some 500 dealers in Northwood, Lee, Epsom and Chichester.

Where to...
Be Entertained

The **Maine Bureau of Parks and Lands** (tel: 207/287-3821; www.maine.gov/doc/parks) provides hiking maps for parks.

Cyclists can meander along quiet back roads or go mountain biking at four-season resorts such as **Sugarloaf** (tel: 207/237-2000; www.sugarloaf.com) and **Sunday River** (tel: 207/824-3000; www.sundayriver.com). Find trails at www.bikemaine.org.

Watersports

For a taste of the Maine of yesteryear, take a three- or six-day cruise aboard a windjammer (a traditional sailing ship). Contact the **Maine Windjammer Association** (www.sailmainecoast.com) for

details. In Camden, the schooner *Appledore* offers 2-hour daily sailings and sunset cruises in summer (tel: 207/236-8353).

Former Coast Guard captain Rich Woodman organizes cruises aboard the schooner *Eleanor* (tel: 207/967-8809). In Bar Harbor, **Coastal Kayaking Tours** (tel: 207/288-9605; www.acadiafun.com) offers guided tours along the coast.

Skiing

Maine's ski resorts are growing in popularity, thanks to well-priced packages and less-crowded slopes. Both snow boarders and skiers love **Sunday River**, near Bethel, and the hugely challenging **Sugarloaf** in northern Maine, with its long season and trails for all abilities, is also very popular.

New Hampshire has a well-organized network of trails and campsites, outfitters and marinas. For details contact **general park information** (tel: 603/271-3556; www.nhparks.state.nh.us).

Fishing

Nonresidents require a license: contact **New Hampshire Fish and Game Department** (tel: 603/271-3421; www.wildlife.state.nh.us). Fishing is hugely popular on Lake Winnipesaukee, and nearby ponds and streams. Most small towns have an agent who sells fishing licenses, and will know the nearest outfitter.

Watersports

At Holderness, the **Squam Lakes Natural Science Center** (www.nhnature.org), organizes wildlife cruises to see the loons on Squam Lake (Golden Pond) between May and October. For canoe rental and instruction,

contact **Wild Meadow Canoes and Kayaks**, Center Harbor (www.wildmeadowcanoes.com). For details on cruises, river trips and more, contact the **Lakes Region Association** (www.lakesregion.org).

Bicycling

Ski resorts such as **Loon Mountain** run summer cycling centers. Bicycle riders can take a shuttle to Echo Lake for the dramatic downhill trip through scenic Franconia Notch past Flume Gorge and other natural attractions.

Skiing

New Hampshire was the cradle of American skiing, with a club dating back to 1872. The first trails were cut at Cannon Mountain in 1930. Both cross-country and downhill skiing are well priced at the resorts strung along I-93: Tenney Mountain, Waterville Valley, Loon Mountain, Cannon and Bretton Woods. Contact **Ski New Hampshire** (www.skinh.com).

Walks and Tours

1 BOSTON'S BEACON HILL AND BACK BAY

Walk

Boston is relatively compact and you can easily stroll from one end of the city to the other. In fact, there are times when this is the fastest way around town. The historical Beacon Hill neighborhood is where the upper echelons of Boston society once lived, and many still do today, though you'll also see plenty of ordinary folks out walking their dogs or bringing home groceries to their red-brick town houses.

Until the 1830s, the Back Bay was under water. A massive landfill project lasting nearly 50 years turned it into Boston's most easily navigable neighborhood. The streets lie perpendicular to each other, unlike the meandering streets in other parts of the city, and the cross streets even go in alphabetical order. Home to Boston's premier shopping street, Newbury Street (▶ 71), the Back Bay is crowded on sunny summer Sundays, with almost everyone looking for an outdoor table.

DISTANCE 1.7 miles (2.7km) (one way) **TIME** 1.5 hours or all day if you linger
T STOP Red Line to Charles/MGH or Blue Line to Bowdoin **START POINT** Otis House
Museum, Beacon Hill ✛ 196 C3 **END POINT** The Back Bay ✛ 196 A1

1–2

Start your tour in Beacon Hill at the **Otis House Museum**. Colonial architect Charles Bulfinch built the home in 1796 for his friend Otis, an aspiring young lawyer who later became a member of Congress and later still the mayor of Boston.

Cross Cambridge Street and walk downhill one block to Joy Street, turn left and walk uphill, into the **Museum of African-American History and**

Abiel Smith School. There are several ways to visit this area: take a free guided tour of the **Black Heritage Trail**, or pick up a brochure and visit the 14 sites on your own. On Joy Street, the **Museum of African-American History** is in the **Abiel Smith School**; in Smith Court is the **African Meeting House** next door (under reconstruction), a half block away from the visitor center. Once known as "the Black Faneuil Hall," this 1806 building is the oldest black church in the United States still in existence. In 1832, William Lloyd Garrison founded the New England Anti-Slavery Society at this historic spot.

onto Pinckney and follow it downhill, then turn left on **Louisburg Square**, home to some fine old Beacon Hill homes. Most of these town houses have been lovingly restored, making this one of Boston's priciest addresses. The park is private and you need a key to get in, so is more for looking at than for doing.

3–4

Continue, crossing Mount Vernon Street, and enter Willow Street. Turn right on **Acorn Street.** The street appears in many photographs of Beacon Hill, perhaps not so much because it is the most picturesque, but because cobblestones prevent all but the most intrepid from driving down the narrow passageway. With its gas lamps and brick sidewalk, you feel you are right back in days gone by.

Turn left at West Cedar Street and right at Chestnut. Cross busy Charles Street (or explore the antiques shops) and continue to Brimmer Street. Turn left and walk to Beacon Street. At the corner you'll see the **Cheers** pub, formerly the Bull and Finch, on which the bar from the TV show *Cheers* was modeled.

Cobblestoned Acorn Street looks today as it did in the 19th century

Frog Pond

Boston Common

CHARLES STREET

Public Garden

Washington Monument

ARLINGTON STREET

BERKELEY STREET

BACK BAY

COMMONWEALTH AVENUE

NEWBURY STREET

CLARENDON ST

The Tortoise & the Hare

Trinity Church

Copley Square

DARTMOUTH STREET

John Hancock Tower

BOYLSTON STREET

Boston Public Library

EXETER STREET

HUNTINGTON AVE

5

6

7

8

0   200 metres
0   200 yards

2–3

Follow Smith Court to the end. Then proceed along the narrow alley to the left, and follow it as it bends right and deposits you on Russell Street. You've just retraced a part of the route that fugitive slaves took in the 19th century on the Underground Railroad (the network of safe houses that provided shelter for escapees).

Turn left onto Russell Street, and then right on Myrtle Street. Go two blocks to Anderson Street and turn left. Then take the first right

The exterior is the one seen at the opening of every episode, but walk inside and you won't recognize the furnishings (the show's interior scenes were shot on a soundstage in Hollywood and do not look at all alike). These days, the "gang at Cheers" is made up mostly of visitors to the city rather than Bostonians.

4–5

Cross Beacon Street and walk a half block left to the entrance to the **Public Garden** (▶ 58). If you're in town at the right time of year and in the mood for a ride on one of the **swan boats**, go clockwise around the lagoon. Otherwise, stroll counterclockwise toward the Washington Monument. Exit the Public Garden at Arlington Street and walk a block left to exclusive **Newbury Street** (▶ 71).

5–6

Chanel, Armani, Versace, Ann Taylor and Burberry are just some of the exclusive brands in the high-rent blocks closest to the Public Garden, but equally intriguing and less familiar retailers line both sides of this popular shopping boulevard. If it's a sunny day, there's nothing better than stopping for a coffee or a leisurely lunch at one of Newbury

Street's excellent restaurants or myriad outdoor cafes. Shop your way as far as Exeter Street (or farther, and then double back; the quirkier shops are farthest from the Public Garden) and turn left. Continue one block to Boylston Street and then turn left again.

6–7

Boylston between Exeter and Dartmouth is home to the old and new buildings of the **Boston Public Library**. The old, an 1895 Renaissance Revival by architects McKim, Mead and White, has been widely imitated throughout the United States. It boasts relief panels on its facade by Saint-Gaudens, bronze doors sculpted by Daniel Chester French, and interior murals by John Singer Sargent and Edwin Abbey. The new, a stark 1972 creation by Philip Johnson, is constructed from the same color granite as the original, but that is about all that the two buildings have in common. The old building has the added benefit of facing **Copley Square** and its pleasant open lawn.

7–8

Cross Dartmouth Street (be careful of the traffic) and walk across the lawn to **Trinity**

Church, built in 1877 by Henry H. Richardson, the dean of American architecture. This granite and sandstone building introduced the popular style that became known

Exclusive Newbury Street, *the* place to shop

as Richardson Romanesque. On Fridays (September to May), there is an organ recital at 12:15pm.

As you face Trinity Church, to your left you will see two low bronze statues, which are likely to be bearing at least one or two small children. This is **The Tortoise and the Hare at Copley Square**, a Nancy Schön sculpture that pays tribute to the thousands of runners who take part in and complete the Boston Marathon (the finish line is actually a block away on Boylston Street between Exeter and Dartmouth streets). Near the statues the **Bostix** booth sells half-price theater tickets (cash only).

Towering above Copley Square, and reflecting Trinity Church's glory to the rest of Boston, is the glass-sheathed **John Hancock Tower**. From some angles, the building's unusual shape and mirrored exterior make it look no wider than a flagpole. Just a short walk away is the **Prudential Center** (► 58–59), another Boston icon. From the Skywalk Observatory, more than 750 feet (230m) up on the 50th floor, you have views over the city and, on a clear day, you can see as far as neighboring New England states. It's just a short walk away.

The 19th-century Trinity Church mirrored in the 20th-century John Hancock Tower

TAKING A BREAK

Otis House Museum

✚ 196 C3 ⊠ 141 Cambridge Street at Lynde Street ☎ 617/994-5920; www.historicnewengland.com ◷ Tours Wed–Sun 11–4:30; tours every 30 min 💲 Moderate

Museum of African-American History/Abiel Smith School

✚ 196 C3 ⊠ 46 Joy Street ☎ 617/720-2991; www.afroammuseum.org ◷ Mon–Sat 10–4 💲 Inexpensive

Boston African American National Historic Site

✚ 196 C3 ⊠ Information desk at Museum of African American History/Abiel Smith School ☎ 617/742-5415; www.nps.gov/boaf ◷ Mon–Sat 10–4 💲 Inexpensive

Boston Public Library

✚ 195 F3 ⊠ 700 Boylston Street ☎ 617/536-5400; www.bpl.org ◷ Mon–Thu 9–9, Fri–Sat 9–5 (also Oct–May Sun 1–5) 💲 Free

Trinity Church

✚ 196 A1 ⊠ Copley Square ☎ 617/536-0944; www.trinitychurchboston.org ◷ Mon–Sat 9–5, Sun 1–6 💲 Inexpensive

Prudential Center Skywalk

✚ 195 E2 ⊠ 800 Boylston Street ☎ 617/859-0648; www.prudentialcenter.com ◷ Mar–Oct daily 10–10; Nov–Feb 10–8 💲 Moderate

2 OLD KING'S HIGHWAY
Tour

Though today's SR 6A linked the colonial towns of Provincetown and Plymouth in the 17th century (hence the name, the Old King's Highway), there was a trail here used by Native Americans long before European settlers arrived. It may no longer be the fastest way to get from one end of the Cape to the other – what scenic

DISTANCE 40 miles (64km)
TIME 1.5 hours, longer if you stop en route **START POINT** Sagamore Bridge ✚ 202 D2
END POINT Cape Cod National Seashore Salt Pond Visitor Center ✚ 202 E2

route is? – but it is the prettiest. Along the way, keep your eyes open for tree-lined avenues, picturesque New England towns and 18th- to 19th-century houses.

1–2
Start your trip just as you cross the

Sagamore Bridge onto Cape Cod. Take exit 1 and turn right at the traffic light onto SR 6A. Follow it to the town of Sandwich and turn right onto SR 130 south into the center of town. After about 2 miles (3km), you'll see the turnoff for **Heritage Museums & Gardens** (▶ 87–88). This is an unusual hodgepodge of a museum – antique cars, military memorabilia, fine art and luxurious gardens – but each collection is top-notch. Young children will love the old-style 1912 carousel.

Cape Cod is a good hunting ground for antiques

2-3

Double back to 6A and turn right to resume the route east. This is the beginning of what is known as "Antiques Alley," which continues as far as Eastham. A map/guide to the shops in the area produced by the dealers is available, though not all the shops are listed. If you're looking for something specific, you may just have to hunt until you've exhausted all the possibilities.

Just past the 11-mile (17km) mark (you'll see green mile-marker signs on the right-hand side of the road), the road splits. Stay left on 6A; don't take SR 132.

3-4

At about the 14-mile (22km) mark, you'll pass through the town of **Barnstable,** which has a concentration of antiques shops and one-of-a-kind stores. Drive on for 3 miles (5km) until you come to **Yarmouth Port.** Blink twice and you could miss this collection of shops, restaurants and antiques dealers. Stop here for a visit to Design Works (159 Main Street, tel: 508/362-9698), which sells candles, linens, soaps and towels in a historic 19th-century dry-goods mercantile, or order a cool root beer at the 120-year-old Hallet's Store (139 Main Street, tel: 508/362-3362), the oldest family-owned, old-fashioned soda fountain in the United States.

4-5

From Yarmouth, continue to the **Antiques Center of Cape Cod** in Dennis, just before the 21-mile/34km marker (243 Main Street, tel: 508/385-6400). With more than 250 dealers housed in old warehouses, serious antiques hounds could easily spend the entire day here.

Theater enthusiasts should stop at the Cape Playhouse in nearby **Dennis Village.** Producer Raymond Moore desperately wanted to have his own theater, so in 1927 he moved a 19th-century Unitarian meetinghouse to this location and attracted big-name stars of stage and screen to perform. Basil Rathbone starred in the opening-night production, and since then the theater claims "almost every well-known star of stage, screen and TV has walked the stage of the Cape Playhouse" – Helen Hayes, Humphrey Bogart, Gregory Peck, Lana Turner and a young acting student named Jane Fonda, to name just a few. The theater is still going strong, and the original pews, now with cushions, still serve as seats.

The adjacent Cape Cinema, which is also housed in a replica of a church, shows a program of independent movies. Continue on toward **Brewster**.

5–6

Just before the 27-mile (43km) mark, you'll find the **Cape Cod Museum of Natural History** (869 Main Street, tel: 508/896-3867). It has some interesting displays on the local flora and fauna and walking trails out to the beach. If you are planning a whale-watching trip, this is a good place to learn about whales. The museum shop sells souvenirs and books on Cape Cod (▶ 89).

Just before the 31-mile (50km) mark in Brewster, you'll pass Cobie's (3620 Main Street, tel: 508/896-7021), an old-fashioned clam shack and ice-cream stand. Stop for a bite to eat here and enjoy something of the very essence of Cape Cod. With your energy levels replenished, look for signs a few hundred yards (meters) ahead on the right for the **Cape Cod Rail Trail** (▶ 86–87). This is about the midpoint of the 26-mile (40km)

paved bicycle route, which follows the path of an abandoned railroad bed from Dennis to Wellfleet. You can rent bicycles at the Idle Times hut (tel: 508/255-8281) and then head off whichever way you like to explore the trail.

A half mile (800m) farther on the right is **Nickerson State Park**, also ideal for biking, as well as many other outdoor activities including hiking, fishing and horseback riding. You will need to call as far as possible in advance if you would like to stay overnight at a campsite, however.

TAKING A BREAK

Antiques Center of Cape Cod
✚ 202 E2 ⊠ 243 SR 6A, Dennis, MA
☎ 508/385-6400;
www.antiquecenterofcapecod.com
🕔 Mon–Sat 10–5, Sun 11–5

Cape Playhouse
✚ 202 E2 ⊠ 820 SR 6A, Dennis, MA
☎ 508/385-3911

Nickerson State Park
✚ 202 E2 ⊠ 3488 Main Street, SR 6A, Brewster, MA ☎ 508/896-3491 🕔 Day use: daily 8–8. Camping permitted. Closed in winter 🟥 Inexpensive

Finally, SR 6A peters out in the town of **Orleans**, where the more commercial and less scenic US 6 joins it.

6–7

It is worth continuing from Orleans on US 6/ SR 6A to Eastham, home of **Cape Cod National Seashore Salt Pond Visitor Center** (▶ 78–80). You can learn all about this beautiful seashore, or simply park your car and spend the rest of the day lazing about on the beach.

Cycling is a popular way to see the Cape

SOUTHERN VERMONT

3

Tour

This drive takes you past the rolling hills, leafy forests, meandering streams and peaceful farms of southern Vermont. It begins in Manchester, ranges north to Woodstock, and then completes a loop back to Manchester. Come in October during the foliage season to see the countryside at its best, but be prepared for the road to be crowded and the drive slow.

DISTANCE 134 miles (216km)
TIME 3.5 hours, longer if you stop en route
START/END POINT Manchester Center ✚ 200 A2

1–2

Begin the tour in Manchester Center, where SRs 11, 30 and 7A all intersect. Drive east on SR 11 toward Londonderry. In about 6 miles (10km), you'll see a turnoff left leading to the **Long Trail** (▶121), the hiking path that stretches across the spine of the Green Mountain range from Massachusetts to Canada. Stop here if you want a hike.

2–3

Continue along SR 11 east to Londonderry. Turn left onto SR 100 north. It may be the prettiest road in all of Vermont and leads to almost every major ski area in the state, including Mount Snow, Killington and Stowe, but few towns extend more than a block or two.

The first such town on this tour is **Weston**, around 5 miles (8km) north of Londonderry.

Spectacular fall foliage near the town of Weston

Vermont prides itself on maintaining age-old traditions

Stop at the Weston Village Store (660 Main Street, tel: 802/824-5477), a particularly good example of an old-fashioned general store that is still making a go of it. Dating to 1891, it features all things Vermont, from the original wooden floorboards to the local maple

syrup, cheese and fudge. Pick up a picnic lunch here; eat it on the town green, with its bandstand, benches and soft grass.

3–4

From Weston, SR 100 twists and turns, but every turn is marked, so you won't get lost. Stay on SR 100 for 21 miles (34km) to SR 100A, which forks to the right. Follow SR 100A a mile (1.6km) to the **President Calvin Coolidge State Historic Site**, in Plymouth. On the death of Warren Harding, Vice President Coolidge was sworn in as 30th President by his father in the family homestead, on August 3, 1923; Vermont's only president. As well as visiting the house, take time to see the 1892 Plymouth Cheese Factory, America's second oldest cheese operation.

4–5

Continue northeast along SR 100A for 5.8 miles (9.3km) to US 4, turn right and follow it to the center of **Woodstock**. This is the halfway point of the trip. However, don't turn around quite yet; stop and spend some time here even if you're not staying the night. Woodstock has lovely shops, good restaurants and

several attractions of its own, including the nearby Marsh-Billings-Rockefeller National Historical Park (▶ 118–120).

5–6

To begin the second half of the trip, loop around the town green to get to SR 106 south. Turn right and follow it 23 miles (37km) to SR 10 west. Turn right onto SR 10 west and stay on it until it reaches Gassetts.

6–7

Turn left to SR 103 south and follow it to Chester. Take SR 35 south by bearing right at the fork; at the next intersection take the soft

Spectacular fall landscape near Woodstock

left on SR 35 for about 7 miles (11km) until you reach the intersection with the SR 121. Turn right into **Grafton** (▶ panel,

on your left. Stay on SR 121 as it turns from dirt to pavement to dirt again, for a total of 10 miles (16km) until it ends at Route 11. Turn left onto SR 11 west and take it 4 miles (6km) to Londonderry.

8–9

Turn left onto SR 100 south to Bondville. At Bondville, turn right onto SR 30 north. After about 3 miles (5km), you'll see the access road to **Stratton Mountain** on your left next to the convenience store. In winter, this is a popular downhill ski area. Summertime activities include hiking and biking.

From the Stratton access road, it's 9 miles (14.5km) on SR 30 north to the intersection with SR 11 west. The two roads overlap for the 6.5-mile (10.5km) return to Manchester.

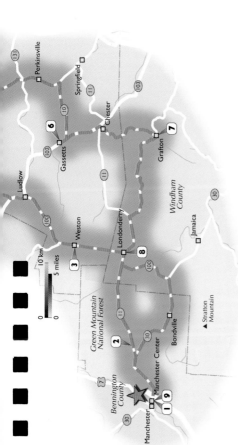

page 122). The village fell on hard times in the 20th century, but has been lovingly restored by the Windham Foundation.
Step back to the 19th-century: eat at The Old Tavern and taste award-winning cheddar at the Grafton Village Cheese Company, visit the small historical museum, nature museum and mineral museum, and browse the art galleries and the old Fire Station, where they make furniture.

7–8

Stay on SR 121 west from Grafton; the road soon turns to dirt. During rainy or snowy weather, it floods, but on clear summer or fall days, it may be the most beautiful part of the whole trip. (If the weather is inclement, take SR 35 north back to Chester, then turn left onto SR 11, continuing west back to Manchester.) About a mile (1.6km) after Grafton, you will pass a Christmas tree farm

TAKING A BREAK

President Calvin Coolidge State Historic Site
➕ 200 A2 ⊠ 3780 Route 100A,
Plymouth Notch, VT ☎ 802/672-3773;
www.historicvermont.org/coolidge
🕐 Late May to mid-Oct daily 9:30–5
💲 Inexpensive; parking: free

4 NEWPORT'S CLIFF WALK

Walk

DISTANCE Short walk 1 mile (1.6km), full walk 6 miles (9.5km)
TIME About 3 hours for the full walk (wear practical shoes)
START/END POINT Narragansett Avenue ☩ 202 C2

Newport's Cliff Walk, a path bordered by the Atlantic on one side and the majestic mansions of Bellevue Avenue on the other, is a lovely way to see the best of what Newport has to offer. It was developed by the owners of some of these estates between 1880 and 1920, and has survived efforts by subsequent owners to destroy it: when landowners tried to barricade their stretches of the walk, Newporters simply ripped up the obstacles and hurled them into the ocean. The walk was restored in 1975 and designated a National Recreation Trail.

The entire Cliff Walk is 3.5 miles (5.5km) long, but you can do as little or as much of it as you like. There aren't any restaurants or public restrooms along the way, and though on hot summer days some enterprising youngsters may set up a lemonade stand on the route, you should take plenty of water. The last 2 miles (3km) of the route are the least traveled (and also the most difficult), but they are filled with idyllic spots for an alfresco lunch.

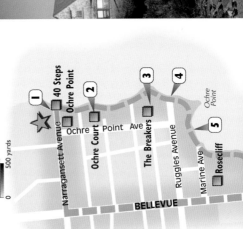

The Cliff Walk passes some of Newport's finest mansions

1–2

Begin your walk at the Narragansett Avenue entrance, where there is limited free street parking. Below you, you'll see the **40 Steps**, which lead from the path almost down into the water. Each of the steps was donated by a Newport resident. At weekends, back in the late 19th century, this was a meeting point for homesick servants and workers from the grand mansions, who danced and played Irish music. Turn right onto the path, where you'll pass **Ochre Point**, an 1882 Queen Anne mansion. Depending on the season, you may have a hard time seeing it behind the high hedges.

There are fine views from the Cliff Walk

Sheep Point

Marble House

AVENUE

⑦

⑥ Rough Point

Bailey's Beach

Land's End

The Waves

owner. The next two buildings, one a gorgeous brownstone with a red-tile roof, are also part of Salve Regina's campus.

3–4

The last building before Ruggles Avenue is the highlight of the walk: Cornelius Vanderbilt II's 1895 **The Breakers** (▶136–137). It's the biggest, the most opulent and the most extravagant of all the mansions in Newport. The massive lawns fronting the ocean (as well as the 70 rooms inside the house) are open only to those paying for the house tour. The view that the Vanderbilts enjoyed each summer is absolutely free. There are even some benches here overlooking the ocean.

2–3

A bit farther along is **Ochre Court**, an early example of Richard Morris Hunt's Beaux Arts grand estates. It is now a part of the campus of Salve Regina University. Unlike the fenced-in topiary gardens separating the private estates from the Cliff Walk, the large, open lawns around the university are open to the public, so you can relax on the lush green grass and pretend you're a 19th-century estate

4–5

After Ruggles Avenue, the trail turns to dirt and then to rocks. Those with mobility problems should turn right onto Ruggles Avenue, then right again onto Ochre Point Avenue and stroll through one of Newport's loveliest neighborhoods (and to see several of the same mansions from the front). Turn right again on Narragansett to get back to your car.

The energetic, however, should continue, as several of the most interesting mansions

lie ahead. Just before Marine Avenue is a small public beach in front of a simple wooden home. It is a lovely place to stop but, unfortunately, this is no secret so you may have to share the sand.

5–6

From Marine Avenue, it's another 2 miles (3km) to the end of the walk, over similarly rocky terrain. If you continue this far, you'll be rewarded with glimpses of (in order) **Rosecliff** (▲ 143), Beechwood and **Marble House** (▲ 143). **Rosecliff**, a white terracotta edifice, is shielded from the Cliff Walk by an imposing balustrade at the end of the lawn. Beechwood, a pale white stucco building with stone dog statues standing sentry over the lawn, was the home of *the* Mrs Caroline Astor (now a

private home). **Marble House** was the estate of Mrs William K. Vanderbilt, who commissioned the rather jarring Chinese Tea House that overlooks the ocean.

Four of the major mansions on this trail are open to visitors (▲ 137), so if you want to see inside, pop in at any one that piques your interest. Or just wander along leafy Bellevue Avenue back to Narragansett Avenue and your car.

6–7

The remainder of the Cliff Walk is rocky. Don't attempt it in foul weather, or without good walking shoes. If you do proceed, the next mansion you'll pass is **Rough Point** (▲ 138–139), a red sandstone building that was the summer home of heiress Doris Duke, once the richest woman in America. You will have to clamber across more rocks to reach **Land's End**, a yellow stucco home with a gray cedar-shingle roof, that once belonged to author Edith Wharton. Around the next bend you will find **The Waves**, a 1927 half-timbered Tudor-style building.

From here, the end is in sight: **Bailey's Beach**, a private enclave with luxurious cabanas. Don't worry about the exclusivity: there is a section of the beach known to locals

as **Reject's Beach** where the general public is allowed. There are no lifeguards or facilities here, but you can swim or picnic, and enjoy the same view as the folks at Bailey's Beach without having to pay for the privilege. From the beach, you can walk back along the Cliff Walk, or take a 3-mile (5km) stroll beneath the trees on Bellevue Avenue to Narragansett Avenue and your car.

Left: The Breakers, Cornelius Vanderbilt II's 1895 mansion. Below: The paved path of the Cliff Walk

Practicalities

BEFORE YOU GO

WHAT YOU NEED

● Required ○ Suggested ▲ Not required △ Not applicable	Visitors to the US have to complete the ESTA (Electronic System of Travel Authorization) online (https://esta.cbp.dhs.gov) before traveling.	UK	Germany	USA	Canada	Australia	Ireland	Netherlands	Spain
Passport/National Identity Card		●	●	▲	▲	●	●	●	●
Visa (regulations can change – check before you travel)		▲	▲	▲	▲	▲	▲	▲	▲
Onward or Return Ticket		●	●	▲	▲	●	●	●	●
Health Inoculations		▲	▲	▲	▲	▲	▲	▲	▲
Health Documentation (► 192, Health)		▲	▲	▲	▲	▲	▲	▲	▲
Travel Insurance		○	○	○	○	○	○	○	○
Drivers License (national)		●	●	●	●	●	●	●	●
Car Insurance Certificate		△	△	●	●	△	△	△	△
Car Registration Document		△	△	●	●	△	△	△	△

WHEN TO GO

Boston & New England

High season   Low season

JAN	FEB	MAR	APR	MAY	JUN	JUL	AUG	SEP	OCT	NOV	DEC
36°F	38°F	46°F	56°F	67°F	76°F	82°F	80°F	73°F	63°F	52°F	40°F
2°C	3°C	8°C	13°C	19°C	24°C	28°C	27°C	23°C	17°C	11°C	4°C
❄	❄	❄	☁	☀	☀	☀	☀	⛅	☀	☁	❄

☀ Sun   ☁ Cloud   🌧 Wet   ⛅ Sun/Showers   ❄ Snow

The temperatures listed above are the **average daily maximum** for each month. New England has many different climates. It is often said that if you don't like the weather in New England, just wait half an hour.

Summer (June–August) is the preferred time to visit, as many of the outdoor activities are in full swing. September is not as reliably warm as summer, but there are frequent beach days, and it's seldom too cool for a hike, a bike ride or a picnic.

October is **fall foliage season**, when all the leaves turn from green to red, orange and yellow. **Skiing season** begins as early as October (but usually November) and ends sometime in mid-April. Late March and early April are known as mud season in the northern states, during which it rains a lot.

GETTING ADVANCE INFORMATION
Websites
- Connecticut Commission on Culture & Tourism: www.ctvisit.com
- Maine Office of Tourism: www.visitmaine.com
- Massachusetts Office of Travel & Tourism: www.massvacation.com
- New Hampshire Division of Travel & Tourism   www.visitnh.gov
- Rhode Island Tourism Division: www.VisitRhodeIsland.com
- Vermont Department of Tourism & Marketing   www.vermontvacation.com

GETTING THERE

From the UK New England's principal gateway is Boston's Logan International Airport. Flying time from London to Boston is approximately 6.5 hours. American Airlines, British Airways, Continental and Virgin Atlantic fly from London Heathrow. Alternative gateways to New England include New York's JFK Airport and Newark Liberty International (for southern New England), and Montréal and Toronto airports (for northern New England).

From Australia and New Zealand Qantas, Air New Zealand, American and United Airlines fly to Boston from both Sydney and Auckland, with a change of planes either in Los Angeles or San Francisco. Flying time to the West Coast of the US is 12 hours from Auckland and 14 hours from Sydney. The length of the layover can vary from 2 to 4 hours; the flight between the West Coast and Boston is about 5 hours.

From Canada Flying time to Boston is just over an hour from Montréal, an hour and a half from Toronto and 5 hours from Vancouver.

From the US All the major US carriers serve Boston's Logan International Airport. US Airways and Delta Airlines both operate a shuttle service between New York's La Guardia Airport and Boston; flights leave each city every hour from 6am to 9pm (weekdays).

Ticket prices The most popular times to visit are usually when airfares are highest and seats scarcest, so make your flight arrangements as soon as you know your travel dates. Travel mid-week for the lowest rate, but stay over at least one Saturday night before you return.

By Rail or Bus Intercity **Amtrak** trains from major US cities arrive at Boston's South Station. For more information call Amtrak at 800/872-7245, or look at their website www.amtrak.com. **Greyhound** (tel: 800/229-9424 or www.greyhound.com) provides nationwide bus service and has information on services throughout New England.

TIME

All of New England is on **Eastern Standard Time**, five hours behind Greenwich Mean Time (GMT −5). Between the second Sunday in March and the first Sunday in November, clocks are set ahead 1 hour for **Daylight Saving**.

CURRENCY AND FOREIGN EXCHANGE

Currency The monetary unit of the United States is the dollar ($), divided into 100 cents (¢). **Coins** come in 1 cent (penny), 5 cents (nickel), 10 cents (dime), 25 cents (quarter), and the very rare 50-cent pieces (half dollars) and one-dollar coins. **Bills** come in denominations of $1, $5, $10, $20, $50, $100 and seldom-seen denominations higher than $100.

Exchange The airport, banks and most large city hotels have facilities for changing foreign currencies and travelers' checks. **Cash withdrawals** can be made at ATMs (automatic teller machines) throughout New England, but check with your bank for details of where your card is accepted and to find out if your personal identification number (PIN) is internationally valid. **Debit cards** may be accepted at retail outlets that are validated for international access. **Credit cards** are widely accepted – the most commonly accepted credit cards are MasterCard, Visa and American Express. Less common, but accepted by many establishments, are Discover and Diners Club.

In the USA	Greater Boston Convention & Visitors Bureau
	☎ Toll free 888/SEE BOSTON (888/733 2678); www.bostonusa.com
Worldwide	Discover New England (www.discovernewengland.org) represents all six New England states for both overseas and US visitors. Their website gives a good overview of the region, with useful information on everything from drives to shopping.

WHEN YOU ARE THERE

NATIONAL HOLIDAYS

Jan 1	New Year's Day
Third Mon Jan	Martin Luther King Day
Third Mon Feb	President's Day
Last Mon May	Memorial Day
Jul 4	Independence Day
First Mon Sep	Labor Day
Second Mon Oct	Columbus Day
Nov 11	Veterans' Day
Fourth Thu Nov	Thanksgiving
Dec 25	Christmas Day

Massachusetts/Maine also celebrate Patriot's Day on the third Monday of April. Banks and post offices close on national holidays, but most major stores are open.

ELECTRICITY

 The power supply is 110/120 volts AC, 60 cycles. Most sockets take two-pronged or three-pronged plugs.

Visitors from Europe, or anywhere that uses 220/240 volt power, will need to bring a converter and a plug adaptor.

OPENING HOURS

○ Stores
● Offices
● Banks
● Post Offices
● Museums/Monuments
● Pharmacies

8am 9am 10am noon 1pm 2pm 4pm 5pm 7pm

☐ Day   ☐ Midday   ☐ Evening

Stores Larger stores are generally open between 9 and 9 weekdays; 10 and 8 on weekends. In Connecticut, liquor stores close on Sunday.
Banks Most are open weekdays from 9 to 4:30, and Saturday 9 to 12:30.
Post Offices usually open from 9 to 5 weekdays, and some open Saturday morning.
Museums Hours vary. Some are closed on Monday.

TIPS/GRATUITIES

Tipping is expected for all services. As a guide:
Yes ✓   No ✗

Restaurants (service not included)	✓	15–20%
Bar service	✓	$1–$2
Tour guides	✓	15–20%
Cabs	✓	15%
Chambermaids	✓	$1–$2 per day
Porters	✓	$1 per bag

DISCOUNT PASSES

Get unlimited travel on the "T" transportation system with a CharlieCard (www.mbta.com). Boston CityPass gives discounts to five major attractions (www.citypass.com); Go Boston covers 70 attractions (www.goboston.com).

TIME DIFFERENCES

GMT	Boston	USA New York	Germany	Spain	Australia
12 noon	7am	7am	1pm	1pm	10pm

STAYING IN TOUCH

Post Boston's main post office is at Fort Point, 25 Dorchester Avenue, MA (near South Station); it is open 24 hours. Yellow Pages lists other post offices. Larger branches open Mon–Fri 8–6, Sat 9–1. Blue mail-boxes are on street corners.

Public telephones Most payphones in public areas are coin operated. From public phones dial 0 for the operator and give the country, city and number you are calling. You will need at least $6 in quarters for an overseas call. Some phones take prepaid phone cards, available at drugstores and newsstands, and some take credit cards. Dial 1 plus the area code for numbers within the US and Canada. Dial 411 to find US and Canadian numbers. Note that toll-free numbers are only free of charge when dialed in the US and Canada.

International Dialing Codes Dial 011 followed by	
UK:	44
Ireland:	353
Australia:	61
Germany:	49
Netherlands:	31
Spain:	34

Cell providers and services Although cell (mobile) phones work in Boston, coverage can be poor or non-existent deep in the countryside. Quad-band phones work in the US, but international calls are expensive. One solution is to buy a cheap pay-as-you go phone at stores such as Radio Shack (www.radioshack.com). Warning: Most states restrict the use of cell phones while driving, both for talking and texting. It is safer not to use a cell phone while driving in New England.

WiFi and internet As well as being business and student communities, Boston and Cambridge kick-started the computer revolution. Therefore, WiFi is widespread, from hotels and bookstores to cafes and ice-cream parlors. Find free WiFi around Faneuil Hall Marketplace, at Logan International Airport and the centrally located Boston Public Library. Use a website such as www.jiwire.com to find WiFi hotspots.

PERSONAL SAFETY

Boston is a walking city and a safe city. The crime rate is far lower than the US national average. New England, in general, is very safe. However, always take the usual precautions:

- Hold on to your purse or bag or wallet.
- Even the safest cities have pickpockets, especially during holidays or major sales in stores.
- The "T," the Boston area metro, streetcar and bus system is safe, but it is always wise to ride in the busier cars.
- Always be aware of your surroundings. Avoid walking around alone at night; avoid quiet side streets and parks.
- Carry minimal cash; leave valuables in the hotel safe. Don't flaunt jewelry.
- Lock your door at night or when you are out of your room.
- If you are robbed, always report the theft or mugging to the police and get a reference number/form for any insurance claim.

Police assistance:
☎ 911 from any phone

POLICE 911

FIRE 911

AMBULANCE 911

HEALTH

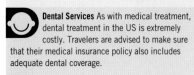

Insurance The US lacks comprehensive medical or dental coverage; medical services must be paid at the time rendered, either with cash or through insurance. It is strongly recommended that you take out a travel insurance policy that covers medical and dental treatment.

Dental Services As with medical treatment, dental treatment in the US is extremely costly. Travelers are advised to make sure that their medical insurance policy also includes adequate dental coverage.

Weather New England winters can bring subfreezing temperatures, so bring plenty of warm clothing. In summer, you can get a serious sunburn; wear sunscreen and cover up.

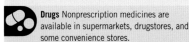

Drugs Nonprescription medicines are available in supermarkets, drugstores, and some convenience stores. Prescription drugs are available only from pharmacies. If you take prescribed medications, bring them with you, plus a copy of your prescription as well, in case you need to refill it while in the US.

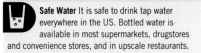

Safe Water It is safe to drink tap water everywhere in the US. Bottled water is available in most supermarkets, drugstores and convenience stores, and in upscale restaurants.

STUDENTS AND SENIOR CITIZENS

Students/Children Hostels are not as common in the US as they are in Europe. Youths should join the **International Youth Hostel Federation** (www.hihostels. com) before leaving home. Most attractions offer discounts on admission for students (with current identification card) and for children under 12.

Senior Citizens Many attractions and some hotels offer senior discounts, some for travelers as young as 50. American travelers over the age of 50 should join the **American Association of Retired Persons** (AARP – tel:888/OUR AARP or internationally 202/243 3525, www.aarp.org), which entitles you to various discounts on hotel rooms, car rentals and some airfares.

TRAVELING WITH A DISABILITY

Major car-rental companies have vehicles adapted for travelers with disabilities. Most Boston hotels are thoroughly wheelchair accessible and many lodgings have made strides to accept travelers with disabilities. If in doubt, call in advance. Mobility International USA (tel: 541/343-1284; www.miusa.org) publishes a book of resources.

CHILDREN

Restaurants are usually child-friendly, and family-style restaurants offer children's menus. Small inns sometimes prohibit children under 12. Baby-changing facilities are available in most large public restrooms.

RESTROOMS

Free public lavatories are a rarity in the US. Department stores, hotels and fast-food restaurants have public restrooms which can be used, especially if you make a small purchase.

CUSTOMS

Importing souvenirs from rare or endangered species may be illegal or require a permit. You should check your home country's customs regulations before purchase.

CONSULATES

UK	Ireland	Canada	Australia	New Zealand
617/245-4500	617/267-9330	617/247-5100	212/351-6500	603/225-8228

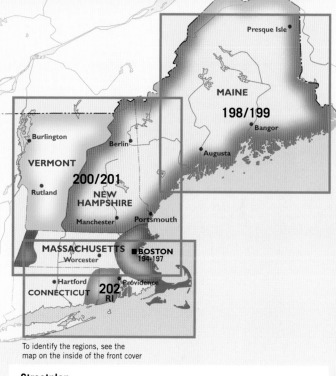

Presque Isle

MAINE
198/199

Bangor

Augusta

Burlington

Berlin

VERMONT
200/201

Rutland

NEW
HAMPSHIRE

Manchester

Portsmouth

MASSACHUSETTS   ■BOSTON
Worcester   194-197

Hartford   Providence
CONNECTICUT **202**
RI

To identify the regions, see the
map on the inside of the front cover

Streetplan

════ Freeway	▨ Important building
──── Main road/Other road	▨ Park/garden
──── Railway	◨ Featured place of interest
──── Freedom Trail	**i** Tourist Information
	✝ Church

| **194–197** | 0 ━━━━ 250 metres |
| | 0 ━━━━ 250 yards |

● Subway (Metro) station

● Tram/Trolley stop

Regional Maps

⊜── Major route	▪ Featured place of interest
⊜── Interstate highway	▫ City
▣── US highway	▫ Town/village
③── State/county highway	✦ Airport
	• Height in metres

| **198–202** | 0 ━━━━ 40 km |
| | 0 ━━━━ 20 miles |

Atlas

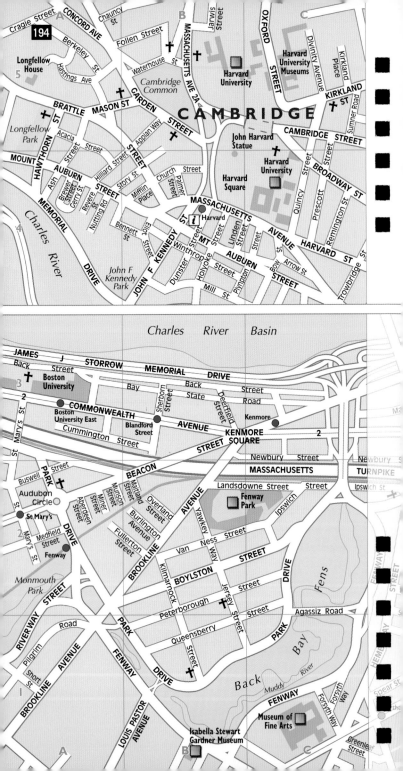

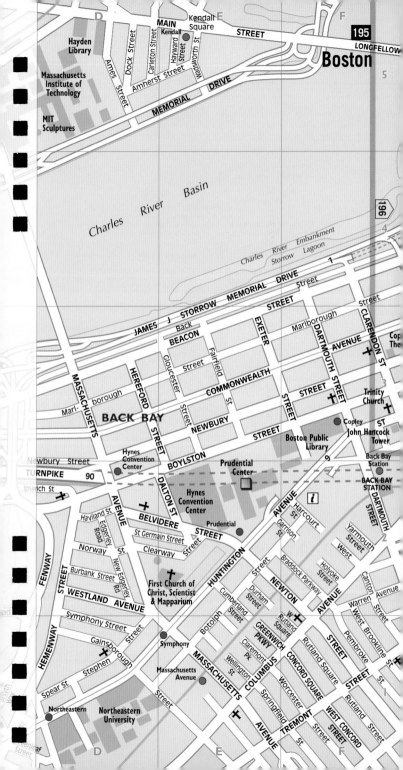

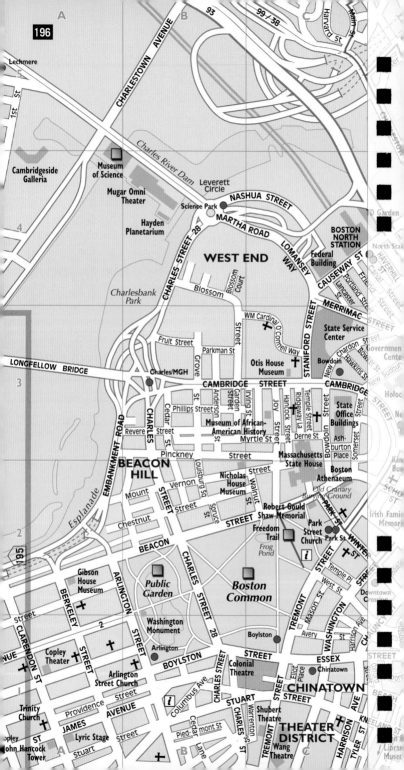

A   B   C

93   99 / 38   Harvard St   Main St

Lechmere

1st St

Charlestown Avenue

Charles River Dam

Cambridgeside Galleria

Museum of Science

Mugar Omni Theater

Hayden Planetarium

Leverett Circle

Science Park

NASHUA STREET

MARTHA ROAD

WEST END

LOMANSEY WAY

BOSTON NORTH STATION

North Sta

Federal Building

CAUSEWAY ST

Portland Street

Lancaster Street

MERRIMAC

D Garden

HAVERHILL

Friend Street

Canal Street

Charlesbank Park

Blossom Court

Blossom Street

Fruit Street

Parkman St

Grove Street

WM Cardinal O'Connell Way

STANIFORD STREET

State Service Center

Governmen Cente

Chardon St

New

Hawkins St

Bowdoin

Holoc

LONGFELLOW BRIDGE

Charles/MGH

Otis House Museum

CAMBRIDGE   STREET   CAMBRIDGE   STREET

New Sudbur

EMBANKMENT ROAD

CHARLES

Cedar St

Revere Street

Phillips Street

Anderson St

Garden Street

Irving St

Joy Street

Hancock Street

Ridgeway La

Temple Street

Derne St

Museum of African-American History

Myrtle St

State Office Buildings

Bowdoin

Somerset Street

Ash-burton Place

Ne

BEACON HILL

Mount Vernon Street

Louisburg Sq

Pinckney Street

Walnut St

Spruce St

Nicholas House Museum

Massachusetts State House

Boston Athenaeum

Kin Bu

SCHC ST

Esplanade

Chestnut Street

BEACON   STREET

Robert Gould Shaw Memorial

Freedom Trail

Park Street Church

Old Granary Burying Ground

Park Street

PARK ST

WINTER

Irish Fami Memori

195

Gibson House Museum

ARLINGTON STREET

Public Garden

CHARLES STREET

Boston Common

Frog Pond

i

Temple Pl

West St

TREMONT STREET

Downtown Crossing

BERKELEY Street

CLARENDON ST

Washington Monument

Arlington

Mason St

Avery St

Boylston

WASHINGTON STREET

Harrison Ave

Copley Theater

Arlington Street Church

BOYLSTON STREET

CHARLES STREET

Colonial Theatre

STREET

Eliot St

ESSEX STREET

Chinatown

CHINATOWN

STREET

Trinity Church

Columbus Ave

PROVIDENCE AVENUE

JAMES AVE

Lyric Stage

opley ST

ohn Hancock Tower

Stuart St

STUART STREET

Cedar Lane

Pied-mont St

Warrenton St

CHARLES ST

Shubert Theatre

Wang Theatre

THEATER DISTRICT

TREMONT STREET

HARRISON AVE

KNEELAND

TYLER ST

Libra Muse

i

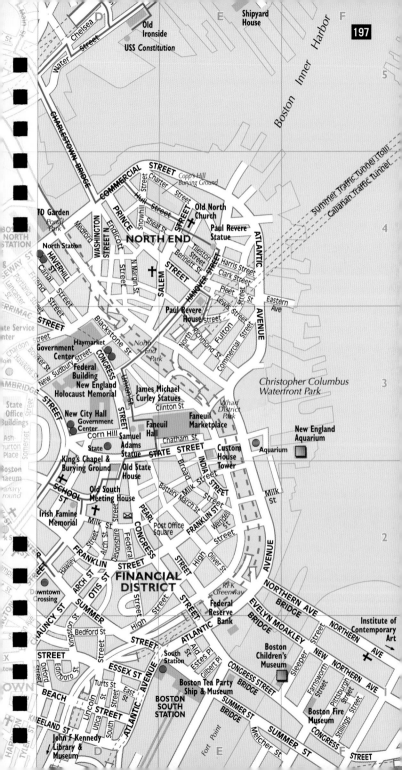

Shipyard House

Old Ironside

USS Constitution

Boston Inner Harbor

Summer Traffic Tunnel (Toll)
Callahan Traffic Tunnel

CHARLESTOWN BRIDGE

COMMERCIAL STREET

Water Street

Chelsea Street

Charter Street

Snowhill Street

Sheaf st

Copp's Hill Burying Ground

Old North Church

Paul Revere Statue

PRINCE STREET

Hull Street

SALEM STREET

NORTH END

HANOVER STREET

ATLANTIC AVENUE

Tileston Street

Bennett Street

Harris Street

Clark Street

Fleet Street

Lewis St

North St

Eastern Ave

TD Garden
Portal Park

BOSTON NORTH STATION

North Station

MEDFORD

WASHINGTON STREET

ENDICOTT STREET

HAVERHILL

Canal Street

Friend Street

N Margin Street

Paul Revere House

Richmond St

Fulton Street

Commercial Street

Portland Street

SEAWAY

Lancaster St

FRIMAC STREET

ate Service enter

Chardon Street

Hawkins St

CAMBRIDGE

Bowker St

Blackstone St

Haymarket

North End Park

Government Center

New Sudbury Street

CONGRESS STREET

Federal Building

New England Holocaust Memorial

James Michael Curley Statues

Clinton St

UNION STREET

Wharf District Park

Christopher Columbus Waterfront Park

New England Aquarium

State Office Buildings

Somerset

Ashburton Place

New City Hall
Government Center

Corn Hill

Faneuil Hall

Faneuil Marketplace

Chatham St

Custom House Tower

Aquarium

Boston Aaeum

anary round

King's Chapel & Burying Ground

State

Samuel Adams Statue

STATE STREET

Broad St

India St

MILK St

Old State House

SCHOOL ST

Old South Meeting House

Battery March St

Milk Street

Franklin St

INDIA STREET

Irish Famine Memorial

Milk St

PEARL

CONGRESS

Post Office Square

Devonshire

Federal

FRANKLIN STREET

High St

Oliver St

Wendell St

AVENUE

Arch St

Hawley

ARCH ST

OTIS ST

FINANCIAL DISTRICT

STREET

High St

RFK Greenway

Federal Reserve Bank

NORTHERN AVE BRIDGE

EVELYN MOAKLEY BRIDGE

Institute of Contemporary Art

Downtown Crossing

SUMMER ST

CHAUNCY ST

Kingston St

Bedford St

ATLANTIC AVENUE

South Station

Aid St

Estes Pl

Gilbert Pl

CONGRESS STREET

Boston Children's Museum

Sleeper Street

NEW NORTHERN AVE

Fid Point

Fansworth Street

Pittsburgh Street

Stillings Street

STREET

Oxford Street

Edinboro St

ESSEX STREET

BEACH STREET

Tufts St

East St

Lincoln Street

Utica St

South Street

BOSTON SOUTH STATION

Boston Tea Party Ship & Museum

SUMMER ST

CONGRESS BRIDGE

SUMMER ST

Boston Fire Museum

CONGRESS

STREET

KNEELAND ST

TYLER

John F Kennedy Library & Museum

Melcher St

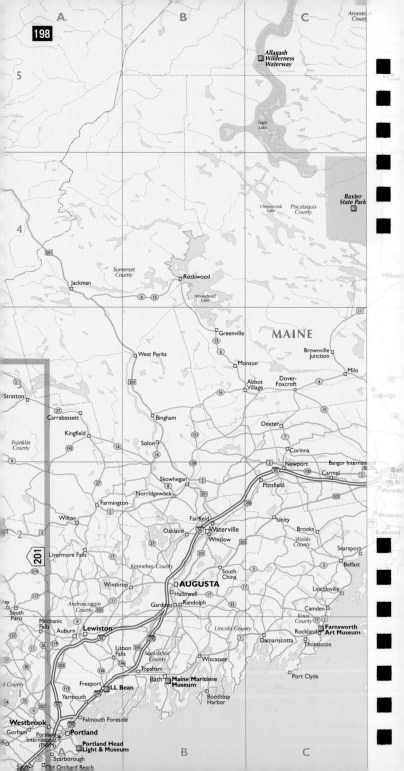

Aroostook
County

D

E

F

Portage

Ashland

Presque Isle

Mars
Hill

St John

689
Peaked Mountain

Knowles Corner

Smyrna Mills

Houlton

Patten

Island Falls

Sherman
Station

Orient

Macwahoc

Danforth

Brookton

Vanceboro

Penobscot

Mattawamkeag

Penobscot County

Lincoln

Springfield

Topsfield

Grand
Lake

Millinocket

Howland

Princeton

Calais

Lagrange

Washington
County

Milo

Milford

Orono

Wesley

Bangor International

Bangor

Beddington

Brewer

Hancock County

East Holden

Hampden

Machias

Winterport

Cherryfield

Harrington

Bucksport

Ellsworth

Milbridge

Jonesport

Belfast

Blue
Hill

Trenton

Bar Harbor

Winter Harbor

Deer Isle

Acadia
National Park

Bass Harbor

Stonington

Acadia
National Park

Penobscot Bay

D

E

F

5

4

3

2

1

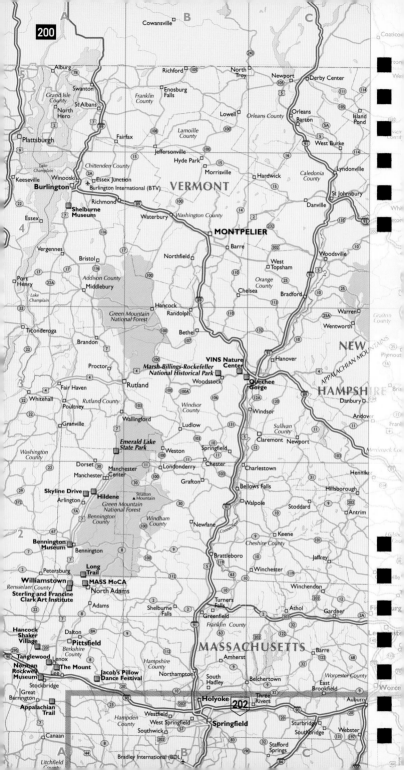

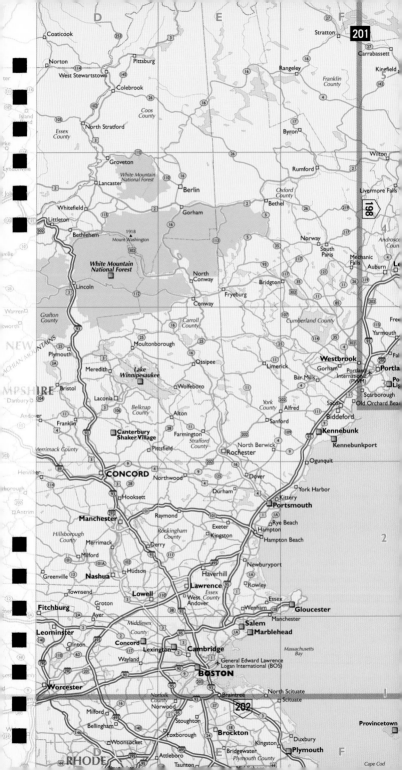

Boston

Cambridge

Picture Credits

The Automobile Association would like to thank the following photographers, companies and picture libraries for their assistance in the preparation of this book.

Abbreviations for the picture credits are as follows: (t) top; (b) bottom; (l) left; (r) right; (c) centre; (AA) AA World Travel Library.

2 (i) AA/J Lynch; 2 (ii) AA/C Coe; 2 (iii) AA/J Nicholson; 2 (iv) AA/C Coe; 2 (v) AA/C Coe; 3 (i) AA/D Clapp; 3 (ii) AA/C Coe; 3 (iii) Danita Delimont/Alamy; 3 (iv) Ian Dagnall/Alamy; 5l AA/J Lynch; 5c AA/M Lynch; 5r Miles Ertman/Masterfile; 6 The Mayflower, engraved and pub. by John A. Lowell, Boston, 1905 (engraving) (b/w photo) by Johnson, Marshall (c.1850-1921), Library of Congress, Washington D.C., USA/ The Bridgeman Art Library; 8 Greater Boston Convention & Visitors Bureau; 9 AA/J Lynch; 10l Danita Delimont/Alamy; 10r Jon Arnold Images Ltd/Alamy; 11l AA/C Coe; 11r culliganphoto/ Alamy; 12 Cindy McIntyre/Photolibrary.com; 12/13 AA/C Coe; 14/15 Rob Tringali/Sportschrome/Getty Images; 16 Mark Rucker/Transcendental Graphics, Getty Images; 18 Franz-Marc Frei/Corbis; 19 Owaki - Kulla/Corbis; 20l Red Cover/ Alamy; 20r America/Alamy; 21 Danita Delimont/Alamy; 23 North Wind Picture Archives/Alamy; 25 AA/D Clapp; 26/27 PCL/ Alamy; 29t Mary Evans Picture Library; 29c Mary Evans Picture Library; 30l Mary Evans Picture Library; 30r Mary Evans Picture Library; 31l AA/C Coe; 31c AA/M Lynch; 31r AA/M Lynch; 39l AA/J Nicholson; 39c AA/C Coe; 39r AA/C Sawyer; 42c Danita Delimont/Alamy; 42b AA/C Coe; 43t AA/C Sawyer; 43b Yoshiki Hase/Museum of Science; 44 AA/J Nicholson; 46 AA/C Sawyer; 48/49 Museum of Fine Arts, Boston; 49 AA/J Nicholson; 50 Dance at Bougival, 1883 (oil on canvas) by Renoir, Pierre Auguste (1841-1919) Museum of Fine Arts, Boston, Massachusetts, USA/ Picture Fund/ The Bridgeman Art Library; 52 AA/C Sawyer; 53 AA/C Sawyer; 54c AA/C Coe; 54b AA/C Coe; 55 John Coletti/Photolibrary.com; 56 AA/C Sawyer; 58t AA/M Lynch; 58b AA/C Coe; 59t Greater Boston Convention & Visitors Bureau; 59c AA/C Sawyer; 60 AA/J Nicholson; 61 AA/D Clapp; 62 AA/C Sawyer; 63t Andre Jenny/Alamy; 63b AA/C Coe; 64l AA/M Lynch; 64r AA/C Sawyer; 73l AA/C Coe; 73c AA/M Lynch; 73r AA/C Coe; 74 AA/D Clapp; 76 Mira/Alamy; 77c Jon Arnold Images Ltd/Alamy; 77b Danita Delimont/Alamy; 78 AA/C Coe; 79t Terry Donnelly/Alamy; 79b AA/D Clapp; 80 AA/M Lynch; 81 Terry Donnelly/Alamy; 82 Rolf Richardson/ Alamy; 83 AA/C Coe; 84t 4Corners/Cozzi Guido/4Corners Images; 84c AA/C Coe; 85 AA/C Coe; 86 Alan Gallery/Alamy; 88 Michael Matthews/Alamy; 89 Jon Arnold Images Ltd/Alamy; 95l AA/C Coe; 95c AA/C Coe; 95r AA/C Coe; 97l Jonathan Blair/Corbis; 97r AA/C Coe; 98c Jeff Greenberg/Alamy; 98b Albert Knapp/Alamy; 99 Mary Steinbacher/Alamy; 100 AA/C Coe; 101 AA/C Coe; 102 Christopher Duggan/Jacob's Pillow Dance Festival; 103 Kelly-Mooney Photography/Corbis; 104 Robert Harding Picture Library Ltd/Alamy; 105 maurice joseph/Alamy; 109l AA/D Clapp; 109c AA/M Lynch; 109r AA/C Coe; 110c AA/D Clapp; 110b AA/D Clapp; 111 Tim Laman/Getty Images; 112l Vespasian/Alamy; 112r AA/C Coe; 113t AA/C Coe; 113b AA/T Lynch; 114 AA/C Coe; 115 Alan Nyiri/Hildene; 116 AA/M Lynch; 117 AA/C Coe; 118 NPS/Ed Sharron; 119 Ed Sharron; 120 Bob Eddy, Courtesy Cabot Creamery Cooperative; 121 Corey Hendrickson/Getty Images; 122 David Lyons/ Alamy; 123l Digital Vision/Alamy; 123r AA/T Lynch; 124 AA/C Coe; 131l AA/C Coe; 131c AA/M Lynch; 131r AA/C Coe; 132 AA/C Coe; 133l AA/M Lynch; 133c AA/M Lynch; 134 AA/C Coe; 135t Andre Jenny/Alamy; 135b Nik Wheeler/Corbis; 136t Patrick O'Connor/The Preservation Society of Newport County; 136c Mary Evans Picture Library; 136b Franco Rossi/The Preservation Society of Newport County; 137 John Corbett/The Preservation Society of Newport County; 138 Visions LLC/ Photolibrary.com; 139 Stan Godlewski/Liaison/Getty; 140t Garry Black/Masterfile; 140c AA/C Coe; 140b AA/C Coe; 141 Andre Jenny/Alamy; 142 Richard Cheek/The Preservation Society of Newport County; 143 John Corbett/The Preservation Society of Newport County; 144 Andre Jenny/Alamy; 145 AA/C Coe; 149l Danita Delimont/Alamy; 149c AA/M Lynch; 149r AA/D Clapp; 151t AA/C Coe; 151c FLPA/Neil Bowman; 152 Andre Jenny/Alamy; 153t Andre Jenny/Alamy; 153b Jon Arnold Images Ltd/Alamy; 154 Peter Horree/Alamy; 155 AA/D Clapp; 156t AA/D Clapp; 156c AA/C Coe; 157t AA/D Clapp; 157c AA/M Lynch; 158 mark sadlier/Alamy; 159t John Shaw/NHPA; 159c Stephan Krasemann/NHPA; 160 mark sadlier/Alamy; 161 Guy Edwards/NHPA; 162/163 AA/C Coe; 164 AA/C Coe; 166l Peter Adams Photography/Alamy; 166r Jeff Greenberg/ Alamy; 167 AA/M Lynch; 173l Ian Dagnall/Alamy; 173c AA/M Lynch; 173r AA/M Lynch; 175 AA/C Coe; 176 Nick Higham/ Alamy; 177 AA/M Lynch; 179 Diane Macdonald/Alamy; 180l AA/M Lynch; 180c Stephen Saks Photography/Alamy; 181l AA/C Coe; 181r AA/C Coe; 182 Karl Rosal/Alamy; 184 AA/C Coe; 185 Visions of America, LLC/Alamy; 186l Ira Block/Getty Images; 186r Visions of America, LLC/Alamy; 187l AA/M Lynch; 187c AA/C Coe; 187r AA/M Lynch; 191t AA/C Coe; 191c AA/R Elliott; 191b AA/C Coe

Every effort has been made to trace the copyright holders, and we apologise in advance for any accidental errors. We would be happy to apply any corrections in the following edition of this publication.

SPIRALGUIDE
Questionnaire

Dear Traveller

Your comments, opinions and recommendations are very important to us. Please help us to improve our travel guides by taking a few minutes to complete this simple questionnaire.

You do not need a stamp (unless posted outside the UK). If you do not want to remove this page from your guide, then photocopy it or write your answers on a plain sheet of paper.

Send to: The Editor, Spiral Guides, AA World Travel Guides, FREEPOST SCE 4598, Basingstoke RG21 4GY.

Your recommendations...

We always encourage readers' recommendations for restaurants, night-life or shopping – if your recommendation is used in the next edition of the guide, we will send you a FREE AA Spiral Guide of your choice. Please state below the establishment name, location and your reasons for recommending it.

_____

_____

_____

_____

_____

Please send me AA Spiral _____

(see list of titles inside the back cover)

About this guide...

Which title did you buy?

_____ AA Spiral

Where did you buy it? _____

When? m m / y y

Why did you choose an AA Spiral Guide? _____

_____

_____

_____

_____

Did this guide meet your expectations?

Exceeded ☐   Met all ☐   Met most ☐   Fell below ☐

Please give your reasons _____

_____

_____

_____

_____

continued on next page...

Were there any aspects of this guide that you particularly liked?

_____

_____

_____

_____

Is there anything we could have done better?

_____

_____

_____

_____

About you...

Name (Mr/Mrs/Ms) _____

Address _____

_____

_____ Postcode _____

Daytime tel no _____ email _____

Please *only* give us your email address and mobile phone number if you wish to hear from us about other products and services from the AA and partners by email or text or mms.

Which age group are you in?

Under 25 ☐   25–34 ☐   35–44 ☐   45–54 ☐   55–64 ☐   65+ ☐

How many trips do you make a year?

Less than one ☐   One ☐   Two ☐   Three or more ☐

Are you an AA member? Yes ☐   No ☐

About your trip...

When did you book? m m / y y   When did you travel? m m / y y

How long did you stay? _____

Was it for business or leisure? _____

Did you buy any other travel guides for your trip?   ☐ Yes ☐ No

If yes, which ones? _____

_____

Thank you for taking the time to complete this questionnaire. Please send it to us as soon as possible, and remember, you do not need a stamp (unless posted outside the UK).